**SUCCESS READING PROGRAM
FOR OLDER STUDENTS**

Learn To Read English With Directions In Haitian Creole
Homework
Color Edition

Homework

ISBN 978-1-945738-55-5
© 2022 – Wendy A. Charles & Alexander J. Charles All
Rights Reserved
Baldwin, New York
www.intellastic.com

All rights reserved. No portion of this book may be reproduced, stored in a retrieval system, or transmitted in any form or by any means – electronic, mechanical, photocopy, recording, video presentation, private instruction, scanning or other – except for brief quotations in critical reviews or articles,
without the prior written permission of the writers.

All Rights Reserved. Printed in the USA.

Homework

Table of Contents

Unit A		
Lesson 1.1	Reading Words with the Letter A/a	1
Lesson 1.2	Reading Words with the Short Vowel "a" Sound	2
Lesson 1.2	Reading & Writing Words with the Short Vowel "a" Sound	3
Lesson 1.3	Reading Words with the Long Vowel "a" Sound	4
Lesson 1.3	Reading & Writing Words with the Long Vowel "a" Sound	5
Lessons 1.2 & 1.3	Reading Short Vowel and Long Vowel Words	6
Lesson 1.4	Reading Words with the "age" Letter Combination	7
Lesson 1.5	Reading Words with the "ai" Vowel Pair	8
Lesson 1.6	Reading Letter "a" Words with the Schwa Sound	9
Lesson 1.7	Reading Words with the "ar" Letter Combination	10
Lesson 1.7	Reading Words with the "ar" Letter Combination	11
Lesson 1.8	Reading Words with a Silent Letter "a"	12
Unit Review	Reading Words with Vowel "a" Sounds: /ă/, /ā/, /ə/ & Silent	13
Lesson 1.9	Reading Multisyllable Words	14
Lesson 1.9	Reading Multisyllable Words	15
Lesson 1.10	Proper and Common Nouns and Adjectives	16

Unit B		
Lesson 2.1	Reading Words with the Letter B/b	17
Lesson 2.2	Reading Words with the "br" Letter Combination	18
Lesson 2.3	Reading Words with the "bl" Letter Combination	19
Lesson 2.3	Reading Words with the "ble" Letter Combination	20
Lesson 2.4	Reading Words with the "mb" Letter Combination	21
Lesson 2.4	Reading Words with the "bt" Letter Combination	22
Lesson 2.5	Reading Words with a Silent Letter "b"	23
Lesson 2.6	Reading Multisyllable Words	24
Lesson 2.6	Reading Multisyllable Words	25
Lesson 2.7	Proper and Common Nouns and Adjectives	26

Homework

Unit C

Lesson 3.1	Reading Words with the Letter C/c	27
Lesson 3.1	Reading Words with the Hard Letter "c"	28
Lesson 3.2	Reading Words with the Soft Letter "c"	29
Lessons 3.1 & 3.2	Reading Hard Letter "c" and Soft Letter "c" Words	30
Lesson 3.3	Reading Words with the "cr" Letter Combination	31
Lesson 3.4	Reading Words with the "cl" Letter Combination	32
Lesson 3.4	Reading Words with the "cle" Letter Combination	33
Lesson 3.5	Reading Words with the "ct" Letter Combination	34
Lesson 3.6	Reading Soft Letter "c" Words	35
Lesson 3.6	Reading Soft Letter "c" Words	36
Lesson 3.7	Reading Words with the "ch" Letter Combination	37
Lesson 3.8	Reading Words with the "cc" Letter Combination	38
Lesson 3.9	Reading Words with a Silent Letter "c"	39
Lesson 3.10	Reading Multisyllable Words	40
Lesson 3.10	Reading Multisyllable Words	41
Lesson 3.11	Proper and Common Nouns and Adjectives	42

Unit D

Lesson 4.1	Reading Words with the Letter D/d	43
Lesson 4.2	Reading Letter "d" Words with the /d/ Sound & /j/ Sound	44
Lesson 4.2	Reading Words with the "dr" Letter Combination	45
Lesson 4.3	Reading Words with the "ed" Suffix/ Past Tense Verbs	46
Lesson 4.4	Reading Words with a Silent Letter "d"	47
Lesson 4.5	Reading Multisyllable Words	48
Lesson 4.5	Reading Multisyllable Words	49
Lesson 4.6	Proper and Common Nouns and Adjectives	50

Unit E

Lesson 5.1	Reading Words with the Letter E/e	51
Lesson 5.2	Reading Words with the Short Vowel "e" Sound	52
Lesson 5.2	Reading & Writing Words with the Short Vowel "e" Sound	53

Homework

Lesson 5.3	Reading Words with the Long Vowel "e" Sound	54
Lesson 5.3	Reading & Writing Words with the Long Vowel "e" Sound	55
Lessons 5.2 & 5.3	Reading Short Vowel and Long Vowel Words	56
Lesson 5.4	Reading Words with Letter "e" Vowel Pairs	57
Lesson 5.5	Reading Words with the Final Letter "e"	58
Lesson 5.6	Reading Letter "e" Words with the Schwa Vowel Sound	59
Lesson 5.7	Reading Words with the "er" Letter Combination	60
Lesson 5.8	Reading Words with the "eu" and "ew" Letter Combinations	61
Lesson 5.9	Reading Words with the "ey" Letter Combination	62
Lesson 5.10	Reading Words with a Silent Letter "e"	63
Unit Review	Reading Words with Vowel "e" Sounds: /ĕ/, /ē/, /ə/ & Silent	64
Lesson 5.11	Reading Multisyllable Words	65
Lesson 5.11	Reading Multisyllable Words	66
Lesson 5.12	Proper and Common Nouns and Adjectives	67

Unit F

Lesson 6.1	Reading Words with the Letter F/f	68
Lesson 6.2	Reading Words with the "fr" Letter Combination	69
Lesson 6.3	Reading Words with the "fl" Letter Combination	70
Lesson 6.3	Reading Words with the "fle" Letter Combination	71
Lesson 6.4	Reading Words with the "ft," "lf" and "ff" Letter Combinations	72
Lesson 6.5	Reading Words with a Silent Letter "f"	73
Lesson 6.6	Reading Singular and Plural forms of Words Ending in "-f" & "-fe"	74
Lesson 6.7	Reading Multisyllable Words	75
Lesson 6.7	Reading Multisyllable Words	76
Lesson 6.8	Proper and Common Nouns and Adjectives	77

Unit G

Lesson 7.1	Reading Words with the Letter G/g	78
Lesson 7.1	Reading Words with the Hard Letter "g"	79
Lesson 7.2	Reading Words with the Soft Letter G/g	80
Lessons 7.1 & 7.2	Reading Hard Letter "g" and Soft Letter "g" Words	81

Homework

Lessons 7.1 & 7.2	Reading Hard Letter "g" and Soft Letter "g" Words	82
Lesson 7.3	Reading Words with the "gr" Letter Combination	83
Lesson 7.4	Reading Words with the "gl" Letter Combination	84
Lesson 7.4	Reading Words with the "gle" Letter Combination	85
Lesson 7.5	Reading Words with the "gh" Letter Combination	86
Lesson 7.6	Reading Words with the "gn" Letter Combination	87
Lesson 7.7	Reading Words with a Silent Letter "g"	88
Lesson 7.8	Reading Multisyllable Words	89
Lesson 7.8	Reading Multisyllable Words	90
Lesson 7.9	Proper and Common Nouns and Adjectives	91

Unit H

Lesson 8.1	Reading Words with the Letter H/h	92
Lesson 8.2	Reading Words with the Letter "h" Combinations: "sh," "wh," "ch," "th," "rh," "ph" and "gh"	93
Lesson 8.2	Reading Words with the Letter "h" Combinations: "sh," "wh," "ch," "th," "rh," "ph," "gh" and "sch"	94
Lesson 8.3	Reading Words with a Silent Letter "h"	95
Lesson 8.4	Reading Multisyllable Words	96
Lesson 8.4	Reading Multisyllable Words	97
Lesson 8.5	Proper and Common Nouns and Adjectives	98

Unit I

Lesson 9.1	Reading Words with the Letter I/i	99
Lesson 9.2	Reading Words with the Short Vowel "i" Sound	100
Lesson 9.2	Reading & Writing Words with the Short Vowel "i" Sound	101
Lesson 9.3	Reading Words with the Long Vowel "i" Sound	102
Lesson 9.3	Reading & Writing Words with the Long Vowel "i" Sound	103
Lessons 9.2 & 9.3	Reading Short Vowel and Long Vowel Words	104
Lesson 9.4	Reading Words with Letter "i" Vowel Pairs	105
Lesson 9.5	Reading Words with the Final Letter "i"	106
Lesson 9.6	Reading Letter "i" Words with the Schwa Vowel Sound	107

Lesson 9.7	Reading Words with the "ir" Letter Combination	108
Lesson 9.8	Reading Letter "i" Words with the Long Vowel "e" Sound	109
Lesson 9.9	Reading Words with a Silent Letter "i"	110
Unit Review	Reading Words with Vowel "i" Sounds: /ĭ/, /ī/, /ə/ & Silent	111
Lesson 9.10	Reading Multisyllable Words	112
Lesson 9.10	Reading Multisyllable Words	113
Lesson 9.11	Proper and Common Nouns and Adjectives	114

Unit J

Lesson 10.1	Reading Words with the Letter J/j	115
Lesson 10.2	Reading Multisyllable Words	116
Lesson 10.2	Reading Multisyllable Words	117
Lesson 10.3	Proper and Common Nouns and Adjectives	118

Unit K

Lesson 11.1	Reading Words with the Letter K/k	119
Lesson 11.2	Reading Words with the Letter "k" and "ck" Letter Combination	120
Lesson 11.3	Reading Words with the "kle" Letter Combination	121
Lesson 11.4	Reading Words with a Silent Letter "k"	122
Lesson 11.5	Reading Multisyllable Words	123
Lesson 11.5	Reading Multisyllable Words	124
Lesson 11.6	Proper and Common Nouns and Adjectives	125

Unit L

Lesson 12.1	Reading Words with the Letter L/l	126
Lesson 12.2	Reading Words with the Letter "l" Combinations: "fl," "pl" & "sl"	127
Lesson 12.3	Reading Words with a Silent Letter "l"	128
Lesson 12.4	Reading Multisyllable Words	129
Lesson 12.4	Reading Multisyllable Words	130
Lesson 12.5	Proper and Common Nouns and Adjectives	131

Homework

Unit M

Lesson 13.1	Reading Words with the Letter M/m	132
Lesson 13.2	Reading Words with a Silent Letter "m"	133
Lesson 13.3	Reading Multisyllable Words	134
Lesson 13.3	Reading Multisyllable Words	135
Lesson 13.4	Proper and Common Nouns and Adjectives	136

Unit N

Lesson 14.1	Reading Words with the Letter N/n	137
Lesson 14.2	Reading Words with the "ng" Letter Combination	138
Lesson 14.3	Reading Words with a Silent Letter "n"	139
Lesson 14.4	Reading Multisyllable Words	140
Lesson 14.4	Reading Multisyllable Words	141
Lesson 14.5	Proper and Common Nouns and Adjectives	142

Unit O

Lesson 15.1	Reading Words with the Letter O/o	143
Lesson 15.2	Reading Words with the Short Vowel "o" Sound	144
Lesson 15.2	Reading & Writing Words with the Short Vowel "o" Sound	145
Lesson 15.3	Reading Words with the Long Vowel "o" Sound	146
Lesson 15.3	Reading & Writing Words with the Long Vowel "o" Sound	147
Lessons 15.2 & 15.3	Reading Short Vowel and Long Vowel Words	148
Lesson 15.4	Reading Words with Letter "o" Vowel Pairs	149
Lesson 15.5	Reading Words with the Final Letter "o"	150
Lesson 15.6	Reading Letter "o" Words with the Schwa Vowel Sound	151
Lesson 15.7	Reading Words with Vowel "o" Sounds: /ŏ/, /ō/ & /$\overline{oo}$/	152
Lesson 15.8	Reading Words with the "or" Letter Combination	153
Lesson 15.8	Reading Words with the "or" Letter Combination	154
Lesson 15.9	Reading Words with a Silent Letter "o"	155
Unit Review	Reading Words with Vowel "o" Sounds: /ŏ/, /ō/, /ə/ & Silent	156
Lesson 15.10	Reading Multisyllable Words	157
Lesson 15.10	Reading Multisyllable Words	158

Lesson 15.11	Proper and Common Nouns and Adjectives	159
Unit P		
Lesson 16.1	Reading Words with the Letter P/p	160
Lesson 16.2	Reading Words with the "ph" Letter Combination	161
Lesson 16.3	Reading Words with the "pr" Letter Combination	162
Lesson 16.4	Reading Words with the "pl" Letter Combination	163
Lesson 16.4	Reading Words with the "ple" Letter Combination	164
Lesson 16.5	Reading Words with a Silent Letter "p"	165
Lesson 16.6	Reading Multisyllable Words	166
Lesson 16.6	Reading Multisyllable Words	167
Lesson 16.7	Proper and Common Nouns and Adjectives	168
Unit Q		
Lesson 17.1	Reading Words with the Letter Q/q	169
Lesson 17.2	Reading Words with the Letter "q" and "qu" Letter Combination	170
Lesson 17.2	Reading Words with the "qu" Letter Combination	171
Lesson 17.3	Reading Multisyllable Words	172
Lesson 17.3	Reading Multisyllable Words	173
Lesson 17.4	Proper and Common Nouns and Adjectives	174
Unit R		
Lesson 18.1	Reading Words with the Letter R/r	175
Lesson 18.2	Reading Words with the Letter "r" Combinations: "br," "cr," "dr," "fr," "gr," "pr" and "tr"	176
Lesson 18.3	Reading Multisyllable Words	177
Lesson 18.3	Reading Multisyllable Words	178
Lesson 18.4	Proper and Common Nouns and Adjectives	179
Unit S		
Lesson 19.1	Reading Words with the Letter S/s	180
Lesson 19.1	Reading Words with the Letter S/s	181

Homework

Lesson 19.2	Reading Words with the "sion," "sial" & "scious" Suffixes	182
Lesson 19.3	Reading Words with the "sch" Letter Combination	183
Lesson 19.4	Reading Words with the "scr," "shr," "spr" & "str" Letter Combinations	184
Lesson 19.5	Reading Words with the "sl" & "sle" Letter Combinations	185
Lesson 19.5	Reading Words with the "sle" Letter Combination	186
Lesson 19.6	Reading Words with the "sm" Letter Combination	187
Lesson 19.7	Reading Words with the "ss" Letter Combination	188
Lesson 19.8	Reading Words with a Silent Letter "s"	189
Lesson 19.9	Reading Multisyllable Words	190
Lesson 19.9	Reading Multisyllable Words	191
Lesson 19.10	Proper and Common Nouns and Adjectives	192

Unit T

Lesson 20.1	Reading Words with the Letter T/t	193
Lesson 20.2	Reading Words with the "thm" Letter Combination	194
Lesson 20.3	Reading Words with the "tion," "tial" & "tious" Suffixes	195
Lesson 20.4	Reading Words with the "tr" Letter Combination	196
Lesson 20.5	Reading Words with the "tle" Letter Combination	197
Lesson 20.6	Reading Words with the Letter "t" Sounds	198
Lesson 20.7	Reading Words with a Silent Letter "t"	199
Lesson 20.8	Reading Multisyllable Words	200
Lesson 20.8	Reading Multisyllable Words	201
Lesson 20.9	Proper and Common Nouns and Adjectives	202

Unit U

Lesson 21.1	Reading Words with the Letter U/u	203
Lesson 21.2	Reading Words with the Short Vowel "u" Sound	204
Lesson 21.2	Reading & Writing Words with the Short Vowel "u" Sound	205
Lesson 21.3	Reading Words with the Long Vowel "u" Sound	206
Lesson 21.3	Reading & Writing Words with the Long Vowel "u" Sound	207
Lessons 21.2 & 21.3	Reading Short Vowel and Long Vowel Words	208
Lesson 21.4	Reading Words with Letter "u" Vowel Pairs	209

Lesson 21.5	Reading Words with the Final Letter "u"	210
Lesson 21.6	Reading Letter "u" Words with the Schwa Vowel Sound	211
Lesson 21.7	Reading Words with the "ur" Letter Combination	212
Lesson 21.8	Reading Words with a Silent Letter "u"	213
Unit Review	Reading Words with Vowel "u" Sounds: / ŭ/, / o͞o/, /ə/ & Silent	214
Lesson 21.9	Reading Multisyllable Words	215
Lesson 21.9	Reading Multisyllable Words	216
Lesson 21.10	Proper and Common Nouns and Adjectives	217

Unit V

Lesson 22.1	Reading Words with the Letter V/v	218
Lesson 22.2	Reading Multisyllable Words	219
Lesson 22.2	Reading Multisyllable Words	220
Lesson 22.3	Proper and Common Nouns and Adjectives	221

Unit W

Lesson 23.1	Reading Words with the Letter W/w	222
Lesson 23.2	Reading Words with a Vowel before the Letter "w"	223
Lesson 23.3	Reading Words with a Silent "w" and "wr" Letter Combination	224
Lesson 23.3	Reading Words with a Silent Letter "w"	225
Lesson 23.4	Reading Multisyllable Words	226
Lesson 23.4	Reading Multisyllable Words	227
Lesson 23.5	Proper and Common Nouns and Adjectives	228

Unit X

Lesson 24.1	Reading Words with the Letter X/x	229
Lesson 24.1	Reading Words with the Letter X/x	230
Lesson 24.2	Reading Multisyllable Words	231
Lesson 24.2	Reading Multisyllable Words	232
Lesson 24.3	Proper and Common Nouns and Adjectives	233

Homework

Unit Y

Lesson 25.1	Reading Words with the Letter Y/y	234
Lesson 25.1	Reading Words with the Letter Y/y	235
Lesson 25.2	Reading Words with a Vowel before the Letter "y"	236
Lesson 25.3	Reading Words with the "cy" Letter Combination	237
Lesson 25.4	Reading Words with the Final Letter "y"	238
Lesson 25.5	Reading Words with the "yr" Letter Combination	239
Lesson 25.6	Reading Letter "y" Words with the Schwa Sound	240
Lesson 25.7	Reading Words with a Silent Letter "y"	241
Lesson 25.8	Reading Multisyllable Words	242
Lesson 25.8	Reading Multisyllable Words	243
Lesson 25.9	Proper and Common Nouns and Adjectives	244

Unit Z

Lesson 26.1	Reading Words with the Letter Z/z	245
Lesson 26.1	Reading Words with the Letter Z/z	246
Lesson 26.2	Reading Words with a Silent Letter "z"	247
Lesson 26.3	Reading Multisyllable Words	248
Lesson 26.3	Reading Multisyllable Words	249
Lesson 26.4	Proper and Common Nouns and Adjectives	250

Appendix

Appendix 1.0	Introduction of the Letter A/a	251
Appendix 2.0	Introduction of the Letter B/b	252
Appendix 2.0	Letter Recognition B/b	253
Appendix 3.0	Introduction of the Letter C/c	254
Appendix 3.0	Letter Recognition C/c	255
Appendix 4.0	Introduction of the Letter D/d	256
Appendix 4.0	Letter Recognition D/d	257
Appendix 5.0	Introduction of the Letter E/e	258
Appendix 6.0	Introduction of the Letter F/f	259
Appendix 6.0	Letter Recognition F/f	260

Appendix 7.0	Introduction of the Letter G/g	261
Appendix 7.0	Letter Recognition G/g	262
Appendix 8.0	Introduction of the Letter H/h	263
Appendix 8.0	Letter Recognition H/h	264
Appendix 9.0	Introduction of the Letter I/i	265
Appendix 10.0	Introduction of the Letter J/j	266
Appendix 10.0	Letter Recognition J/j	267
Appendix 11.0	Introduction of the Letter K/k	268
Appendix 11.0	Letter Recognition K/k	269
Appendix 12.0	Introduction of the Letter L/l	270
Appendix 12.0	Letter Recognition L/l	271
Appendix 13.0	Introduction of the Letter M/m	272
Appendix 13.0	Letter Recognition M/m	273
Appendix 14.0	Introduction of the Letter N/n	274
Appendix 14.0	Letter Recognition N/n	275
Appendix 15.0	Introduction of the Letter O/o	276
Appendix 16.0	Introduction of the Letter P/p	277
Appendix 16.0	Letter Recognition P/p	278
Appendix 17.0	Introduction of the Letter Q/q	279
Appendix 17.0	Letter Recognition Q/q	280
Appendix 18.0	Introduction of the Letter R/r	281
Appendix 18.0	Letter Recognition R/r	282
Appendix 19.0	Introduction of the Letter S/s	283
Appendix 19.0	Letter Recognition S/s	284
Appendix 20.0	Introduction of the Letter T/t	285
Appendix 20.0	Letter Recognition T/t	286
Appendix 21.0	Introduction of the Letter U/u	287
Appendix 22.0	Introduction of the Letter V/v	288
Appendix 22.0	Letter Recognition V/v	289
Appendix 23.0	Introduction of the Letter W/w	290
Appendix 23.0	Letter Recognition W/w	291

Homework

Appendix 24.0	Introduction of the Letter X/x	292
Appendix 24.0	Letter Recognition X/x	293
Appendix 25.0	Introduction of the Letter Y/y	294
Appendix 25.0	Letter Recognition Y/y	295
Appendix 26.0	Introduction of the Letter Z/z	296
Appendix 26.0	Letter Recognition Z/z	297

My Cup of Water

Homework

Name: _____ Date: ___/___/_____ Score: _____

Lesson 1.1

Reading Words with the Letter A/a

✓ Lesson Check Point

Directions: Read each target word. Find the letter "a" and put a check (✓) in the column that identifies its position: beginning, within or end.
Direksyons: Li chak mo objektif. Jwenn lèt "a" a epi mete yon tchèck (✓) nan kolòn ki idantifye pozisyon li an: nan kòmansman, ladan oubyen nan finisman.

Target Words	Beginning (First Letter)	Within	End (Last Letter)
1. sofa			
2. basic			
3. April			
4. thankful			
5. formula			

Directions: Read each target word. Read the words in the row and circle the word that has a different vowel "a" sound.
Direksyons: Li chak mo objektif. Li mo yo ki nan ranje a epi antoure mo a ki bay yon son vwayèl "a" ki diferan an.

Target Words				
6. clan	mass	play	can't	camp
7. plant	task	back	ants	plane
8. grass	hand	flame	nap	ask
9. stand	gate	rank	bass	has
10. bran	had	sand	raft	sauce

Learn to Read English With Directions In Haitian Creole

Homework

 Name: _____   Date: ___/___/_____   Score: _____

Lesson 1.2

Reading Words with the Short Vowel "a" Sound

✓ Lesson Check Point

 Directions: Read the words in the four boxes. Circle two words with the short vowel /ă/ sound. The anchor word for the short vowel /ă/ sound is <u>apple</u>.

Direksyons: Li mo yo ki nan kat ti bwat yo. Antoure de mo ki genyen son vwayèl kout /ă/ a. Mo referans pou son vwayèl kout /ă/ a se mo, <u>apple</u>.

sake	track		lay	saw		lad	rattle
wax	nail		pack	pad		plane	car

tap	ram		hat	calm		place	tan
ball	yarn		shape	van		sale	and

 Directions: Read the words in the four boxes. Circle two words that rhyme. Rhyming words have the same ending sound, such as <u>tap</u> and <u>map</u>.

Direksyons: Li mo yo ki nan kat ti bwat yo. Antoure de mo ki rime. De mo oubyen plizyè mo ki rime genyen menm son nan finisman yo, tankou <u>tap</u> ak <u>map</u>.

ape	fan		snack	ball		palm	aunt
mall	can		tape	crack		mass	grass

tax	day		law	fast		glass	class
wax	straw		past	rain		tall	pause

Homework

Name: _____ Date:___/___/_____ Score:_____

Lesson 1.2

Reading & Writing Words with the Short Vowel "a" Sound

✓ Lesson Check Point

Directions: Read each sentence and underline three words with the short vowel /ă/ sound. Then, write the underlined words on the lines below. The anchor word for the short vowel /ă/ sound is <u>apple</u>.

Direksyons: Li chak fraz epi soulinye twa mo ki genyen son vwayèl kout /ă/ a. Answit, ekri mo soulinye yo sou trè sa yo ki anba. Mo referans pou son vwayèl kout /ă/ a se mo, <u>apple</u>.

Model

<u>Ann</u> raised her <u>hand</u> in <u>class</u>.

    Ann   hand   class
   _____   _____   _____

1. The large map is in the black sack.

   _____   _____   _____

2. My father's crystal glasses have cracks.

   _____   _____   _____

3. I can walk faster on the grass in the park.

   _____   _____   _____

4. The man has a large, tasty cake in his bag.

   _____   _____   _____

5. My awesome math teacher gave snacks to the class.

   _____   _____   _____

Learn to Read English With Directions In Haitian Creole

Homework

 Name: _____   Date: ___/___/_____   Score: _____

Lesson 1.3

Reading Words with the Long Vowel "a" Sound

✓ Lesson Check Point

 Directions: Read the words in the four boxes. Circle two words with the long vowel /ā/ sound. The anchor word for the long vowel /ā/ sound is <u>ape</u>.

Direksyons: Li mo yo ki nan kat ti bwat yo. Antoure de mo ki genyen son vwayèl long /ā/ a. Mo referans pou son vwayèl long /ā/ a se mo, <u>ape</u>.

fat	father		soda	hale		pages	nap
tape	ray		man	date		comma	bake

grass	rate		wail	sand		state	cape
pale	plant		scale	map		yam	taps

 Directions: Read the words in the four boxes. Circle two words that rhyme. Rhyming words have the same ending sound, such as <u>wait</u> and <u>date</u>.

Direksyons: Li mo ki nan kat ti bwat yo. Antoure de mo ki rime. De mo oubyen plizyè mo ki rime genyen menm son nan finisman yo, tankou <u>wait</u> ak <u>date</u>.

idea	may		at	cake		taste	waste
fast	sway		take	alike		had	lack

face	sad		pain	asks		and	ago
trace	can't		am	Dane		game	tame

Homework

Name: _____ Date: ___/___/_____ Score: _____

Lesson 1.3

Reading & Writing Words with the Long Vowel "a" Sound

✓ **Lesson Check Point**

Directions: Read each sentence and underline three words with the long vowel /ā/ sound. Then, write the underlined words on the lines below. The anchor word for the long vowel /ā/ sound is <u>ape</u>.

Direksyons: Li chak fraz epi soulinye twa mo ki genyen son vwayèl long /ā/ a. Answit, ekri mo soulinye yo sou trè sa yo ki anba. Mo referans pou son vwayèl long /ā/ a se mo, <u>ape</u>.

Model

Ann has <u>grapes</u> and <u>cake</u> on her <u>plate</u>.

grapes　　　　　　cake　　　　　　plate

1. She said, "It rained all day in Maine."

2. Diane ate two large bagels with grape jam.

3. Dave was brave to go into the dark cave alone.

4. It is not safe to wait on the train platform after dark.

5. Late last night, Alex baked large cakes in square pans.

Homework

Name: _____ Date: ___/___/_____ Score: _____

Review Lessons 1.2 & 1.3

Reading Short Vowel and Long Vowel Words

Directions: Read the target words in the word box. In the first column, write the words that have the short vowel /ă/ sound, as in the word apple. In the second column, write the words that have the long vowel /ā/ sound, as in the word ape.

Direksyons: Li mo yo objektif yo ki nan bwat mo a. Nan premye kolòn nan, ekri mo ki bay son vwayèl kout /ă/ yo, tankou li ye nan mo apple la. Nan dezyèm kolòn nan, ekri mo ki bay son vwayèl long /ā/ yo, tankou li ye nan mo ape la.

Target Word Box				
trap	plane	gram	tape	asked
plant	same	land	snacks	paid
label	packs	cake	safe	late
crack	shape	pass	male	cap

Letter "a" has the /ă/ sound as in the word apple

Letter "a" has the /ā/ sound as in the word ape

Homework

 Name: _____ Date: ___/___/_____ Score: _____

Lesson 1.4

Reading Words with the "age" Letter Combination

✓ Lesson Check Point

 Directions: Read each target word. Find the "age" letter combination and put a check (✓) in the column that correctly identifies its sounds.

Direksyons: Li chak mo objektif. Jwenn konbinezon lèt "age" la epi mete yon tchèk (✓) nan kolòn nan ki idantifye son li yo kòrèkteman.

Target Words	"age" has the /ā/ + /j/ sounds as in the word <u>stage</u>	"age" has the /ĭ/ + /j/ sounds as in the word <u>package</u>	"age" has the /ä/ + /j/ or /ä/ + /zh/ sounds as in the word <u>massage</u>
1. pages			
2. fuselage			
3. average			
4. upstage			
5. entourage			

 Directions: Read each sentence and underline the word that has an "age" letter combination that has the /ĭ/ + /j/ sounds, as in the word <u>package</u>.

Direksyons: Li chak fraz epi soulinye mo a ki genyen konbinezon lèt "age" la ki bay son /ĭ/ + /j/ a, tankou li ye nan mo <u>package</u> la.

6. At my school, teenage students wear vintage shirts.

7. The teenage star and his entourage ate sausages and rice.

8. My agent encouraged everyone to have a relaxing massage.

9. The stage manager scheduled three performances in New York.

10. The search team found the airplane's fuselage in Anchorage, Alaska.

Homework

Name: _____ Date: ___/___/_____ Score: _____

Lesson 1.5

Reading Words with the "ai" Vowel Pair

✓ **Lesson Check Point**

Directions: Read each target word. Circle the word in the column that has the same "ai" sound as the target word.

Direksyons: Li chak mo objektif. Antoure mo a ki nan kolòn nan ki bay menm son "ai" la tankou mo objektif la.

laid	a. face
	b. stand

plaid	a. apple
	b. main

rail	a. plaid
	b. date

brain	a. wage
	b. said

Directions: Read each target word. Put a check (✓) under the correct column heading.

Direksyons: Li chak mo objektif. Mete yon tchèk (✓) anba antèt kolòn ki kòrèk la.

Target Words	Words have the long "a" sound as in the word <u>sail</u>	Words do not have the long "a" sound
1. plaid		
2. gain		
3. said		
4. train		

Homework

 Name: _____ Date:___/___/_____ Score: _____

Lesson 1.6

Reading Letter "a" Words with the Schwa Vowel Sound

✓ Lesson Check Point

 Directions: Read each target word. Circle the word in the column that has the same "a" sound as the target word.
Direksyons: Li chak mo objektif. Antoure mo a ki nan kolòn nan ki bay menm son "a" a tankou mo ojektif la.

aware	a. collar
	b. table

vitamin	a. teenage
	b. about

around	a. circular
	b. apples

regular	a. educate
	b. across

 Directions: Read each sentence and underline the letter "a" word that has the schwa vowel /ə/ sound. The anchor word for the letter "a" schwa vowel sound is sofa.
Direksyons: Li chak fraz epi soulinye mo ki genyen lèt "a" a ki bay son schwa /ə/. Mo referans pou son schwa lèt "a" a se mo, sofa.

1. The large snakes are from Kenya.

2. Alex always adds sugar to his tea.

3. The artist will draw the map of Africa.

4. This Sunday, I will walk in the parade.

5. At the plaza, the cars are tan and black.

6. Mrs. Ansel's math class is very popular.

Homework

Name: _____ Date: ___/___/_____ Score: _____

Lesson 1.7

Reading Words with the "ar" Letter Combination

✓ Lesson Check Point

Directions: Read each target word. Circle the word in the column that has the same "a" + "r" sounds as the target word.
Direksyons: Li chak mo objektif. Antoure mo a ki nan kolòn nan ki bay menm son "a" + "r" yo tankou mo ojektif la.

yarn	a. regular
	b. chart

sugar	a. warn
	b. dollar

carrot	a. arrow
	b. cedar

scholar	a. grammar
	b. artist

Directions: Read each target word. Put a check (✓) under the correct column heading.
Direksyons: Li chak mo objektif. Mete yon tchèk (✓) anba antèt kolòn ki kòrèk la.

Target Words	"ar" has the /ă/ + /r/ sounds as in the word <u>baron</u>	"ar" has the /ə/ + /r/ sounds as in the word <u>dollar</u>	"ar" has the /ä/ + /r/ sounds as in the word <u>car</u>	"ar" has the /ô/ + /r/ sounds as in the word <u>war</u>
1. yarn				
2. sugar				
3. carrot				
4. scholar				

Homework

 Name: _____   Date: ___/___/_____   Score: _____

Lesson 1.7

Reading Words with the "ar" Letter Combination

Dictionary Skills/ Vocabulary

✓ Lesson Check Point

 Directions: Read each target word and its definition. Write the target word on the line in front of its meaning. Use a dictionary or the Internet to check your answers.

Direksyons: Li chak mo objektif ak definisyon yo chak. Ekri mo objektif la sou trè ki devan definisyon li an. Itilize yon diksyonè oubyen entènèt pou tcheke repons ou yo.

Target Word Box				
Argentina	park	married	part	carriage

1. _____ a large South American country
2. _____ a vehicle that is pulled by a horse
3. _____ to have been joined in marriage
4. _____ an assigned role in a performance
5. _____ a place with trees, playgrounds and benches

 Directions: Read each sentence and write the target word that correctly completes the sentence.

Direksyons: Li chak fraz epi ekri mo objektif ki konplete fraz la kòrèkteman.

6. Arnold is having a family barbecue at the _____.

7. Arsenio and I are getting _____ on March 31st.

8. The couple will have a _____ ride around the park.

9. My classmate, Arty, has a major _____ in the musical drama.

10. Do you know that Spanish is the official language of _____?

Homework

Name: _____ Date: ___/___/_____ Score: _____

Lesson 1.8

Reading Words with a Silent Letter "a"

✓ Lesson Check Point

Directions: Read the target words in the word box. Write the words that have a silent letter "a" in the first column. Write the words that do not have a silent letter "a" in the second column.

Direksyons: Li mo objektif yo ki nan ti bwat mo a. Ekri mo yo ki genyen lèt "a" ki pa pwononse a nan premye kolòn nan. Ekri mo yo ki pa genyen lèt "a" ki pa pwononse a nan dezyèm kolòn nan.

Target Word Box				
heating	landing	chart	breadbox	many
assist	beautify	East	floating	oatmeal
camp	hand	coat	ready	teams
boar	flake	cars	half	sand

Letter "a" is silent

_____
_____
_____
_____
_____
_____
_____
_____

Letter "a" has a letter "a" sound

_____
_____
_____
_____
_____
_____
_____
_____

Learn to Read English With Directions In Haitian Creole

Homework

 Name: _____ Date: ___/___/_____ Score: _____

Unit Review - A/a

Reading Words with Vowel "a" Sounds: /ă/, /ā/, /ə/ & Silent

✓ **Lesson Check Point**

 Directions: Read each target word. Circle the word in the column that has the same "a" sound as the target word.

Direksyons: Li chak mo objektif. Antoure mo a ki nan kolòn nan ki bay menm son "a" a tankou mo ojektif la.

plane	a. zebras
	b. grapes

made	a. race
	b. past

stanz<u>a</u>	a. umbrella
	b. flat

mamm<u>a</u>	a. comma
	b. place

 Directions: Read each target word. Put a check (✓) under the correct column heading.

Direksyons: Li chak mo objektif. Mete yon tchèk (✓) anba antèt kolòn ki kòrèk la.

Target Words	"a" has the /ă/ sound as in the word <u>apple</u>	"a" has the /ā/ sound as in the word <u>ate</u>	"a" has the /ə/ sound as in the word <u>sofa</u>	"a" is silent as in the word <u>boat</u>
1. plane				
2. made				
3. stanz<u>a</u>				
4. mamm<u>a</u>				

Homework

 Name: _____ Date:___/___/_____ Score:_____

The Reading Challenge

Lesson 1.9

Reading Multisyllable Words

✓ **Lesson Check Point**

 Directions: Read and divide each target word into syllables. Write each word and place a hyphen (-) between the syllables in the second column. Write the number of syllables in the third column. Use a dictionary or the Internet to check your answers.

Direksyons: Li epi divize chak mo objektif an silab. Ekri chak mo epi mete yon tirè (-) ant silab yo nan dezyèm kolòn nan. Ekri kantite silab ke yo genyen an nan twazyèm kolòn nan. Itilize yon diksyonè oubyen entènèt pou tcheke repons ou yo.

Target Words	Words Divided into Syllables	Number of Syllables
1. giant	_____	_____
2. constantly	_____	_____
3. observant	_____	_____
4. pregnancy	_____	_____
5. mousetrap	_____	_____
6. eyelashes	_____	_____
7. implanted	_____	_____
8. democrat	_____	_____
9. eggplant	_____	_____
10. servant	_____	_____

Unit A
Lesson 1.9

Learn to Read English With Directions In Haitian Creole   Copyrighted Material

Homework

 Name: _____ Date: ___/___/_____ Score: _____

The Reading Challenge

Lesson 1.9

Reading Multisyllable Words

✓ **Lesson Check Point**

 Directions: Read each target word. Circle the word in the row that is divided correctly into syllables. Use a dictionary or the Internet to check your answers.

Direksyons: Li chak mo objektif. Antoure mo a ki nan ranje a ki divize an silab korèkteman yo. Itilize yon diksyonè oubyen entènèt pou tcheke repons ou yo.

Model

| important | a. im-por-tant | b. im-port-ant | c. im-porta-nt |

1. abundant	a. a-bun-dant	b. ab-un-dant	c. ab-und-ant
2. contestant	a. con-tes-tant	b. cont-es-tant	c. con-test-ant
3. advocate	a. ad-vo-cate	b. a-dvoc-ate	c. ad-voc-ate
4. dependent	a. dep-en-dent	b. de-pen-dent	c. de-pend-ent
5. elegant	a. e-leg-ant	b. el-e-gant	c. e-le-gant
6. answering	a. ans-wer-ing	b. a-nswe-ring	c. an-swer-ing
7. flamboyant	a. flam-boy-ant	b. flam-bo-yant	c. flam-boya-nt
8. ascendant	a. a-scen-dant	b. asc-en-dant	c. as-cen-dant

Unit A
Lesson 1.9

Learn to Read English With Directions In Haitian Creole

Homework

Name: _____ Date: ___/___/_____ Score: _____

Lesson 1.10

Reading and Writing

Proper and Common Nouns and Adjectives

Directions: Read the words in the word box. Put an (X) on the line next to each word that is written incorrectly. Remember that all proper nouns and proper adjectives are capitalized. Use a dictionary or the Internet to check your answers.

Direksyons: Li chak mo yo ki nan bwat mo a. Met yon (X) sou ti trè a ki bò kote mo ki pa kri byen yo. Sonje ke tout non pwòp ak adjektif pwop ekri avèk yon lèt majiskil nan kòmansman yo. Itilize yon diksyonè oubyen entènèt pou tcheke repons ou yo.

Word Box					
__	africa	__	april	__	Alarming
__	apple Inc.	__	airport	__	alabama
__	angel	__	attraction	__	American
__	Afghanistan	__	Australian	__	Above

Directions: Read each unedited sentence and underline the word that is written incorrectly. Write each sentence correctly on the line.

Direksyons: Li chak fraz ki pa edite yo epi soulinye mo ki pa ekri byen an. Ekri chak fraz korèkteman sou liy lan.

Model

Andrew has a view of the <u>atlantic</u> Ocean from his apartment.
<u>Andrew has a view of the Atlantic Ocean from his apartment.</u>

1. Anna always Asks challenging questions about Asia.

_____

2. The Author wrote a book about ants and alligators.

_____

3. Our amazing, All-star athletes are competing in Athens.

_____

4. My Aunt said, "Many animals live in the Amazon Rainforest."

_____

Homework

Name: _____   Date: ___/___/_____   Score: _____

Lesson 2.1

Reading Words with the Letter B/b

✓ Lesson Check Point

Directions: Read each target word. Find the letter "b" and put a check (✓) in the column that identifies its position: beginning, within or end.
Direksyons: Li chak mo objektif. Jwenn lèt "b" a epi mete yon tchèck (✓) nan kolòn ki idantifye pozisyon li an: nan kòmansman, ladan oubyen nan finisman.

Target Words	Beginning (First Letter)	Within	End (Last Letter)
1. tab			
2. limb			
3. bring			
4. about			
5. husband			

Directions: Read each sentence and underline the words that begin with the letter "b." Write all the underlined words in alphabetical order on the lines below.
Direksyons: Li chak fraz epi soulinye mo ki kòmanse avèk lèt "b" yo. Ekri tout mo ki soulinye yo nan lòd alfabetik sou trè sa yo ki anba.

6. Adam has a big bat.

7. Ann has a black bag.

8. Andy's boats are blue.

9. The buds have bloomed.

10. The fat bees are by the flowers.

_____   _____   _____

_____   _____   _____

_____   _____   _____

_____

Homework

 Name: _____ Date: ___/___/_____ Score: _____

Lesson 2.2

Reading Words with the "br" Letter Combination

Dictionary Skills/ Vocabulary

✓ **Lesson Check Point**

 Directions: Read each target word and its definition. Write the letter of the definition on the line of each target word. Use a dictionary or the Internet to check your answers.

Direksyons: Li chak mo objektif ak definisyon yo chak. Ekri lèt la ki koresponn ak definisyon an sou trè chak mo objektif yo. Itilize yon diksyonè oubyen entènèt pou tcheke repons ou yo.

Target Words	Definitions
1. __ brakes	a. shiny, glowing reflection of light
2. __ bright	b. baked food product that is made from wheat
3. __ brook	c. separated into pieces as a result of a strong force
4. __ broke	d. a place where water flows along a small path
5. __ bread	e. device that slows down and stops a vehicle

 Directions: Read each sentence. Underline the word in the parentheses that correctly completes each sentence. Then, write the underlined word on the line.

Direksyons: Li chak fraz. Soulinye mo a ki nan parantèz yo ki konplete chak fraz kòrèkteman. Answit, ekri mo soulinye a sou trè a.

6. Bret _____ the baseball bat. (bright, broke)

7. My bike's _____ are bad. (brakes, bright)

8. The sun at the bay is _____. (bread, bright)

9. Brian is sitting by the _____. (brook, brakes)

10. Brad always eats _____ for breakfast. (brook, bread)

Homework

 Name: _____ Date:___/___/_____ Score:_____

Lesson 2.3

Reading Words with the "bl" Letter Combination

Dictionary Skills/ Vocabulary

✓ **Lesson Check Point**

 Directions: Read each target word and its definition. Write the target word on the line in front of its meaning. Use a dictionary or the Internet to check your answers.

Direksyons: Li chak mo objektif ak definisyon yo chak. Ekri mo objektif la sou trè ki devan definisyon li an. Itilize yon diksyonè oubyen entènèt pou tcheke repons ou yo.

Target Word Box				
blames	blouse	blind	blueberry	blanket

1. _____ to assign fault
2. _____ a sweet fruit
3. _____ a long loosely fitting shirt
4. _____ a person or animal's inability to see things
5. _____ a large cloth covering used to cover a bed

 Directions: Read each sentence. Underline the word in the parentheses that correctly completes each sentence. Then, write the underlined word on the line.

Direksyons: Li chak fraz. Soulinye mo a ki nan parantèz yo ki konplete chak fraz kòrèkteman yo. Answit, ekri mo soulinye a sou trè a.

6. The _____ boys have Braille books. (blueberry, blind)

7. Bill's _____ has pictures of bats on it. (blind, blanket)

8. Beth washed her _____ with bleach. (blames, blouse)

9. Bob _____ me for eating the bananas. (blames, blanket)

10. The boys ate _____ bread at brunch. (blouse, blueberry)

Homework

 Name: _____ Date: ___/___/_____ Score: _____

Lesson 2.3

Reading Words with the "ble" Letter Combination

✓ Lesson Check Point

 Directions: Read each target word. Find the "ble" letter combination and put a check (✓) in the column that identifies its position: beginning, within or end.

Direksyons: Li chak mo objektif. Jwenn konbinezon lèt "ble" a epi mete yon tchèk (✓) nan kolòn nan ki idantifye pozisyon li an: nan kòmansman, ladan oubyen nan finisman.

Target Words	Beginning (First 3 Letters)	Within	End (Last 3 Letters)
1. blew			
2. doublet			
3. capable			
4. terrible			
5. assembled			

 Directions: Read each target word. Put a check (✓) in the "yes" column if the "ble" letter combination has the /b/ + /ə/ + /l/ sounds. Put a check (✓) in the "no" column if the "ble" letter combination does not have the /b/ + /ə/ + /l/ sounds.

Direksyons: Li chak mo objektif. Mete yon tchèk (✓) nan kolòn "yes" an si konbinezon let "ble" a bay sons /b/ + /ə/ + /l/. Mete yon tchèk (✓) nan kolòn "no" an si konbinezon let "ble" a pa bay sons /b/ + /ə/ + /l/.

Target Words	Yes	No
6. cable		
7. tablet		
8. emblem		
9. enjoyable		
10. convertible		

Homework

 Name: _____ Date: ___/___/_____ Score: _____

Lesson 2.4

Reading Words with the "mb" Letter Combination

✓ **Lesson Check Point**

 Directions: Read each target word. Circle the word in the column that has the same "mb" sound(s) as the target word.

Direksyons: Li chak mo objektif. Antoure mo a ki nan kolòn nan ki bay menm son "mb" la (yo) tankou mo ojektif la.

lamb	a. remember
	b. entomb

crumb	a. crumble
	b. catacomb

number	a. thrombus
	b. numb

bombard	a. jumbo
	b. womb

 Directions: Read each target word. In the second column, write the number of letters in the word. In the third column, write the number of letters heard in the word.

Direksyons: Li chak mo objektif. Nan dezyèm kolòn nan, ekri kantite lèt ki nan mo a. Nan twazyèm kolòn nan, ekri kantite lèt ou tande nan mo a.

Target Words	Number of letters in the word	Number of letters heard
1. lamb		
2. crumb		
3. number		
4. bombard		

Homework

Name: _____ Date: ___/___/_____ Score: _____

Lesson 2.4

Reading Words with the "bt" Letter Combination

✓ Lesson Check Point

Directions: Read each target word. Circle the word in the column that has the same "bt" sound(s) as the target word.

Direksyons: Li chak mo objektif. Antoure mo a ki nan kolòn nan ki bay menm son "bt" la (yo) tankou mo ojektif la.

debt	a. obtuse
	b. subtle

debtors	a. doubting
	b. subtract

subtract	a. obtrude
	b. subtleness

subtropics	a. doubt
	b. obtain

Directions: Read each target word. In the second column, write the number of letters in the word. In the third column, write the number of letters heard in the word.

Direksyons: Li chak mo objektif. Nan dezyèm kolòn nan, ekri kantite lèt ki nan mo a. Nan twazyèm kolòn na, ekri kantite lèt ou tande nan mo a.

Target Words	Number of letters in the word	Number of letters heard
1. debt		
2. debtors		
3. subtract		
4. subtropics		

Homework

 Name: _____ Date: ___/___/_____ Score: _____

Lesson 2.5

Reading Words with a Silent "b"

✓ Lesson Check Point

 Directions: Read the target words in the word box. Write the words that have a silent letter "b" in the first column. Write the words that do not have a silent letter "b" in the second column.

Direksyons: Li mo objektif yo ki nan ti bwat mo a. Ekri mo yo ki genyen lèt "b" ki pa pwononse a nan premye kolòn nan. Ekri mo yo ki pa genyen lèt "b" ki pa pwononse a nan dezyèm kolòn nan.

Target Word Box				
crumbs	indebted	behave	laboratory	combing
doubt	rebate	plumbing	burger	quibble
basket	beagle	lamb	subtlety	bonding
public	climbers	balance	thumb	beaver

Letter "b" is silent

_____
_____
_____
_____
_____
_____
_____
_____

Letter "b" has the /b/ sound

_____
_____
_____
_____
_____
_____
_____
_____

Unit B
Lesson 2.5

Learn to Read English With Directions In Haitian Creole   Copyrighted Material

Homework

 Name: _____ Date: ___/___/_____ Score: _____

The Reading Challenge

Lesson 2.6

Reading Multisyllable Words

✓ Lesson Check Point

Directions: Read and divide each target word into syllables. Write each word and place a hyphen (-) between the syllables in the second column. Write the number of syllables in the third column. Use a dictionary or the Internet to check your answers.

Direksyons: Li epi divize chak mo objektif an silab. Ekri chak mo epi mete yon tirè (-) ant silab yo nan dezyèm kolòn nan. Ekri kantite silab ke yo genyen an nan twazyèm kolòn nan. Itilize yon diksyonè oubyen entènèt pou tcheke repons ou yo.

Target Words	Words Divided into Syllables	Number of Syllables
1. absent	_____	_____
2. submit	_____	_____
3. table	_____	_____
4. tablet	_____	_____
5. absolutely	_____	_____
6. somebody	_____	_____
7. habitat	_____	_____
8. fabulous	_____	_____
9. observing	_____	_____
10. subtracting	_____	_____

Homework

 Name: _____ Date:___/___/_____ Score: _____

The Reading Challenge

Lesson 2.6

Reading Multisyllable Words

✓ **Lesson Check Point**

 Directions: Read each target word. Circle the word in the row that is divided correctly into syllables. Use a dictionary or the Internet to check your answers.

Direksyons: Li chak mo objektif. Antoure mo a ki nan ranje a ki divize an silab korèkteman yo. Itilize yon diksyonè oubyen entènèt pou tcheke repons ou yo.

Model

| because | a. be-cause (circled) | b. beca-use | c. b-ecause |

1. barbecue	a. bar-b-ecue	b. bar-becue	c. bar-be-cue
2. brainstorm	a. brain-storm	b. brai-nst-orm	c. br-ain-storm
3. belated	a. belat-ed	b. be-lat-ed	c. b-ela-ted
4. barber	a. barb-er	b. bar-ber	c. ba-rber
5. biweekly	a. bi-wee-kly	b. biw-eek-ly	c. bi-week-ly
6. bathroom	a. bath-room	b. ba-throom	c. bathr-oom
7. beagle	a. beag-le	b. bea-gle	c. be-agle
8. background	a. back-ground	b. backgr-ound	c. ba-ckground

Learn to Read English With Directions In Haitian Creole

Homework

Name: _____ Date: ___/___/_____ Score: _____

Lesson 2.7

Reading and Writing

Proper and Common Nouns and Adjectives

Directions: Read the words in the word box. Put an (X) on the line next to each word that is written incorrectly. Remember that all proper nouns and proper adjectives are capitalized. Use a dictionary or the Internet to check your answers.

Direksyons: Li chak mo yo ki nan bwat mo a. Met yon (X) sou ti trè a ki bò kote mo ki pa kri byen yo. Sonje ke tout non pwòp ak adjektif pwop ekri avèk yon lèt majiskil nan kòmansman yo. Itilize yon diksyonè oubyen entènèt pou tcheke repons ou yo.

Word Box		
__ Bronx	__ brazilian	__ British
__ bathtaB	__ biology	__ bulgaria
__ bangladesh	__ Bonanza	__ botswana
__ bittersweet	__ Brother Bob	__ Bonaparte

Directions: Read each unedited sentence and underline the word that is written incorrectly. Write each sentence correctly on the line.

Direksyons: Li chak fraz ki pa edite yo epi soulinye mo ki pa ekri byen an. Ekri chak fraz korèkteman sou liy lan.

Model
<u>brandon's</u> books are about big boats.
Brandon's books are about big boats.

1. Bess and Beth are at the Beach.

   _____

2. The Boy's bike is blue and brown.

   _____

3. bugs and birds are flying by the bay.

   _____

4. baby Ben has a big bear and a black boat.

   _____

Homework

Name: _____ Date: ___/___/_____ Score: _____

Lesson 3.1

Reading Words with the Letter C/c

✓ Lesson Check Point

Directions: Read each target word. Find the letter "c" and put a check (✓) in the column that identifies its position: beginning, within or end.
Direksyons: Li chak mo objektif. Jwenn lèt "c" a epi mete yon tchèck (✓) nan kolòn ki idantifye pozisyon li an: nan kòmansman, ladan oubyen nan finisman.

Target Words	Beginning (First Letter)	Within	End (Last Letter)
1. zinc			
2. carrot			
3. fabric			
4. impacted			
5. protractor			

Directions: Read each sentence and underline the words that begin with the letter "c." Write all the underlined words in alphabetical order on the lines below.
Direksyons: Li chak fraz epi soulinye mo ki kòmanse avèk lèt "c" yo. Ekri tout mo ki soulinye yo nan lòd alfabetik sou trè sa yo ki anba.

6. The clock is on a big chain.

7. Andrew is counting the cats.

8. Bobby will climb up the cliff.

9. All the coins add up to ten cents.

10. Al said, "The chair is by my baby's crib."

_____   _____   _____

_____   _____   _____

_____   _____

_____

Homework

Name: _____ Date: ___/___/_____ Score: _____

Lesson 3.1

Reading Words with the Hard Letter "c"

✓ Lesson Check Point

Directions: Read each target word. Put a check (✓) under the correct column heading.

Direksyons: Li chak mo objektif. Mete yon tchèk (✓) anba antèt kolòn ki kòrèk la.

Target Words	Hard "c" has the /k/ sound as in the word cat	Soft "c" has the /s/ sound as in the word cell
1. cavity		
2. central		
3. century		
4. camping		
5. covering		

Directions: Read each sentence and underline the words that have the hard "c" sound, as in the word cat. Write all the underlined words in alphabetical order on the lines below.

Direksyons: Li chak fraz epi souliye mo ki gen son "c" difisil, tankou nan mo cat la. Ekri tout mo ki soulinye yo nan lòd alfabetik sou trè sa yo ki anba.

6. Cindy likes to eat cake and candy.

7. Cyril is the coolest kid in his class.

8. The climbers did not see the icy cliff.

9. The experienced chemists can study animal cells.

10. My college campus has four large buildings in the city.

_____ _____ _____

_____ _____ _____

_____ _____ _____

_____

Homework

Name: _____ Date: ___/___/_____ Score: _____

Lesson 3.2

Reading Words with the Soft Letter "c"

✓ Lesson Check Point

Directions: Read each target word. Put a check (✓) under the correct column heading.

Direksyons: Li chak mo objektif. Mete yon tchèk (✓) anba antèt kolòn ki kòrèk la.

Target Words	Hard "c" has the /k/ sound as in the word cat	Soft "c" has the /s/ sound as in the word cell
1. cub		
2. cab		
3. city		
4. grace		
5. recite		

Directions: Read each sentence and underline the words that have the soft "c" sound, as in the word cell. Write all the underlined words in alphabetical order on the lines below.

Direksyons: Li chak fraz epi soulinye mo ki bay son dous "c" yo, tankou li ye nan mo cell la. Ekri tout mo ki soulinye yo nan lòd alfabetik sou trè sa yo ki anba.

6. A cyclone is a strong wind that moves in a circle.

7. We will celebrate Cindy's birthday in the country.

8. While in the city, I ate cranberry and cinnamon candy.

9. The ceramic dishes and cereal bowls are in the cabinets.

10. We can repair the ceilings in the Central Street apartments.

_____   _____   _____

_____   _____   _____

_____   _____   _____

_____

Unit C
Lesson 3.2

Homework

Name: _____ **Date:** ___/___/_____ **Score:** _____

Review Lessons 3.1 & 3.2

Reading Hard Letter "c" and Soft Letter "c" Words

Directions: Read the target words in the word box. In the first column, write the words with the letter "c" that have the /k/ sound, as in the word <u>cat</u>. In the second column, write the words with the letter "c" that have the /s/ sound, as in the word <u>cell</u>.

Direksyons: Li mo objektif yo ki nan bwat mo a. Nan premye kolòn nan, ekri mo yo ki genyen lèt "c" ki bay son /k/ yo, tankou li ye nan mo <u>cat</u>. Nan dezyèm kolòn nan, ekri mo yo ki genyen lèt "c" ki bay son /s/ yo, tankou li ye nan mo <u>cell</u>.

Target Word Box				
cyst	car	cold	fence	icy
cider	places	candy	lacy	color
can	curl	come	cute	Tracy
face	cents	curb	cinch	camel

Hard letter "c" has the /k/ sound as in the word <u>cat</u>

Soft letter "c" has the /s/ sound as in the word <u>cell</u>

Homework

 Name: _____ Date:___/___/_____ Score: _____

Lesson 3.3

Reading Words with the "cr" Letter Combination

Dictionary Skills/ Vocabulary

✓ Lesson Check Point

 Directions: Read each target word and its definition. Write the letter of the definition on the line of each target word. Use a dictionary or the Internet to check your answers.

Direksyons: Li chak mo objektif ak definisyon yo chak. Ekri lèt la ki koresponn ak definisyon an sou trè chak mo objektif yo. Itilize yon diksyonè oubyen entènèt pou tcheke repons ou yo.

Target Words	Definitions
1. __ crabs	a. to have collided violently with another vehicle
2. __ crashed	b. shelled animals that live by and in water
3. __ creek	c. brittle texture of something that is easily broken
4. __ crispy	d. to have walked from one side to the other side
5. __ crossed	e. a stream of water that is smaller than a river

 Directions: Read each sentence. Underline the word in the parentheses that correctly completes each sentence. Then, write the underlined word on the line.

Direksyons: Li chak fraz. Soulinye mo a ki nan parantèz yo ki konplete chak fraz kòrèkteman. Answit, ekri mo soulinye a sou trè a.

6. The children _____ the street. (crossed, creek)

7. My mommy's cookies are _____. (crispy, crashed)

8. Cindy and Chad had a picnic by the _____. (crispy, creek)

9. The big _____ live in a cold water creek. (crossed, crabs)

10. In the city, the cars _____ into one another. (crashed, crabs)

Homework

Name: _____ Date: ___/___/_____ Score: _____

Lesson 3.4

Reading Words with the "cl" Letter Combination

Dictionary Skills/ Vocabulary

✓ **Lesson Check Point**

Directions: Read each target word and its definition. Write the target word on the line in front of its meaning. Use a dictionary or the Internet to check your answers.

Direksyons: Li chak mo objektif ak definisyon yo chak. Ekri mo objektif la sou trè ki devan definisyon li an. Itilize yon diksyonè oubyen entènèt pou tcheke repons ou yo.

Target Word Box				
clapped	cleans	clock	close	clothes

1. _____ a near position
2. _____ a device used to indicate and display time
3. _____ to have hit the palms of one's hands together
4. _____ the process of removing dirt off of something
5. _____ garments used to cover and adorn a person's body

Directions: Read each sentence. Underline the word in the parentheses that correctly completes each sentence. Then, write the underlined word on the line.

Direksyons: Li chak fraz. Soulinye mo a ki nan parantèz yo ki konplete chak fraz kòrèkteman. Answit, ekri mo soulinye a sou trè a.

6. Cecil _____ the cabinets with bleach. (clock, cleans)

7. Cindy hangs her _____ in the closet. (clothes, close)

8. The audience _____ for the choir. (clapped, clothes)

9. Chad lives _____ to the country's capital. (cleans, close)

10. The _____ in the cabin tells the correct time. (clock, clapped)

Homework

 Name: _____ Date: ___/___/_____ Score: _____

Lesson 3.4

Reading Words with the "cle" Letter Combination

✓ **Lesson Check Point**

Directions: Read each target word. Find the "cle" letter combination and put a check (✓) in the column that identifies its position: beginning, within or end.

Direksyons: Li chak mo objektif. Jwenn konbinezon lèt "cle" a epi mete yon tchèk (✓) nan kolòn nan ki idantifye pozisyon li an: nan kòmansman, ladan oubyen nan finisman.

Target Words	Beginning (First 3 Letters)	Within	End (Last 3 Letters)
1. clerk			
2. cleave			
3. vehicle			
4. bicycle			
5. inclemently			

Directions: Read each target word. Put a check (✓) in the "yes" column if the "cle" letter combination has the /k/ + /ə/ + /l/ sounds. Put a check (✓) in the "no" column if the "cle" letter combination does not have the /k/ + /ə/ + /l/ sounds.

Direksyons: Li chak mo objektif. Mete yon tchèk (✓) nan kolòn "yes" an si konbinezon let "cle" a bay sons /k/ + /ə/ + /l/. Mete yon tchèk (✓) nan kolòn "no" an si konbinezon let "cle" a pa bay sons /k/ + /ə/ + /l/.

Target Words	Yes	No
6. clerk		
7. cleave		
8. vehicle		
9. bicycle		
10. inclemently		

Homework

 Name: _____ Date: ___ / ___ / _____ Score: _____

Lesson 3.5

Reading Words with the "ct" Letter Combination

✓ Lesson Check Point

 Directions: Read each target word. Circle the word in the column that has the same "ct" sound(s) as the target word.
Direksyons: Li chak mo objektif. Antoure mo a ki nan kolòn nan ki bay menm son "ct" la (yo) tankou mo objektif la.

affect	a. actual
	b. factor

product	a. abduction
	b. compact

practicing	a. acting
	b. induction

Connecticut	a. indict
	b. section

 Directions: Read each target word. Put a check (✓) under the correct column heading.
Direksyons: Li chak mo objektif. Mete yon tchèk (✓) anba antèt kolòn ki kòrèk la.

Target Words	"ct" has the /k/ + /t/ sounds as in the word <u>fact</u>	"ct" has the silent "c" + /t/ sound as in the word <u>indict</u>
1. affect		
2. product		
3. practicing		
4. Connecticut		

Homework

 Name: _____ Date: ___/___/_____ Score: _____

Lesson 3.6

Reading Soft Letter "c" Words

Directions: Read each target word. Circle the word in the column that has the same "cean," "cian," "cial," "cious" or "cient" sound as the target word.

Direksyons: Li chak mo objektif. Antoure mo a ki nan kolòn nan ki bay menm son "cean," "cian," "cial," "cious" oubyen "cient" yo tankou mo objektif la.

| crucial | a. practical |
| | b. commercial |

| capricious | a. physician |
| | b. delicious |

| proficient | a. optician |
| | b. ancient |

| crustacean | a. clinician |
| | b. facial |

 Directions: Read each target word. Put a check (✓) in the column that identifies the same "cean," "cian," "cial," "cious" or "cient" sound within the target word.

Direksyons: Li chak mo objektif. Mete yon tchèk (✓) nan kolòn nan ki idantifye menm son "cean," "cian," "cial," "cious" oubyen "cient" yo nan mo objektif la.

Target Words	"cean" has the /sh/+/ə/+/n/ sounds as in the word <u>ocean</u>	"cial" has the /sh/+/ə/+/l/ sounds as in the word <u>special</u>	"cious" has the /sh/+/ə/+/s/ sounds as in the word <u>delicious</u>	"cient" has the /sh/+/ə/+/n/+/t/ sounds as in the word <u>ancient</u>
1. crucial				
2. capricious				
3. proficient				
4. crustacean				

Homework

Name: _____ Date: ___/___/_____ Score: _____

Lesson 3.6

Reading Soft Letter "c" Words

Directions: Read the target words in the word box. In the first column, write the words with the letter "c" that have the /s/ sound, as in the word <u>cell</u>. In the second column, write the words with the letter "c" that have the /sh/ sound, as in the word <u>ocean</u>.

Direksyons: Li mo objektif yo ki nan bwat la. Nan premye kolòn nan, ekri mo yo ki avèk lèt "c" ki bay son /s/ yo, tankou li ye nan mo <u>cell</u>. Nan dezyèm kolòn nan, ekri mo ki avèk lèt "c" ki bay son /sh/ yo, tankou li ye nan mo <u>ocean</u>.

Target Word Box				
politician	fancy	deficient	musician	cider
ferocious	special	fence	nice	social
bicycle	excited	spicy	facial	cents
crustacean	circle	sufficient	city	magician

Soft Letter "c" has the /s/ sound as in the word <u>cell</u>

Soft Letter "c" has the /sh/ sound as in the word <u>ocean</u>

Homework

Name: _____ Date: ___/___/_____ Score: _____

Lesson 3.7

Reading Words with the "ch" Letter Combination

✓ Lesson Check Point

Directions: Read each target word. Circle the word in the column that has the same "ch" sound as the target word.

Direksyons: Li chak mo objektif. Antoure mo a ki nan kolòn nan ki bay menm son "ch" a tankou mo objektif la.

teach	a. speech
	b. chronic

character	a. choir
	b. ache

fuchsia	a. school
	b. yacht

chauffeur	a. chaos
	b. chef

Directions: Read each target word. Put a check (✓) under the correct column heading.

Direksyons: Li chak mo objektif. Mete yon tchèk (✓) anba antèt kolòn ki kòrèk la.

Target Words	"ch" has the /ch/ sound as in the word chain	"ch" has the /sh/ sound as in the word chef	"ch" has the /k/ sound as in the word chaos	"ch" is silent as in the word yacht
1. teach				
2. character				
3. fuchsia				
4. chauffeur				

Homework

Name: _____ Date: ___/___/_____ Score: _____

Lesson 3.8

Reading Words with the "cc" Letter Combination

✓ Lesson Check Point

Directions: Read each target word. Circle the word in the column that has the same "cc" sound(s) as the target word.

Direksyons: Li chak mo objektif. Antoure mo a ki nan kolòn nan ki bay menm son "cc" la (yo) tankou mo objektif la.

succinct	a. occupy
	b. accept

success	a. access
	b. accomplish

acclaim	a. accord
	b. accident

account	a. broccoli
	b. accent

Directions: Read each target word. Put a check (✓) under the correct column heading.

Direksyons: Li chak mo objektif. Mete yon tchèk (✓) anba antèt kolòn ki kòrèk la.

Target Words	"cc" has the /k/ sound as in the word <u>soccer</u>	"cc" has the /k/ + /s/ sounds as in the word <u>accept</u>
1. succinct		
2. success		
3. acclaim		
4. account		

Homework

 Name: _____ Date: ___/___/_____ Score: _____

Lesson 3.9

Reading Words with a Silent Letter "c"

✓ Lesson Check Point

 Directions: Read the target words in the word box. Write the words that have a silent letter "c" in the first column. Write the words that do not have a silent letter "c" in the second column.

Direksyons: Li mo objektif yo ki nan ti bwat mo a. Ekri mo yo ki genyen lèt "c" ki pa pwononse a nan premye kolòn nan. Ekri mo yo ki pa genyen lèt "c" ki pa pwononse a nan dezyèm kolòn nan.

Target Word Box				
corner	scuba	scent	cycle	score
essence	domestic	clocks	collar	acquit
abscess	descend	fascinate	ascent	scene
adolescent	escalator	disciple	recruit	fuchsia

Letter "c" is silent   **Letter "c" has the /k/, /s/ or /sh/ sound**

Learn to Read English With Directions In Haitian Creole

Homework

Name: _____   Date: ___/___/_____   Score: _____

The Reading Challenge

Lesson 3.10

Reading Multisyllable Words

✓ **Lesson Check Point**

Directions: Read and divide each target word into syllables. Write each word and place a hyphen (-) between the syllables in the second column. Write the number of syllables in the third column. Use a dictionary or the Internet to check your answers.

Direksyons: Li epi divize chak mo objektif an silab. Ekri chak mo epi mete yon tirè (-) ant silab yo nan dezyèm kolòn nan. Ekri kantite silab ke yo genyen an nan twazyèm kolòn nan. Itilize yon diksyonè oubyen entènèt pou tcheke repons ou yo.

Target Words	Words Divided into Syllables	Number of Syllables
1. cardinal	_____	_____
2. chamber	_____	_____
3. cockroach	_____	_____
4. cauliflower	_____	_____
5. cylinder	_____	_____
6. conjunction	_____	_____
7. casual	_____	_____
8. complexion	_____	_____
9. category	_____	_____
10. California	_____	_____

Unit C Lesson 3.10

Learn to Read English With Directions In Haitian Creole

Homework

Name: _____ Date: ___/___/_____ Score: _____

The Reading Challenge

Lesson 3.10

Reading Multisyllable Words

✓ **Lesson Check Point**

Directions: Read each target word. Circle the word in the row that is divided correctly into syllables. Use a dictionary or the Internet to check your answers.

Direksyons: Li chak mo objektif. Antoure mo a ki nan ranje a ki divize an silab korèkteman yo. Itilize yon diksyonè oubyen entènèt pou tcheke repons ou yo.

Model

| calculus | a. calcu-lus | b. cal-cu-lus (circled) | c. cal-culus |

1. clinical	a. clin-i-cal	b. clini-cal	c. clin-ic-al
2. cockatoo	a. co-ck-atoo	b. cock-a-too	c. cocka-too
3. coconut	a. coco-nut	b. co-conut	c. co-co-nut
4. clerical	a. cler-i-cal	b. cleri-cal	c. cle-ri-cal
5. citizen	a. cit-izen	b. cit-i-zen	c. ci-tiz-en
6. condition	a. con-di-tion	b. cond-i-tion	c. co-ndi-tion
7. congruent	a. co-ngru-ent	b. con-gru-ent	c. con-g-ruent
8. constitute	a. cons-tit-ute	b. const-i-tute	c. con-sti-tute

Unit C Lesson 3.10

Learn to Read English With Directions In Haitian Creole

Homework

Name: _____ Date: ___/___/_____ Score: _____

Lesson 3.11

Reading and Writing

Proper and Common Nouns and Adjectives

Directions: Read the words in the word box. Put an (X) on the line next to each word that is written incorrectly. Remember that all proper nouns and proper adjectives are capitalized. Use a dictionary or the Internet to check your answers.

Direksyons: Li chak mo yo ki nan bwat mo a. Met yon (X) sou ti trè a ki bò kote mo ki pa kri byen yo. Sonje ke tout non pwòp ak adjektif pwop ekri avèk yon lèt majiskil nan kòmansman yo. Itilize yon diksyonè oubyen entènèt pou tcheke repons ou yo.

Word Box		
___ City	___ closet	___ Curtain
___ capital	___ CriCket	___ Cutting
___ Columbus	___ canyon	___ Costa Rica
___ Cousin Charles	___ cherokee	___ carson city

Directions: Read each unedited sentence and underline the word that is written incorrectly. Write each sentence correctly on the line.

Direksyons: Li chak fraz ki pa edite yo epi soulinye mo ki pa ekri byen an. Ekri chak fraz korèkteman sou liy lan.

Model
The <u>Camp</u> in Cleveland is closed.
<u>The camp in Cleveland is closed.</u>

1. chad is carrying his bag of rice.

   _____

2. The climate in central America is not cold.

   _____

3. The Coffee and cocoa in our cups are cold.

   _____

4. Charles and Cecil are Characters in my cool book.

   _____

Homework

Name: _____ Date: ___/___/_____ Score: _____

Lesson 4.1

Reading Words with the Letter D/d

✓ Lesson Check Point

Directions: Read each target word. Find the letter "d" and put a check (✓) in the column that identifies its position: beginning, within or end.
Direksyons: Li chak mo objektif. Jwenn lèt "d" a epi mete yon tchèck (✓) nan kolòn ki idantifye pozisyon li an: nan kòmansman, ladan oubyen nan finisman.

Target Words	Beginning (First Letter)	Within	End (Last Letter)
1. hold			
2. dollar			
3. holiday			
4. darling			
5. kingdom			

Directions: Read each sentence and underline the words that begin with the letter "d." Write all the underlined words in alphabetical order on the lines below.
Direksyons: Li chak fraz epi soulinye mo ki kòmanse avèk lèt "d" yo. Ekri tout mo ki soulinye yo nan lòd alfabetik sou trè sa yo ki anba.

6. My daughter is an excellent doctor.

7. Fred ate deep-fried chicken for dinner.

8. The detective drives his blue car to the city.

9. My mom drove directly to the college campus.

10. I asked about the dangers of the hot desert sun.

_____   _____   _____
_____   _____   _____
_____   _____   _____
              _____

Learn to Read English With Directions In Haitian Creole

Homework

Name: _____ Date: ___/___/_____ Score: _____

Lesson 4.2

Reading Letter "d" Words with the /d/ Sound & /j/ Sound

✓ Lesson Check Point

Directions: Read each target word. Circle the word in the column that has the same "d" sound as the target word.

Direksyons: Li chak mo objektif. Antoure mo a ki nan kolòn nan ki bay menm son "d" a tankou mo objektif la.

cordial	a. schedule
	b. dental

indirect	a. education
	b. model

advance	a. doctor
	b. nodule

glandular	a. bedrock
	b. educated

Directions: Read each target word. Put a check (✓) under the correct column heading.

Direksyons: Li chak mo objektif. Mete yon tchèk (✓) anba antèt kolòn ki kòrèk la.

Target Words	"d" has the /d/ sound as in the word <u>doctor</u>	"d" has the /j/ sound as in the word <u>educate</u>
1. cordial		
2. indirect		
3. advance		
4. glandular		

Homework

 Name: _____ Date:___/___/_____ Score:_____

Lesson 4.2

Reading Words with the "dr" Letter Combination

Dictionary Skills/ Vocabulary

✓ Lesson Check Point

 Directions: Read each target word and its definition. Write the letter of the definition on the line of each target word. Use a dictionary or the Internet to check your answers.

Direksyons: Li chak mo objektif ak definisyon yo chak. Ekri lèt la ki koresponn ak definisyon an sou trè chak mo objektif yo. Itilize yon diksyonè oubyen entènèt pou tcheke repons ou yo.

Target Words	Definitions
1. __ dress up	a. a musical instrument
2. __ drive	b. to operate a car, train or bus
3. __ drum	c. pictures made with an artist's tool
4. __ dramatic	d. to wear fancy clothes for a special event
5. __ drawings	e. the act of showing feelings during a performance

 Directions: Read each sentence. Underline the word in the parentheses that correctly completes each sentence. Then, write the underlined word on the line.

Direksyons: Li chak fraz. Soulinye mo a ki nan parantèz yo ki konplete chak fraz kòrèkteman. Answit, ekri mo soulinye a sou trè a.

6. We will _____ out of the driveway. (dress up, drive)

7. Danny's _____ were skillfully done. (drive, drawings)

8. David played the _____ at the concert. (drum, dramatic)

9. At the show, Diana did a _____ dance. (dramatic, drive)

10. Everyone in my class will _____ for the dance. (dress up, drawings)

Homework

 Name: _____ Date:___/___/_____ Score:_____

Lesson 4.3

Reading Words with the "ed" Suffix/ Past Tense Verbs

✓ Lesson Check Point

 Directions: Read each target word. Circle the word in the column that has the same "ed" sound(s) as the target word.

Direksyons: Li chak mo objektif. Antoure mo a ki nan kolòn nan ki bay menm son "ed" a tankou mo objektif la.

| fixed | a. framed |
| | b. ripped |

| saved | a. cooked |
| | b. tamed |

| started | a. plotted |
| | b. produced |

| stopped | a. rested |
| | b. licked |

 Directions: Read each target word. Put a check (✓) under the correct column heading.

Direksyons: Li chak mo objektif. Mete yon tchèk (✓) anba antèt kolòn ki kòrèk la.

Target Words	"ed" has the /ĭ/ + /d/ sounds as in the word <u>rested</u>	"ed" has the /d/ sound as in the word <u>hugged</u>	"ed" has the /t/ sound as in the word <u>tipped</u>
1. fixed			
2. saved			
3. started			
4. stopped			

Homework

Name: _____   Date: ___/___/_____   Score: _____

Lesson 4.4

Reading Words with a Silent Letter "d"

✓ Lesson Check Point

Directions: Read the target words in the word box. Write the words that have a silent letter "d" in the first column. Write the words that do not have a silent letter "d" in the second column.

Direksyons: Li mo objektif yo ki nan ti bwat mo a. Ekri mo yo ki genyen yon lèt "d" ki pa pwononse a nan premye kolòn nan. Ekri mo yo ki pa genyen yon lèt "d" ki pa pwononse a nan dezyèm kolòn nan.

Target Word Box				
sedge	candy	saddle	fridge	fade
dollar	deck	radiant	radish	drink
bridge	denim	adjective	doctor	nudge
cartridge	pendant	knowledge	Windsor	Wednesday

Letter "d" is silent   **Letter "d" has the /d/ sound**

Unit D
Lesson 4.4

Learn to Read English With Directions In Haitian Creole   47   Copyrighted Material

Homework

Name: _____ Date:___/___/_____ Score:_____

The Reading Challenge

Lesson 4.5

Reading Multisyllable Words

✓ Lesson Check Point

Directions: Read and divide each target word into syllables. Write each word and place a hyphen (-) between the syllables in the second column. Write the number of syllables in the third column. Use a dictionary or the Internet to check your answers.

Direksyons: Li epi divize chak mo objektif an silab. Ekri chak mo epi mete yon tirè (-) ant silab yo nan dezyèm kolòn nan. Ekri kantite silab ke yo genyen an nan twazyèm kolòn nan. Itilize yon diksyonè oubyen entènèt pou tcheke repons ou yo.

Target Words	Words Divided into Syllables	Number of Syllables
1. dentistry	_____	_____
2. dialect	_____	_____
3. development	_____	_____
4. disembark	_____	_____
5. denominate	_____	_____
6. department	_____	_____
7. description	_____	_____
8. demanding	_____	_____
9. designer	_____	_____
10. dependent	_____	_____

Homework

 Name: _____ Date: ___/___/_____ Score: _____

The Reading Challenge

Lesson 4.5

Reading Multisyllable Words

✓ Lesson Check Point

 Directions: Read each target word. Circle the word in the row that is divided correctly into syllables. Use a dictionary or the Internet to check your answers.

Direksyons: Li chak mo objektif. Antoure mo a ki nan ranje a ki divize an silab korèkteman yo. Itilize yon diksyonè oubyen entènèt pou tcheke repons ou yo.

Model

dictionary	a. di-ction-ary	b. dic-tion-ar-y (circled)	c. dic-tiona-ry

1. deception	a. dec-ep-tion	b. de-cep-tion	c. de-ce-ption

2. database	a. da-ta-base	b. dat-a-base	c. da-tab-ase

3. delinquent	a. del-in-quent	b. de-lin-quent	c. delin-qu-ent

4. disengage	a. dis-en-gage	b. di-sen-gage	c. dis-eng-age

5. drapery	a. dra-pe-ry	b. drap-er-y	c. drape-r-y

6. decided	a. de-cide-d	b. de-ci-ded	c. de-cid-ed

7. duplicate	a. du-pli-cate	b. dup-li-cate	c. du-plic-ate

8. diagnosis	a. dia-gno-sis	b. di-ag-no-sis	c. diagn-o-sis

Unit D
Lesson 4.5

Homework

Name: _____ Date: ___/___/_____ Score: _____

Lesson 4.6

Reading and Writing

Proper and Common Nouns and Adjectives

Directions: Read the words in the word box. Put an (X) on the line next to each word that is written incorrectly. Remember that all proper nouns and proper adjectives are capitalized. Use a dictionary or the Internet to check your answers.

Direksyons: Li chak mo yo ki nan bwat mo a. Met yon (X) sou ti trè a ki bò kote mo ki pa kri byen yo. Sonje ke tout non pwòp ak adjektif pwop ekri avèk yon lèt majiskil nan kòmansman yo. Itilize yon diksyonè oubyen entènèt pou tcheke repons ou yo.

Word Box		
__ dr.	__ Dove	__ Desk
__ dutch	__ Delhi	__ driver
__ Detroit	__ Dominica	__ distant
__ Dessert	__ december	__ Damascus

Directions: Read each unedited sentence and underline the word that is written incorrectly. Write each sentence correctly on the line.

Direksyons: Li chak fraz ki pa edite yo epi soulinye mo ki pa ekri byen an. Ekri chak fraz korèkteman sou liy lan.

Model
Dan said, "My daughter's name is <u>donna</u>."
<u>Dan said, "My daughter's name is Donna."</u>

1. After dinner, I ate dad's donuts.

_____

2. dina designed a cute denim dress.

_____

3. Daniel dug a Ditch by the bushes.

_____

4. detroit Diner has delicious dishes.

_____

Homework

 Name: _____ Date:___/___/_____ Score:_____

Lesson 5.1

Reading Words with the Letter E/e

✓ Lesson Check Point

 Directions: Read each target word. Find the letter "e" and put a check (✓) in the column that identifies its position: beginning, within or end.
Direksyons: Li chak mo objektif. Jwenn lèt "e" a epi mete yon tchèck (✓) nan kolòn ki idantifye pozisyon li an: nan kòmansman, ladan oubyen nan finisman.

Target Words	Beginning (First Letter)	Within	End (Last Letter)
1. east			
2. alive			
3. exact			
4. heater			
5. annex			

 Directions: Read each target word. Read the words in the row and circle the word that has a different vowel "e" sound.
Direksyons: Li chak mo objektif. Li mo yo ki nan ranje a epi antoure mo a ki bay yon son vwayèl "e" ki diferan an.

Target Words				
6. help	tend	he	sell	rent
7. check	bell	rest	cent	she
8. shell	west	clef	me	step
9. bless	be	get	red	sent
10. French	self	the	dent	desk

Learn to Read English With Directions In Haitian Creole

Homework

 Name: _____ Date: ___/___/_____ Score: _____

Lesson 5.2

Reading Words with the Short Vowel "e" Sound

✓ **Lesson Check Point**

 Directions: Read the words in the four boxes. Circle two words with the short vowel /ĕ/ sound. The anchor word for the short vowel /ĕ/ sound is <u>egg</u>.

Direksyons: Li mo yo ki nan kat ti bwat yo. Antoure de mo ki genyen son vwayèl kout /ĕ/ a. Mo referans pou son vwayel kout /ĕ/a se mo, <u>egg</u>.

were	send		great	dean		please	bred
dwell	scheme		peg	belt		we	spend

blend	sea		bet	these		spell	Ted
rend	she		take	den		leaf	be

 Directions: Read the words in the four boxes. Circle two words that rhyme. Rhyming words have the same ending sound, such as <u>set</u> and <u>wet</u>.

Direksyons: Li mo yo ki nan kat ti bwat yo. Antoure de mo ki rime. De mo oubyen plizyè mo ki rime genyen menm son nan finisman yo, tankou <u>set</u> ak <u>wet</u>.

Ben	leap		lead	they		nest	heat
her	ten		wreck	peck		west	break

meal	sell		tend	send		smell	melt
tell	where		these	bent		bend	felt

Homework

Name: _____ Date: ___/___/_____ Score: _____

Lesson 5.2

Reading & Writing Words with the Short Vowel "e" Sound

✓ **Lesson Check Point**

Directions: Read each sentence and underline three words with the short vowel /ĕ/ sound. Then, write the underlined words on the lines below. The anchor word for the short vowel /ĕ/ sound is egg.

Direksyons: Li chak fraz epi soulinye twa mo ki genyen son vwayèl kout /ĕ/ a. Answit, ekri mo soulinye yo sou trè sa yo ki anba. Mo referans pou son vwayèl kout /ĕ/ a se mo, egg.

Model

She placed her legs on the wet deck.

    legs   wet   deck

    _____   _____   _____

1. At the campsite, he fell into the deep red well.

    _____   _____   _____

2. Do you know whether Beth ironed her blue dress?

    _____   _____   _____

3. At Mr. Eastman's house, the pets made a mess in the den.

    _____   _____   _____

4. On Tuesday, the men slept in the green and orange tents.

    _____   _____   _____

5. In December, I saw Lewis with ten extremely large emblems.

    _____   _____   _____

Homework

 Name: _____ Date: ___/___/_____ Score: _____

Lesson 5.3

Reading Words with the Long Vowel "e" Sound

✓ Lesson Check Point

 Directions: Read the words in the four boxes. Circle two words with the long vowel /ē/ sound. The anchor word for the long vowel /ē/ sound is <u>me</u>.

Direksyons: Li mo yo ki nan kat ti bwat yo. Antoure de mo ki genyen son vwayèl long /ē/ a. Mo referans pou son vwayèl long /ē/ a se mo, <u>me</u>.

pelt	text		great	weak		best	crease
tree	meat		wet	three		peace	fear

grease	belt		knee	peck		eels	team
pearl	cleave		bear	teal		spell	lent

 Directions: Read the words in the four boxes. Circle two words that rhyme. Rhyming words have the same ending sound, such as <u>beep</u> and <u>reap</u>.

Direksyons: Li mo yo ki nan kat ti bwat yo. Antoure de mo ki rime. De mo oubyen plizyè mo ki rime genyen menm son nan finisman yo, tankou <u>beep</u> ak <u>reap</u>.

peak	crest		speck	apples		blest	cream
beard	seek		real	peel		heart	dream

meal	spent		please	ease		lets	cheat
deal	tear		smell	head		treat	stress

Homework

Name: _____ Date: ___/___/_____ Score: _____

Lesson 5.3

Reading & Writing Words with the Long Vowel "e" Sound

✓ Lesson Check Point

Directions: Read each sentence and underline three words with the long vowel /ē/ sound. Then, write the underlined words on the lines below. The anchor word for the long vowel /ē/ sound is me.

Direksyons: Li chak fraz epi soulinye twa mo ki genyen son vwayèl long /ē/ a. Answit, ekri mo soulinye yo sou trè sa yo ki anba. Mo referans pou son vwayèl long /ē/ a se mo, me.

Model

We are reading an article entitled, "Eagles Bird of Prey."

  We   reading   Eagles
 _____   _____   _____

1. The dean is speaking about our ten athletic teams.

 _____   _____   _____

2. At three o'clock, she began to eat bread and eggs.

 _____   _____   _____

3. Sheila and Peter are reading interesting articles.

 _____   _____   _____

4. Steve said, "One pound of meat has more protein than ten eggs."

 _____   _____   _____

5. My teacher began her lesson with three facts about the planet Venus.

 _____   _____   _____

Learn to Read English With Directions In Haitian Creole   Copyrighted Material

Unit E Lesson 5.3

Homework

Name: _____ Date: ___/___/_____ Score: _____

Review Lessons 5.2 & 5.3

Reading Short Vowel and Long Vowel Words

Directions: Read the target words in the word box. In the first column, write the words that have the short vowel /ĕ/ sound, as in the word <u>egg</u>. In the second column, write the words that have the long vowel /ē/ sound, as in the word <u>me</u>.

Direksyons: Li mo objektif yo ki nan bwat mo a. Nan premye kolòn nan, ekri mo ki bay son vwayèl kout /ĕ/ yo, tankou li ye nan mo <u>egg</u> la. Nan dezyèm kolòn nan, ekri mo ki bay son vwayèl long /ē/ yo, tankou li ye nan mo <u>me</u> la.

Target Word Box				
defeat	stem	supreme	stream	press
coffee	never	flesh	between	stress
help	speech	next	dress	ceiling
ever	complete	deplete	check	asleep

Letter "e" has the /ĕ/ sound as in the word <u>egg</u>

Letter "e" has the /ē/ sound as in the word <u>me</u>

Homework

 Name: _____ Date:___/___/_____ Score:_____

Lesson 5.4

Reading Words with Letter "e" Vowel Pairs

✓ **Lesson Check Point**

 Directions: Read each target word. Circle the word in the column that has the same vowel "ea," "ee," "ei," "eo" or "eu" sound as the target word.

Direksyons: Li chak mo objektif. Antoure mo a ki nan kolòn nan ki bay menm son vwayèl "ea," "ee," "ei," "eo" oubyen "eu" a tankou mo objektif la.

ream	a. health
	b. teal

heat	a. peel
	b. bread

protein	a. asleep
	b. hear

streusel	a. mean
	b. Europe

 Directions: Read each target word. Put a check (✓) under the correct column heading.

Direksyons: Li chak mo objektif. Mete yon tchèk (✓) anba antèt kolòn ki kòrèk la.

Target Words	Words have the long "e" sound as in the word <u>tea</u>	Words do not have the long "e" sound
1. ream		
2. heat		
3. protein		
4. streusel		

Homework

Name: _____   Date: ___/___/_____   Score: _____

Lesson 5.5

Reading Words with the Final Letter "e"

✓ **Lesson Check Point**

Directions: Read each target word. Find the letter "e" and put a check (✓) in the column that identifies its position within the syllable.

Direksyons: Li chak mo objektif. Jwenn lèt "e" a epi mete yon tchèk (✓) nan kolòn ki idantifye pozisyon li an nan silab la.

Target Words	"e" is at the end of a one syllable word	"e" is at the end of the first syllable	"e" is at the end of a multi-syllable word
1. he			
2. me			
3. hero			
4. r<u>e</u>fresh			
5. becom<u>e</u>			

Directions: Read each target word. Put a check (✓) under the correct column heading.

Direksyons: Li chak mo objektif. Mete yon tchèk (✓) anba antèt kolòn ki kòrèk la.

Target Words	"e" has the /ĕ/ sound as in the word <u>egg</u>	"e" has the /ē/ sound as in the word <u>me</u>	"e" has the /ə/ sound as in the word <u>item</u>	"e" is silent as in the word <u>great</u>
6. either				
7. pollen				
8. resting				
9. Europe				
10. urgently				

Homework

 Name: _____ Date: ___/___/_____ Score: _____

Lesson 5.6

Reading Letter "e" Words with the Schwa Vowel Sound

✓ Lesson Check Point

 Directions: Read each target word. Circle the word in the column that has the same "e" sound as the target word.

Direksyons: Li chak mo objektif. Antoure mo a ki nan kolòn nan ki bay menm son "e" a tankou mo objektif la.

letter	a. systems
	b. eggplant

celebrate	a. reap
	b. answer

elephant	a. father
	b. eating

problem	a. labels
	b. beeping

 Directions: Read each sentence and underline the letter "e" word that has the schwa vowel /ə/ sound. The anchor word for the letter "e" schwa vowel sound is <u>item</u>.

Direksyons: Li chak fraz epi soulinye mo ki genyen lèt "e" ki bay son schwa /ə/ a. Mo referans pou son schwa lèt "e" a se mo, <u>item</u>.

1. You will benefit from reading this book.

2. Today, Emma began to shiver from fear.

3. Curried chicken with rice tastes very good.

4. My friend, Pete, made a profound statement.

5. Eddie painted an elephant for his art project.

6. There is oxygen in the large blue and white tank.

Homework

 Name: _____ Date:___/___/_____ Score: _____

Lesson 5.7

Reading Words with the "er" Letter Combination

Dictionary Skills/ Vocabulary

✓ **Lesson Check Point**

Directions: Read each target word and its definition. Write the letter of the definition on the line of each target word. Use a dictionary or the Internet to check your answers.

Direksyons: Li chak mo objektif ak definisyon yo chak. Ekri lèt la ki koresponn ak definisyon an sou trè chak mo objektif yo. Itilize yon diksyonè oubyen entènèt pou tcheke repons ou yo.

Target Words	Definitions
1. ___ ferry	a. sweet fruit
2. ___ brother	b. meal eaten in the evening
3. ___ periscope	c. a boat that sails across a body of water
4. ___ supper	d. a viewing instrument that has a system of lenses
5. ___ blackberries	e. a male person who has the same parent(s) as another

Directions: Read each sentence and write the target word that correctly completes the sentence.
Direksyons: Li chak fraz epi ekri mo objektif ki konplete fraz la kòrèkteman.

6. The _____ is floating under the city bridge.

7. Are you going to put _____ on your cereal?

8. Jerry always looks through his big _____.

9. My sister and _____ like to eat sweet cherries.

10. Tonight, we are going to have herring for _____.

Homework

 Name: _____ Date: ___/___/_____ Score: _____

Lesson 5.8

Reading Words with the "eu" and "ew" Letter Combinations

✓ Lesson Check Point

 Directions: Read each sentence and underline the word that has a silent letter "e."

Direksyons: Li chak fraz epi soulinye mo a ki genyen lèt "e" ki pa pwononse a.

Model
My father said, "The apricot <u>streusel</u> is very tasty."

1. The eulogy at Eddie's funeral was very touching.
2. Lieutenant Glen has been a soldier for ten years.
3. Eleven of my friends went to Europe for an exciting vacation.
4. Prior to the wedding, Edwina will sew my white bridal gown.

 Directions: Read each sentence and underline the word with an "eu" or "ew" letter combination that has the long vowel /yo͞o/ or /o͞o/ sound, as in the words <u>feud</u> and <u>flew</u>.

Direksyons: Li chak fraz epi soulinye mo a ki genyen yon konbinezon lèt "eu" oubyen "ew" ki bay son vwayèl long /yo͞o/ oubyen /o͞o/ a, tankou li ye nan mo <u>feud</u> ak <u>flew</u>.

5. Emily likes to wear neutral colors.
6. Edward chews his baked granola bar very slowly.
7. The artist drew a picture of an eagle and her eaglets.
8. Eugene's favorite television show is "The Price is Right."
9. The patients in the hospital are being treated for rheumatic fever.
10. Dr. Edmond said that Annie's rheumatism is a very painful condition.

Homework

Name: _____ Date: ___/___/_____ Score: _____

Lesson 5.9

Reading Words with the "ey" Letter Combination

✓ **Lesson Check Point**

Directions: Read each target word. Put a check (✓) under the correct column heading.

Direksyons: Li chak mo objektif. Mete yon tchèk (✓) anba antèt kolòn ki kòrèk la.

Target Words	"ey" has the long /ē/ sound as in the word <u>honey</u>	"ey" has the long /ā/ sound as in the word <u>hey</u>
1. they're		
2. journey		
3. odyssey		
4. obeyed		

Directions: Read each sentence and underline the word with the "ey" letter combination. Put a check (✓) under the correct column heading.

Direksyons: Li chak fraz epi soulinye mo a ki genyen konbinezon lèt "ey" la. Mete yon tchèk (✓) anba antèt kolòn ki kòrèk la.

	"ey" has the long /ē/ sound as in the word <u>honey</u>	"ey" has the long /ā/ sound as in the word <u>hey</u>
5. I completed an extremely long survey.	_____	
6. He should obey the class rules.		_____
7. They like to eat eggs for breakfast.	_____	_____
8. The new medley sounds very good.	_____	_____
9. I like parsley flakes on my sandwich.	_____	_____
10. It is difficult to convey the message.	_____	_____

Name: _____ Date:___/___/_____ Score:_____

Homework

Lesson 5.10

Reading Words with a Silent Letter "e"

✓ Lesson Check Point

 Directions: Read the target words in the word box. Write the words that have a silent letter "e" in the first column. Write the words that do not have a silent letter "e" in the second column.

Direksyons: Li mo objektif yo ki nan ti bwat mo a. Ekri mo yo ki genyen yon lèt "e" ki pa pwononse a nan premye kolòn nan. Ekri mo yo ki pa genyen yon lèt "e" ki pa pwononse a nan dezyèm kolòn nan.

Target Word Box				
beat	intake	water	cube	denting
ate	tea	blue	mule	life
bone	wife	the	lively	reading
sea	me	space	meat	elephant

Letter "e" is silent   Letter "e" has a letter "e" sound

Homework

 Name: _____ Date: ___/___/_____ Score: _____

Unit Review - E/e

Reading Words with Vowel "e" Sounds: /ĕ/, /ē/, /ə/ & Silent

✓ **Lesson Check Point**

Directions: Read each target word. Circle the word in the column that has the same "e" sound as the target word.

Direksyons: Li chak mo objektif. Antoure mo a ki nan kolòn nan ki bay menm son "e" a tankou mo objektif la.

belts	a. cakes
	b. legs

peanuts	a. cheese
	b. edge

eating	a. asleep
	b. melt

oxygen	a. bled
	b. label

Directions: Read each target word. Put a check (✓) under the correct column heading.

Direksyons: Li chak mo objektif. Mete yon tchèk (✓) anba antèt kolòn ki kòrèk la.

Target Words	"e" has the /ĕ/ sound as in the word <u>egg</u>	"e" has the /ē/ sound as in the word <u>me</u>	"e" has the /ə/ sound as in the word <u>item</u>	"e" is silent as in the word <u>great</u>
1. belts				
2. peanuts				
3. eating				
4. oxygen				

Homework

 Name: _____ Date: ___/___/_____ Score: _____

The Reading Challenge

Lesson 5.11

Reading Multisyllable Words

✓ Lesson Check Point

Directions: Read and divide each target word into syllables. Write each word and place a hyphen (-) between the syllables in the second column. Write the number of syllables in the third column. Use a dictionary or the Internet to check your answers.

Direksyons: Li epi divize chak mo objektif an silab. Ekri chak mo epi mete yon tirè (-) ant silab yo nan dezyèm kolòn nan. Ekri kantite silab ke yo genyen an nan twazyèm kolòn nan. Itilize yon diksyonè oubyen entènèt pou tcheke repons ou yo.

Target Words	Words Divided into Syllables	Number of Syllables
1. nutshell	_____	_____
2. increasing	_____	_____
3. emblem	_____	_____
4. stairwell	_____	_____
5. exceeding	_____	_____
6. airmen	_____	_____
7. drunken	_____	_____
8. eggshell	_____	_____
9. repeated	_____	_____
10. fasten	_____	_____

Homework

 Name: _____ Date: ___/___/_____ Score: _____

The Reading Challenge

Lesson 5.11

Reading Multisyllable Words

✓ **Lesson Check Point**

Directions: Read each target word. Circle the word in the row that is divided correctly into syllables. Use a dictionary or the Internet to check your answers.

Direksyons: Li chak mo objektif. Antoure mo a ki nan ranje a ki divize an silab korèkteman yo. Itilize yon diksyonè oubyen entènèt pou tcheke repons ou yo.

Model

| megabyte | a. me-ga-byte | b. meg-a-byte (circled) | c. me-gaby-te |

1. ecosystem	a. eco-sys-tem	b. e-co-sys-tem	c. eco-syst-em
2. segregate	a. se-gre-gate	b. se-greg-ate	c. seg-re-gate
3. countrymen	a. coun-trym-en	b. count-ry-men	c. coun-try-men
4. woodpecker	a. wood-peck-er	b. wood-pec-ker	c. woo-dpeck-er
5. gardening	a. gard-en-ing	b. gar-de-ning	c. gar-den-ing
6. legislate	a. leg-is-late	b. le-gis-late	c. leg-isl-ate
7. comprehend	a. comp-re-hend	b. com-preh-end	c. com-pre-hend
8. dividend	a. div-i-dend	b. di-vid-end	c. div-id-end

Homework

Name: _____ Date: ___/___/_____ Score: _____

Lesson 5.12
Reading and Writing
Proper and Common Nouns and Adjectives

Directions: Read the words in the word box. Put an (X) on the line next to each word that is written incorrectly. Remember that all proper nouns and proper adjectives are capitalized. Use a dictionary or the Internet to check your answers.

Direksyons: Li chak mo yo ki nan bwat mo a. Met yon (X) sou ti trè a ki bò kote mo ki pa kri byen yo. Sonje ke tout non pwòp ak adjektif pwop ekri avèk yon lèt majiskil nan kòmansman yo. Itilize yon diksyonè oubyen entènèt pou tcheke repons ou yo.

Word Box		
___ EssEx	___ edition	___ elbow
___ English	___ elaborate	___ ecuador
___ Eskimo	___ Egyptology	___ Education
___ eastern european	___ erie Channel	___ Middle east

Directions: Read each unedited sentence and underline the word that is written incorrectly. Write each sentence correctly on the line.

Direksyons: Li chak fraz ki pa edite yo epi soulinye mo ki pa ekri byen an. Ekri chak fraz korèkteman sou liy lan.

Model
All my friends are <u>Excited</u> about the class trip to Europe.
<u>All my friends are excited about the class trip to Europe.</u>

1. My friend, Elias, speaks english extremely well.
   _____

2. Mr. edison developed a battery for the electric car.
   _____

3. This evening, Dr. Edwards Examined Elliot's eyes.
   _____

4. Eileen's e-ticket to edinburgh will expire on April eleventh.
   _____

Homework

Name: _____ Date:___/___/_____ Score:_____

Lesson 6.1

Reading Words with the Letter F/f

✓ **Lesson Check Point**

Directions: Read each target word. Find the letter "f" and put a check (✓) in the column that identifies its position: beginning, within or end.
Direksyons: Li chak mo objektif. Jwenn lèt "f" a epi mete yon tchèck (✓) nan kolòn ki idantifye pozisyon li an: nan kòmansman, ladan oubyen nan finisman.

Target Words	Beginning (First Letter)	Within	End (Last Letter)
1. leaf			
2. fresh			
3. flipped			
4. comfort			
5. defrost			

Directions: Read each sentence and underline the words that begin with the letter "f." Write all the underlined words in alphabetical order on the lines below.
Direksyons: Li chak fraz epi soulinye mo ki kòmanse avèk lèt "f" yo. Ekri tout mo ki soulinye yo nan lòd alfabetik sou trè sa yo ki anba.

6. Did you know the fox had fleas?

7. Annie said, "The field is far away."

8. Last January, Bobby ate a lot of fast food.

9. The children like to have fun at the fountain.

10. In the afternoon, the flock of birds flew away.

_____   _____   _____
_____   _____   _____
_____   _____
_____

Homework

 Name: _____ Date:___/___/_____ Score:_____

Lesson 6.2

Reading Words with the "fr" Letter Combination

Dictionary Skills/ Vocabulary

✓ Lesson Check Point

 Directions: Read each target word and its definition. Write the letter of the definition on the line of each target word. Use a dictionary or the Internet to check your answers.

Direksyons: Li chak mo objektif ak definisyon yo chak. Ekri lèt la ki koresponn ak definisyon an sou trè chak mo objektif yo. Itilize yon diksyonè oubyen entènèt pou tcheke repons ou yo.

Target Words	Definitions
1. __ frames	a. facial expression indicating displeasure
2. __ French	b. language spoken in France
3. __ front	c. the first or forward position
4. __ frowns	d. something made solid by extreme cold
5. __ frozen	e. borders around an object, such as a picture

 Directions: Read each sentence. Underline the word in the parentheses that correctly completes each sentence. Then, write the underlined word on the line.

Direksyons: Li chak fraz. Soulinye mo a ki nan parantèz yo ki konplete chak fraz kòrèkteman. Answit, ekri mo soulinye a sou trè a.

6. The food in the freezer is _____. (frame, frozen)

7. Flo puts her drawings in beautiful _____. (frames, frozen)

8. Freda speaks _____ and Finnish fluently. (frowns, French)

9. The whiteboard is in _____ of the classroom. (front, French)

10. Happy clowns do not have _____ on their faces. (frowns, frames)

Homework

Name: _____ Date: ___/___/_____ Score: _____

Lesson 6.3

Reading Words with the "fl" Letter Combination

Dictionary Skills/ Vocabulary

✓ **Lesson Check Point**

Directions: Read each target word and its definition. Write the target word on the line in front of its meaning. Use a dictionary or the Internet to check your answers.

Direksyons: Li chak mo objektif ak definisyon yo chak. Ekri mo objektif la sou trè ki devan definisyon li an. Itilize yon diksyonè oubyen entènèt pou tcheke repons ou yo.

Target Word Box				
flag	flavor	flu	flute	flying

1. _____ the taste of food
2. _____ a woodwind instrument
3. _____ to travel through the air with wings
4. _____ a sickness caused by an acute viral infection
5. _____ a designed fabric used as a country's symbol

Directions: Read each sentence. Underline the word in the parentheses that correctly completes each sentence. Then, write the underlined word on the line.

Direksyons: Li chak fraz. Soulinye mo a ki nan parantèz yo ki konplete chak fraz kòrèkteman. Answit, ekri mo soulinye a sou trè a.

6. Fred is in bed with the bad _____. (flag, flu)

7. Francis enjoys _____ in the airplane. (flying, flavor)

8. The Japanese _____ is white and red. (flag, flute)

9. Flossy is learning to play the _____ in class. (flute, flu)

10. Flex's fried chicken is full of _____. (flavor, flying)

Homework

 Name: _____ Date: ___/___/_____ Score: _____

Lesson 6.3

Reading Words with the "fle" Letter Combination

✓ Lesson Check Point

 Directions: Read each target word. Find the "fle" letter combination and put a check (✓) in the column that identifies its position: beginning, within or end.

Direksyons: Li chak mo objektif. Jwenn konbinezon lèt "fle" a epi mete yon tchèk (✓) nan kolòn nan ki idantifye pozisyon li an: nan kòmansman, ladan oubyen nan finisman.

Target Words	Beginning (First 3 Letters)	Within	End (Last 3 Letters)
1. fled			
2. baffle			
3. waffle			
4. deflect			
5. inflexed			

 Directions: Read each target word. Put a check (✓) in the "yes" column if the "fle" letter combination has the /f/ + /ə/ + /l/ sounds. Put a check (✓) in the "no" column if the "fle" letter combination does not have the /f/ + /ə/ + /l/ sounds.

Direksyons: Li chak mo objektif. Mete yon tchèk (✓) nan kolòn "yes" an si konbinezon lèt "fle" a bay sons /f/ + /ə/ + /l/. Mete yon tchèk (✓) nan kolòn "no" an si konbinezon lèt "fle" a pa bay sons /f/ + /ə/ + /l/.

Target Words	Yes	No
6. fled		
7. baffle		
8. waffle		
9. deflect		
10. inflexed		

Learn to Read English With Directions In Haitian Creole

Homework

Name: _____ Date:___/___/_____ Score:_____

Lesson 6.4

Reading Words with the "ft," "lf" and "ff" Letter Combinations

Dictionary Skills/ Vocabulary

✓ Lesson Check Point

Directions: Read each target word and its definition. Write the letter of the definition on the line of each target word. Use a dictionary or the Internet to check your answers.

Direksyons: Li chak mo objektif ak definisyon yo chak. Ekri lèt la ki koresponn ak definisyon an sou trè chak mo objektif yo. Itilize yon diksyonè oubyen entènèt pou tcheke repons ou yo.

Target Words	Definitions
1. __ staff	a. not hard or firm
2. __ golf	b. an athletic game
3. __ cliff	c. people who work for a company
4. __ soft	d. vehicles driving along the road
5. __ traffic	e. a high and steep area of overhanging soil and rock

Directions: Read each sentence and write the target word that correctly completes the sentence.

Direksyons: Li chak fraz epi ekri mo objektif ki konplete fraz la kòrèkteman.

6. My family enjoys sleeping on _____ beds.

7. The _____ on the road is backed up to Main Street.

8. My dad's company is hiring new _____ members.

9. Fred and Francis are playing _____ on the course.

10. During the camping trip, the boys climbed up a high _____.

Homework

 Name: _____ Date: ___/___/_____ Score: _____

Lesson 6.5

Reading Words with a Silent Letter "f"

✓ Lesson Check Point

 Directions: Read the target words in the word box. Write the words that have a silent letter "f" in the first column. Write the words that do not have a silent letter "f" in the second column.

Direksyons: Li mo objektif yo ki nan ti bwat mo a. Ekri mo yo ki genyen lèt "f" ki pa pwononse a nan premye kolòn nan. Ekri mo yo ki pa genyen lèt "f" ki pa pwononse a nan dezyèm kolòn nan.

Target Word Box				
effort	infant	off	friend	afraid
buffer	before	stiff	figure	rainfall
official	graffiti	waffle	confront	stuffy
suffer	effect	fitting	filter	refer

Letter "f" is silent	Letter "f" has the /f/ sound

Learn to Read English With Directions In Haitian Creole   73   Copyrighted Material

Homework

 Name: _____ Date:___/___/_____ Score:_____

Lesson 6.6

Reading Singular and Plural forms of Words Ending in "-f" & "-fe"

 Lesson Check Point

Directions: Read each target word. Put a check (✓) in the second column if the plural form of the target word ends with "-ves." Put a check (✓) in the third column if the plural form of the target word ends with "-s" or "-es."

Direksyons: Li chak mo objektif. Mete yon tchèck (✓) nan dezyèm kolòn nan si fòm priryèl mo objektif la fini avek "-ves." Mete yon tchèck (✓) nan twazyèm kolòn nan si fòm priryèl mo objektif la fini avek "-s" oubyen "-es."

Target Words	The plural form of the target word ends with "-ves"	The plural form of the target word ends with "-s" or "-es"
1. roof		
2. calf		
3. knife		
4. chief		
5. belief		

 Directions: Read each sentence. Complete each sentence by writing the plural form of the word on the line.

Direksyons: Li chak fraz. Konplete chak fraz pandan ou ap ekri fòm priryèl korèk mo a sou trè a.

6. In autumn, the _____ change color. (leaf)

7. The two dull _____ cannot cut the bread. (knife)

8. On Friday, five bold _____ robbed the bank. (thief)

9. Lifeguards are stationed by the pool to save _____. (life)

10. During the storm, the shingles on the _____ blew away. (roof)

Homework

 Name: _____ Date:___/___/_____ Score: _____

The Reading Challenge

Lesson 6.7

Reading Multisyllable Words

✓ Lesson Check Point

 Directions: Read and divide each target word into syllables. Write each word and place a hyphen (-) between the syllables in the second column. Write the number of syllables in the third column. Use a dictionary or the Internet to check your answers.

Direksyons: Li epi divize chak mo objektif an silab. Ekri chak mo epi mete yon tirè (-) ant silab yo nan dezyèm kolòn nan. Ekri kantite silab ke yo genyen an nan twazyèm kolòn nan. Itilize yon diksyonè oubyen entènèt pou tcheke repons ou yo.

Target Words	Words Divided into Syllables	Number of Syllables
1. finalist	_____	_____
2. facade	_____	_____
3. flowery	_____	_____
4. folding	_____	_____
5. formula	_____	_____
6. failure	_____	_____
7. fluctuate	_____	_____
8. foolish	_____	_____
9. freedom	_____	_____
10. frequency	_____	_____

Learn to Read English With Directions In Haitian Creole   Copyrighted Material

Homework

Name: _____ Date:___/___/_____ Score:_____

The Reading Challenge

Lesson 6.7

Reading Multisyllable Words

✓ **Lesson Check Point**

Directions: Read each target word. Circle the word in the row that is divided correctly into syllables. Use a dictionary or the Internet to check your answers.

Direksyons: Li chak mo objektif. Antoure mo a ki nan ranje a ki divize an silab korèkteman yo. Itilize yon diksyonè oubyen entènèt pou tcheke repons ou yo.

Model

| factory | a. fac-tor-y | b. fac-to-ry (circled) | c. fa-cto-ry |

1. forgetful	a. for-get-ful	b. fo-rget-ful	c. forg-et-ful
2. faculty	a. fac-u-lty	b. fa-cult-y	c. fac-ul-ty
3. fabulous	a. fab-u-lous	b. fa-bul-ous	c. fab-ulo-us
4. financial	a. fi-nan-cial	b. fin-an-cial	c. fin-anc-ial
5. foliage	a. fo-li-age	b. fol-i-age	c. fo-lia-ge
6. foreigner	a. fore-ign-er	b. fore-ig-ner	c. for-eign-er
7. focusing	a. fo-cus-ing	b. foc-us-ing	c. foc-u-sing
8. falsify	a. fal-sif-y	b. fals-i-fy	c. fal-si-fy

Homework

Name: _____ Date: ___/___/_____ Score: _____

Lesson 6.8

Reading and Writing

Proper and Common Nouns and Adjectives

Directions: Read the words in the word box. Put an (X) on the line next to each word that is written incorrectly. Remember that all proper nouns and proper adjectives are capitalized. Use a dictionary or the Internet to check your answers.

Direksyons: Li chak mo yo ki nan bwat mo a. Met yon (X) sou ti trè a ki bò kote mo ki pa kri byen yo. Sonje ke tout non pwòp ak adjektif pwop ekri avèk yon lèt majiskil nan kòmansman yo. Itilize yon diksyonè oubyen entènèt pou tcheke repons ou yo.

Word Box		
___ Farmer	___ frog	___ france
___ Friend	___ female	___ fingers
___ french	___ frankfort	___ finnish
___ Fort Lee	___ Franklin	___ Fred's Diner

Directions: Read each unedited sentence and underline the word that is written incorrectly. Write each sentence correctly on the line.

Direksyons: Li chak fraz ki pa edite yo epi soulinye mo ki pa ekri byen an. Ekri chak fraz korèkteman sou liy lan.

Model
Fiji is my <u>Florist's</u> favorite holiday destination.
<u>Fiji is my florist's favorite holiday destination.</u>

1. Flo said, "China is in the far East."

   _____

2. Frank is visiting Aunt flossy in Florida.

   _____

3. franklin and Francis were born in Frankfort.

   _____

4. On friday, Florence wore a fancy dress to the dance.

   _____

Homework

Name: _____ Date: ___/___/_____ Score: _____

Lesson 7.1

Reading Words with the Letter G/g

✓ **Lesson Check Point**

Directions: Read each target word. Find the letter "g" and put a check (✓) in the column that identifies its position: beginning, within or end.

Direksyons: Li chak mo objektif. Jwenn lèt "g" a epi mete yon tchèck (✓) nan kolòn ki idantifye pozisyon li an: nan kòmansman, ladan oubyen nan finisman.

Target Words	Beginning (First Letter)	Within	End (Last Letter)
1. judge			
2. loving			
3. sibling			
4. grammar			
5. hamburger			

Directions: Read each sentence and underline the words that begin with the letter "g." Write all the underlined words in alphabetical order on the lines below.

Direksyons: Li chak fraz epi soulinye mo ki kòmanse avèk lèt "g" yo. Ekri tout mo ki soulinye yo nan lòd alfabetik sou trè sa yo ki anba.

6. The goldfish is in a glass bowl.

7. On Saturday, I am going to the art gallery.

8. On Sundays, Grace enjoys singing gospel music.

9. Annie is growing beautiful flowers in her garden.

10. The graphic designer drew a great logo for my business card.

_____   _____   _____
_____   _____   _____
_____   _____   _____

Homework

 Name: _____ Date: ___/___/_____ Score: _____

Lesson 7.1

Reading Words with the Hard Letter "g"

✓ Lesson Check Point

 Directions: Read each target word. Put a check (✓) under the correct column heading.

Direksyons: Li chak mo objektif. Mete yon tchèk (✓) anba antèt kolòn ki kòrèk la.

Target Words	Hard "g" has the /g/ sound as in the word <u>gum</u>	Soft "g" has the /j/ sound as in the word <u>gem</u>
1. girls		
2. giant		
3. glossy		
4. gender		
5. garden		

 Directions: Read each sentence and underline the words that have the hard "g" sound. The anchor word for the hard "g" sound is <u>gum</u>. Write all the underlined words in alphabetical order on the lines below.

Direksyons: Li chak fraz epi soulinye mo yo ki bay son "g" di a. Mo referans pou son "g" di a se mo, <u>gum</u>. Ekri tout mo ki soulinye yo nan lòd alfabetik sou trè sa yo ki anba.

6. Ginny's gift was a colorful globe.

7. George is guilty of grabbing the balloons.

8. The giant likes to eat grapes and garlic cloves.

9. In Guyana, the skilled gymnasts are very gracious.

10. Two groups of students are going to visit Germany.

_____   _____   _____
_____   _____   _____
_____   _____   _____
                  _____

Homework

Name: _____ Date: ___/___/_____ Score: _____

Lesson 7.2

Reading Words with the Soft Letter "g"

✓ Lesson Check Point

Directions: Read each target word. Put a check (✓) under the correct column heading.

Direksyons: Li chak mo objektif. Mete yon tchèk (✓) anba antèt kolòn ki kòrèk la.

Target Words	Soft "g" has the /j/ or /zh/ sound as in the words gem & massage	Hard "g" has the /g/ sound as in the word gum	Both soft "g" and hard "g" sounds as in the word gauge
1. give			
2. emerge			
3. apology			
4. garages			
5. geographical			

Directions: Read each sentence and underline the words that have the soft "g" sound. The anchor word for the soft "g" sound is gem. Write all the underlined words in alphabetical order on the lines below.

Direksyons: Li chak fraz epi soulinye mo yo ki bay son "g" dous lan. Mo referans pou son "g" dous lan se mo, gem. Ekri tout mo ki soulinye yo nan lòd alfabetik sou trè sa yo ki anba.

6. The gentle giant did not break the gate.

7. Gilbert gave me two oranges and a big gyro.

8. Mr. Green said, "The two geese are in a huge cage."

9. My guest took a guided tour of Genie's gymnasium.

10. There is a picture of a gigantic gorilla on the next page.

_____   _____   _____
_____   _____   _____
_____   _____   _____
                _____

Homework

Name: _____ Date: ___/___/_____ Score: _____

Review Lessons 7.1 & 7.2

Reading Hard Letter "g" and Soft Letter "g" Words

Directions: Read each target word. Put a check (✓) under the correct column heading.

Direksyons: Li chak mo objektif. Mete yon tchèk (✓) anba antèt kolòn ki kòrèk la.

Target Words	Soft "g" has the /j/ or /zh/ sound as in the words gem & massage	Hard "g" has the /g/ sound as in the word gum	Both soft "g" and hard "g" sounds as in the word gauge
1. griddle			
2. change			
3. analogy			
4. girlfriend			
5. geography			

Directions: Read each sentence and underline the words that have the hard "g" sound. The anchor word for the hard "g" sound is gum. Write all the underlined words in alphabetical order on the lines below.

Direksyons: Li chak fraz epi soulinye mo yo ki bay son "g" di a. Mo referans pou son "g" di a se mo, gum. Ekri tout mo ki souliye yo nan lòd alfabetik sou trè sa yo ki anba.

6. George gave each child a toy kangaroo.

7. Gina designed a great maze in the garden.

8. Geron received golf clubs as a birthday gift.

9. Gene is allergic to an ingredient in orange gum.

10. Grandma said, "The magic gel is in a gold bottle."

_____   _____   _____

_____   _____   _____

_____   _____   _____

                _____

Homework

Name: _____ Date: ___/___/_____ Score: _____

Review Lessons 7.1 & 7.2

Reading Hard Letter "g" and Soft Letter "g" Words

Directions: Read the target words in the word box. In the first column, write the words with the letter "g" that have the /g/ sound, as in the word gum. In the second column, write the words with the letter "g" that have the /j/ sound, as in the word gem.

Direksyons: Li mo objektif yo ki nan bwat mo a. Nan premye kolòn nan, ekri mo yo ki genyen lèt "g" ki bay son /g/ a, tankou li ye nan mo gum nan. Nan dezyèm kolòn nan, ekri mo yo ki genyen lèt "g" ki bay son /j/ a, tankou li ye nan mo gem nan.

Target Word Box				
page	gesture	good	gene	green
garden	gills	ginger	gift	gentle
cage	ago	orange	gypsy	grade
gulp	bag	large	figure	German

Hard Letter "g" has the /g/ sound as in the word gum

Soft Letter "g" has the /j/ sound as in the word gem

Learn to Read English With Directions In Haitian Creole

Homework

 Name: _____ Date:___/___/_____ Score:_____

Lesson 7.3

Reading Words with the "gr" Letter Combination

Dictionary Skills/ Vocabulary

✓ Lesson Check Point

 Directions: Read each target word and its definition. Write the letter of the definition on the line of each target word. Use a dictionary or the Internet to check your answers.

Direksyons: Li chak mo objektif ak definisyon yo chak. Ekri lèt la ki koresponn ak definisyon an sou trè chak mo objektif yo. Itilize yon diksyonè oubyen entènèt pou tcheke repons ou yo.

Target Words	Definitions
1. __ grilled	a. the color of leaves and plant stems
2. __ gravity	b. characteristic of distinction and importance
3. __ great	c. force that keeps things grounded
4. __ green	d. kindness and politeness in a person's character
5. __ gracious	e. to have cooked food on parallel bars over a fire

 Directions: Read each sentence. Underline the word in the parentheses that correctly completes each sentence. Then, write the underlined word on the line.

Direksyons: Li chak fraz. Soulinye mo a ki nan parantèz yo ki konplete chak fraz kòrèkteman. Answit, ekri mo soulinye a sou trè a.

6. The _____ grass is growing. (grilled, green)

7. At the barbecue, my dad _____ the chicken. (great, grilled)

8. Gloria is always _____ and charming. (gracious, green)

9. The _____ citizens received service awards. (gravity, great)

10. _____ stops things from floating upward. (Gracious, Gravity)

Homework

Name: _____ Date: ___/___/_____ Score: _____

Lesson 7.4

Reading Words with the "gl" Letter Combination

Dictionary Skills/ Vocabulary

✓ Lesson Check Point

Directions: Read each target word and its definition. Write the target word on the line in front of its meaning. Use a dictionary or the Internet to check your answers.

Direksyons: Li chak mo objektif ak definisyon yo chak. Ekri mo objektif la sou trè ki devan definisyon li an. Itilize yon diksyonè oubyen entènèt pou tcheke repons ou yo.

Target Word Box				
glamorous	glass	glasses	gloves	glows

1. _____ having glamour
2. _____ protective coverings for hands
3. _____ to reflect light through an object
4. _____ a container used for drinking hot or cold beverages
5. _____ a pair of lenses fitted into a frame that a person wears to see

Directions: Read each sentence. Underline the word in the parentheses that correctly completes each sentence. Then, write the underlined word on the line.

Direksyons: Li chak fraz. Soulinye mo a ki nan parantèz yo ki konplete chak fraz kòrèkteman. Answit, ekri mo soulinye a sou trè a.

6. My doctor always wears latex _____. (glows, gloves)

7. The computer screen _____ in the dark. (gloves, glows)

8. Greg wears _____ to see things at a distance. (glasses, glass)

9. Gloria likes to drink her coffee with a crystal _____. (glows, glass)

10. The girls bought _____ dresses for the concert. (glamorous, glasses)

Homework

 Name: _____ Date: ___/___/_____ Score: _____

Lesson 7.4

Reading Words with the "gle" Letter Combination

✓ Lesson Check Point

 Directions: Read each target word. Find the "gle" letter combination and put a check (✓) in the column that identifies its position: beginning, within or end.

Direksyons: Li chak mo objektif. Jwenn konbinezon lèt "gle" a epi mete yon tchèk (✓) nan kolòn nan ki idantifye pozisyon li an: nan kòmansman, ladan oubyen nan finisman.

Target Words	Beginning (First 3 Letters)	Within	End (Last 3 Letters)
1. ringlet			
2. dangle			
3. bungle			
4. gleamed			
5. Glenwood			

 Directions: Read each target word. Put a check (✓) in the "yes" column if the "gle" letter combination has the /g/ + /ə/ + /l/ sounds. Put a check (✓) in the "no" column if the "gle" letter combination does not have the /g/ + /ə/ + /l/ sounds.

Direksyons: Li chak mo objektif. Mete yon tchèk (✓) nan kolòn "yes" an si konbinezon let "gle" a bay sons /g/ + /ə/ + /l/. Mete yon tchèk (✓) nan kolòn "no" an si konbinezon let "gle" a pa bay sons /g/ + /ə/ + /l/.

Target Words	Yes	No
6. ringlet		
7. dangle		
8. bungle		
9. gleamed		
10. Glenwood		

Homework

 Name: _____ Date: ___/___/_____ Score: _____

Lesson 7.5

Reading Words with the "gh" Letter Combination

✓ **Lesson Check Point**

 Directions: Read each target word. Circle the word in the column that has the same "gh" sound as the target word.

Direksyons: Li chak mo objektif. Antoure mo a ki nan kolòn nan ki bay menm son "gh" la tankou mo objektif la.

ghost	a. ghastly
	b. rough

weight	a. enough
	b. thigh

insight	a. laughing
	b. weigh

coughing	a. mighty
	b. tougher

 Directions: Read each target word. Put a check (✓) under the correct column heading.

Direksyons: Li chak mo objektif. Mete yon tchèk (✓) anba antèt kolòn ki kòrèk la.

Target Words	"gh" has the /g/ sound as in the word <u>ghetto</u>	"gh" has the /f/ sound as in the word <u>laugh</u>	"gh" is silent as in the word <u>light</u>
1. ghost			
2. weight			
3. insight			
4. coughing			

Homework

Name: _____ Date: ___/___/_____ Score: _____

Lesson 7.6

Reading Words with the "gn" Letter Combination

 Lesson Check Point

Directions: Read each target word. Circle the word in the column that has the same "gn" sound(s) as the target word.

Direksyons: Li chak mo objektif. Antoure mo a ki nan kolòn nan ki bay menm son "gn" la (yo) tankou mo objektif la.

| ignore | a. aligned |
| | b. recognition |

| ignition | a. diagnostic |
| | b. alignment |

| vignette | a. magnified |
| | b. benign |

| champagne | a. ignorant |
| | b. designer |

Directions: Read each target word. Put a check (✓) under the correct column heading.

Direksyons: Li chak mo objektif. Mete yon tchèk (✓) anba antèt kolòn ki kòrèk la.

Target Words	"gn" has the /g/ + /n/ sounds as in the word <u>ignite</u>	"gn" has the silent "g" + /n/ sound as in the word <u>sign</u>
1. ignore		
2. ignition		
3. vignette		
4. champagne		

Homework

Name: _____ Date: ___/___/_____ Score: _____

Lesson 7.7

Reading Words with a Silent Letter "g"

✓ **Lesson Check Point**

Directions: Read the target words in the word box. Write the words that have a silent letter "g" in the first column. Write the words that do not have a silent letter "g" in the second column.

Direksyons: Li mo objektif yo ki nan ti bwat mo a. Ekri mo yo ki genyen lèt "g" ki pa pwononse a nan premye kolòn nan. Ekri mo yo ki pa genyen lèt "g" ki pa pwononse a nan dezyèm kolòn nan.

Target Word Box				
signal	ago	Ghana	goat	campaign
clog	thigh	bright	gloves	foreign
design	program	magic	sign	tight
bologna	good	goggle	smug	snuggle

Letter "g" is silent	Letter "g" has the /g/ or /j/ sound

Homework

 Name: _____ Date:___/___/_____ Score: _____

The Reading Challenge

Lesson 7.8

Reading Multisyllable Words

✓ **Lesson Check Point**

 Directions: Read and divide each target word into syllables. Write each word and place a hyphen (-) between the syllables in the second column. Write the number of syllables in the third column. Use a dictionary or the Internet to check your answers.

Direksyons: Li epi divize chak mo objektif an silab. Ekri chak mo epi mete yon tirè (-) ant silab yo nan dezyèm kolòn nan. Ekri kantite silab ke yo genyen an nan twazyèm kolòn nan. Itilize yon diksyonè oubyen entènèt pou tcheke repons ou yo.

Target Words	Words Divided into Syllables	Number of Syllables
1. goalkeeper	_____	_____
2. government	_____	_____
3. gasoline	_____	_____
4. guarantee	_____	_____
5. gelatin	_____	_____
6. glorified	_____	_____
7. gathering	_____	_____
8. Grenada	_____	_____
9. generalize	_____	_____
10. glamorous	_____	_____

Homework

 Name: _____ Date: ___/___/_____ Score: _____

The Reading Challenge

Lesson 7.8

Reading Multisyllable Words

✓ **Lesson Check Point**

 Directions: Read each target word. Circle the word in the row that is divided correctly into syllables. Use a dictionary or the Internet to check your answers.

Direksyons: Li chak mo objektif. Antoure mo a ki nan ranje a ki divize an silab korèkteman yo. Itilize yon diksyonè oubyen entènèt pou tcheke repons ou yo.

Model

| galaxy | a. ga-lax-y | b. gal-ax-y | c. gal-a-xy |

| 1. generate | a. ge-ner-ate | b. gen-er-ate | c. gen-era-te |

| 2. gigabyte | a. gig-a-byte | b. gi-ga-byte | c. gig-aby-te |

| 3. gardenia | a. ga-rde-nia | b. gar-de-nia | c. gar-den-ia |

| 4. gondola | a. go-ndo-la | b. go-ndol-a | c. gon-do-la |

| 5. generous | a. gen-er-ous | b. ge-ner-ous | c. gen-ero-us |

| 6. gradual | a. grad-u-al | b. gra-du-al | c. grad-ua-l |

| 7. gasoline | a. gas-o-line | b. ga-soline | c. gas-oli-ne |

| 8. gestation | a. gest-a-tion | b. ge-stat-ion | c. ges-ta-tion |

Homework

Name: _____ Date: ___/___/_____ Score: _____

Lesson 7.9

Reading and Writing

Proper and Common Nouns and Adjectives

Directions: Read the words in the word box. Put an (X) on the line next to each word that is written incorrectly. Remember that all proper nouns and proper adjectives are capitalized. Use a dictionary or the Internet to check your answers.

Direksyons: Li chak mo yo ki nan bwat mo a. Met yon (X) sou ti trè a ki bò kote mo ki pa kri byen yo. Sonje ke tout non pwòp ak adjektif pwop ekri avèk yon lèt majiskil nan kòmansman yo. Itilize yon diksyonè oubyen entènèt pou tcheke repons ou yo.

Word Box		
__ Guyana	__ Greek	__ guam
__ georgia	__ Glacier	__ great
__ Gesture	__ guardian	__ Guitar
__ Grandfather	__ Gentleman	__ Germany

Directions: Read each unedited sentence and underline the word that is written incorrectly. Write each sentence correctly on the line.

Direksyons: Li chak fraz ki pa edite yo epi soulinye mo ki pa ekri byen an. Ekri chak fraz korèkteman sou liy lan.

Model
Ginger and gene are going to Georgetown, Guyana.
Ginger and Gene are going to Georgetown, Guyana.

1. The Gorgeous gymnast is from Gibraltar.

   _____

2. On Friday, gina was gossiping about Gene.

   _____

3. Ginger bought a glamorous Gold ring from Guatemala.

   _____

4. I saw a gracious gazelle at the famous Golden gate Zoo.

   _____

Homework

Name: _____ Date:___/___/_____ Score: _____

Lesson 8.1

Reading Words with the Letter H/h

✓ Lesson Check Point

Directions: Read each target word. Find the letter "h" and put a check (✓) in the column that identifies its position: beginning, within or end.
Direksyons: Li chak mo objektif. Jwenn lèt "h" a epi mete yon tchèck (✓) nan kolòn ki idantifye pozisyon li an: nan kòmansman, ladan oubyen nan finisman.

Target Words	Beginning (First Letter)	Within	End (Last Letter)
1. Utah			
2. teach			
3. horse			
4. helper			
5. Fahrenheit			

Directions: Read each sentence and underline the words that begin with the letter "h." Write all the underlined words in alphabetical order on the lines below.
Direksyons: Li chak fraz epi soulinye mo ki kòmanse avèk lèt "h" yo. Ekri tout mo ki soulinye yo nan lòd alfabetik sou trè sa yo ki anba.

6. Pat's high chair is very heavy.

7. Henry broke Samantha's heart.

8. Ashley is holding a very big hammer.

9. Brenda puts green herbs in the hummus.

10. The hacker accessed Harry's email account.

_____   _____   _____
_____   _____   _____
_____   _____   _____
             _____

Homework

 Name: _____ Date: ___/___/_____ Score: _____

Lesson 8.2

Reading Words with the Letter "h" Combinations:
"sh," "wh," "ch," "th," "rh," "ph" and "gh"

✓ Lesson Check Point

 Directions: Read the target words in the word box. Identify the words with the following letter combinations: "sh," "wh," "ch," "th," "rh," "ph" and "gh." Write the word on the line that shows the position of the letter combination: beginning, within or end.

Direksyons: Li mo objektif yo ki nan ti bwat mo a. Idantifye mo yo ki genyen konbinezon lèt sa yo: "sh," "wh," "ch," "th," "rh," "ph" ak "gh". Ekri mo a sou liy ki montre pozisyon konbinezon lèt la: kòmansman, ladan oubyen finisman.

Target Word Box				
white	myrrh	phonics	echo	laughed
birthday	shake	letterhead	triumph	rich
rhetoric	chorus	theme	north	tough
flywheel	finish	telephone	ghetto	wishes

	Beginning	Within	End
sh	1. _____	2. _____	3. _____
wh	4. _____	5. _____	
ch	6. _____	7. _____	8. _____
th	9. _____	10. _____	11. _____
rh	12. _____	13. _____	14. _____
ph	15. _____	16. _____	17. _____
gh	18. _____	19. _____	20. _____

Homework

Name: _____ Date: ___/___/_____ Score: _____

Lesson 8.2

Reading Words with the Letter "h" Combinations: "sh," "wh," "ch," "th," "rh," "ph," "gh" and "sch"

✓ **Lesson Check Point**

Directions: Read the target words in the word box. Identify the words with the following letter combinations: "sh," "wh," "ch," "th," "rh," "ph," "gh" and "sch." Write the target word that correctly completes each sentence on the line.

Direksyons: Li mo objektif yo ki nan ti bwat mo a. Idantifye mo yo ki genyen konbinezon lèt sa yo: "sh," "wh," "ch," "th," "rh," "ph," "gh"ak "sch". Ekri mo objektif la ki konplete chak fraz korèkteman sou liy lan.

Target Word Box		
white	school	laughed
teacher	ship	elephant
through		rhombus
shortbread		phone

1. My family and I saw a big _____ at the circus.

2. My science _____ wrote three facts on the board.

3. Sharon wore her new _____ shoes to school.

4. My parents bought me three notebooks for _____.

5. The diamond-shaped figure is called a _____.

6. The cruise _____ sailed from New York to Florida.

7. Everyone _____ at Grandma's funny jokes.

8. The children walked _____ the rain without umbrellas.

9. Alexandria is unable to sync her _____ to the computer.

10. The bakers baked _____ cookies with three ingredients.

Unit H
Lesson 8.2

Learn to Read English With Directions In Haitian Creole

Homework

Name: _____ Date: ___/___/_____ Score: _____

Lesson 8.3

Reading Words with a Silent Letter "h"

✓ Lesson Check Point

Directions: Read the target words in the word box. Write the words that have a silent letter "h" in the first column. Write the words that do not have a silent letter "h" in the second column.

Direksyons: Li mo objektif yo ki nan ti bwat mo a. Ekri mo yo ki genyen lèt "h" ki pa pwononse a nan premye kolòn nan. Ekri mo yo ki pa genyen lèt "h" ki pa pwononse a nan dezyèm kolòn nan.

Target Word Box				
manhood	behind	honest	prohibit	ought
overhaul	whisk	honorarium	inherit	helpful
bought	right	spaghetti	houses	manhole
shorthand	heirs	rehearse	exhume	rhyme

Letter "h" is silent   Letter "h" has the /h/ sound

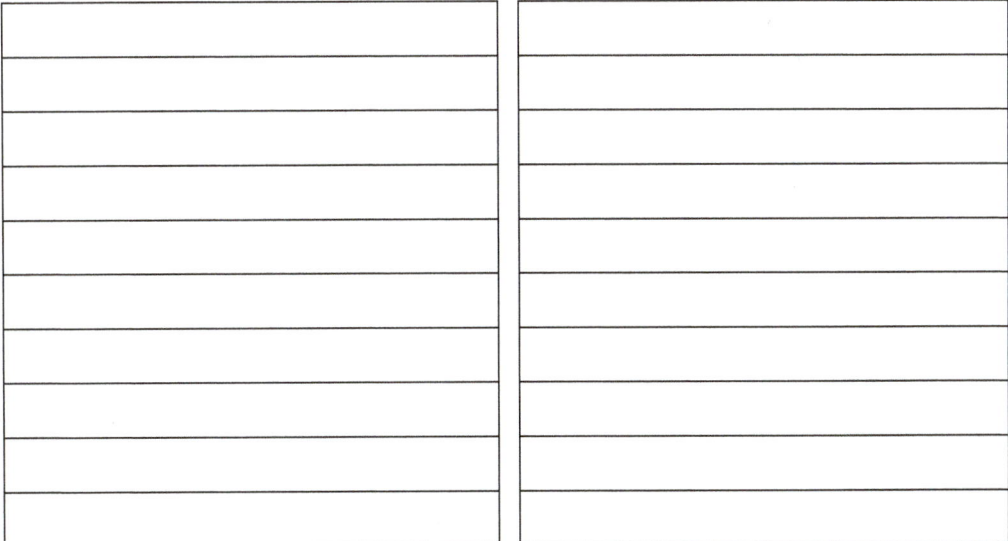

Homework

Name: _____   Date: ___/___/_____   Score: _____

The Reading Challenge

Lesson 8.4

Reading Multisyllable Words

✓ **Lesson Check Point**

Directions: Read and divide each target word into syllables. Write each word and place a hyphen (-) between the syllables in the second column. Write the number of syllables in the third column. Use a dictionary or the Internet to check your answers.

Direksyons: Li epi divize chak mo objektif an silab. Ekri chak mo epi mete yon tirè (-) ant silab yo nan dezyèm kolòn nan. Ekri kantite silab ke yo genyen an nan twazyèm kolòn nan. Itilize yon diksyonè oubyen entènèt pou tcheke repons ou yo.

Target Words	Words Divided into Syllables	Number of Syllables
1. hibernate	_____	_____
2. hallway	_____	_____
3. helicopter	_____	_____
4. holdover	_____	_____
5. headstrong	_____	_____
6. hazardous	_____	_____
7. historic	_____	_____
8. humorous	_____	_____
9. heartbroken	_____	_____
10. homework	_____	_____

Homework

 Name: _____ Date: ___/___/_____ Score: _____

The Reading Challenge

Lesson 8.4

Reading Multisyllable Words

✓ **Lesson Check Point**

 Directions: Read each target word. Circle the word in the row that is divided correctly into syllables. Use a dictionary or the Internet to check your answers.

Direksyons: Li chak mo objektif. Antoure mo a ki nan ranje a ki divize an silab korèkteman yo. Itilize yon diksyonè oubyen entènèt pou tcheke repons ou yo.

Model

heroic	a. he-roi-c	b. her-o-ic	c. he-ro-ic

1. histogram	a. his-to-gram	b. hi-sto-gram	c. his-tog-ram
2. hab-i-tat	a. ha-bi-tat	b. ha-bit-at	c. hab-i-tat
3. hospital	a. hos-pi-tal	b. hos-pit-al	c. ho-spi-tal
4. hamburger	a. ham-burg-er	b. hamb-urg-er	c. hamb-ur-ger
5. habitual	a. hab-it-ual	b. hab-i-tual	c. ha-bit-u-al
6. handicap	a. hand-i-cap	b. han-di-cap	c. hand-ic-ap
7. holiday	a. hol-i-day	b. ho-lid-ay	c. ho-li-day
8. humorous	a. hum-or-ous	b. hum-o-rous	c. hu-mor-ous

Homework

Name: _____ Date: ___/___/_____ Score: _____

Lesson 8.5

Reading and Writing

Proper and Common Nouns and Adjectives

Directions: Read the words in the word box. Put an (X) on the line next to each word that is written incorrectly. Remember that all proper nouns and proper adjectives are capitalized. Use a dictionary or the Internet to check your answers.

Direksyons: Li chak mo yo ki nan bwat mo a. Met yon (X) sou ti trè a ki bò kote mo ki pa kri byen yo. Sonje ke tout non pwòp ak adjektif pwop ekri avèk yon lèt majiskil nan kòmansman yo. Itilize yon diksyonè oubyen entènèt pou tcheke repons ou yo.

Word Box		
__ Haiti	__ hawk	__ Hotel
__ Horizon	__ House	__ herself
__ Heather	__ holland	__ horses
__ hinduism	__ Hannah	__ honduras

Directions: Read each unedited sentence and underline the word that is written incorrectly. Write each sentence correctly on the line.

Direksyons: Li chak fraz ki pa edite yo epi soulinye mo ki pa ekri byen an. Ekri chak fraz korèkteman sou liy lan.

Model
Mr. Hitt has a big house on hope Avenue.
Mr. Hitt has a big house on Hope Avenue.

1. Hadia and Henry are standing in the Hallway.

   _____

2. The best Hamburgers are sold at Harpo's Diner.

   _____

3. Hollywood is producing a movie entitled, "The house of Hearts."

   _____

4. The Hacker broke into Hartford Hospital's computer database.

   _____

Homework

 Name: _____ Date: ___/___/_____ Score: _____

Lesson 9.1

Reading Words with the Letter I/i

✓ Lesson Check Point

 Directions: Read each target word. Find the letter "i" and put a check (✓) in the column that identifies its position: beginning, within or end.
Direksyons: Li chak mo objektif. Jwenn lèt "i" a epi mete yon tchèck (✓) nan kolòn ki idantifye pozisyon li an: nan kòmansman, ladan oubyen nan finisman.

Target Words	Beginning (First Letter)	Within	End (Last Letter)
1. blink			
2. octopi			
3. certify			
4. iceberg			
5. alumni			

 Directions: Read each target word. Read the words in the row and circle the word that has a different vowel "i" sound.
Direksyons: Li chak mo objektif. Li mo yo ki nan ranje a epi antoure mo a ki bay yon son vwayèl "i" ki diferan an.

Target Words				
6. pink	fib	did	him	like
7. ring	bride	kid	bit	fig
8. gift	jig	blip	drive	hint
9. fish	flit	lime	brim	hid
10. pick	cite	kit	fill	silk

Homework

 Name: _____ Date: ___/___/_____ Score: _____

Lesson 9.2

Reading Words with the Short Vowel "i" Sound

✓ **Lesson Check Point**

 Directions: Read the words in the four boxes. Circle two words with the short vowel /ĭ/ sound. The anchor word for the short vowel /ĭ/ sound is <u>insect</u>.

Direksyons: Li mo yo ki nan kat ti bwat yo. Antoure de mo ki genyen son vwayèl kout /ĭ/ a. Mo referans pou son vwayel kout /ĭ/ a se mo, <u>insect</u>.

ripe	did	wish	link	click	vice
lid	five	fine	dime	wipe	bring

wide	size	dish	wing	sing	dive
stick	flint	miles	wild	dine	limp

 Directions: Read the words in the four boxes. Circle two words that rhyme. Rhyming words have the same ending sound, such as <u>hip</u> and <u>dip</u>.

Direksyons: Li mo yo ki nan kat ti bwat yo. Antoure de mo ki rime. De mo oubyen plizyè mo ki rime genyen menm son nan finisman yo, tankou <u>hip</u> ak <u>dip</u>.

trim	fire	hive	grip	tire	pipe
tide	brim	tile	trip	skip	ship

flip	snip	swim	dice	file	gift
wire	pile	skim	ride	lift	hire

Homework

Name: _____ Date: ___/___/_____ Score: _____

Lesson 9.2

Reading & Writing Words with the Short Vowel "i" Sound

✓ Lesson Check Point

Directions: Read each sentence and underline three words with the short vowel /ĭ/ sound. Then, write the underlined words on the lines below. The anchor word for the short vowel /ĭ/ sound is <u>insect</u>.

Direksyons: Li chak fraz epi soulinye twa mo ki genyen son vwayèl kout /ĭ/ a. Answit, ekri mo soulinye yo sou trè sa yo ki anba. Mo referans pou son vwayèl kout /ĭ/ a se mo, <u>insect</u>.

Model

<u>Jim</u> placed a <u>big</u> cup of ice on the <u>windowsill</u>.

    Jim   big   windowsill
   _____   _____   _____

1. Gil's white shirt did not fit.

   _____   _____   _____

2. Isaac drinks white skim milk.

   _____   _____   _____

3. Jim likes to sit on top of the hill.

   _____   _____   _____

4. Will you miss the five kids from Iceland?

   _____   _____   _____

5. My friends, Irene and Tim, ate six tortilla chips.

   _____   _____   _____

Unit I Lesson 9.2

Homework

 Name: _____ Date: ___/___/_____ Score: _____

Lesson 9.3

Reading Words with the Long Vowel "i" Sound

✓ **Lesson Check Point**

 Directions: Read the words in the four boxes. Circle two words with the long vowel /ī/ sound. The anchor word for the long vowel /ī/ sound is <u>ice</u>.

Direksyons: Li mo yo ki nan kat ti bwat yo. Antoure de mo ki genyen son vwayèl long /ī/ a. Mo referans pou son vwayel long /ī/ a se mo, <u>ice</u>.

tile	wing		cling	dine		trick	milk
side	grill		chain	cite		hide	lime

rite	lice		price	click		hive	item
main	brick		disk	pile		sink	Spain

 Directions: Read the words in the four boxes. Circle two words that rhyme. Rhyming words have the same ending sound, such as <u>rice</u> and <u>nice</u>.

Direksyons: Li mo yo ki nan kat ti bwat yo. Antoure de mo ki rime. De mo oubyen plizyè mo ki rime genyen menm son nan finisman yo, tankou <u>rice</u> ak <u>nice</u>.

file	stick		wide	lint		mist	rink
clip	mile		side	mill		mice	dice

trip	tile		nice	wish		limb	skip
pile	king		ski	vice		pipe	ripe

Homework

↳ Name: _____ Date: ___/___/_____ Score: _____

Lesson 9.3

Reading & Writing Words with the Long Vowel "i" Sound

✓ **Lesson Check Point**

Directions: Read each sentence and underline three words with the long vowel /ī/ sound. Then, write the underlined words on the lines below. The anchor word for the long vowel /ī/ sound is <u>ice</u>.

Direksyons: Li chak fraz epi soulinye twa mo ki genyen son vwayèl long /ī/ a. Answit, ekri mo soulinye yo sou trè sa yo ki anba. Mo referans pou son vwayèl long /ī/ a se mo, <u>ice</u>.

Model

David and <u>I</u> flew our big, <u>white</u> <u>kite</u> along the riverbank.

    I   white   kite
_____   _____   _____

1. The child likes to hide in the old mill.

   _____   _____   _____

2. At night, Jim drives his car for miles.

   _____   _____   _____

3. He will win a prize for the ninth time.

   _____   _____   _____

4. At five o'clock, the bride simply smiled at William.

   _____   _____   _____

5. His wife admires the six firefighters for their bravery.

   _____   _____   _____

Homework

Name: _____ Date: ___/___/_____ Score: _____

Review Lessons 9.2 & 9.3

Reading Short Vowel and Long Vowel Words

✓ **Lesson Check Point**

Directions: Read the target words in the word box. In the first column, write the words that have the short vowel /ĭ/ sound, as in the word <u>insect</u>. In the second column, write the words that have the long vowel /ī/ sound, as in the word <u>ice</u>.

Direksyons: Li mo objektif yo ki nan bwat mo a. Nan premye kolòn nan, ekri mo ki bay son vwayèl kout /ĭ/ yo, tankou li ye nan mo <u>insect</u> la. Nan dezyèm kolòn nan, ekri mo ki bay son vwayèl long /ī/ yo, tankou li ye nan mo <u>ice</u> la.

Target Word Box				
lion	blimp	hike	mild	lie
dill	tiger	bring	tried	fine
fish	miss	king	fried	ring
dice	fiber	cinch	spring	click

Letter "i" has the /ĭ/ sound as in the word <u>insect</u>

Letter "i" has the /ī/ sound as in the word <u>ice</u>

Homework

 Name: _____ Date: ___/___/_____ Score: _____

Lesson 9.4

Reading Words with Letter "i" Vowel Pairs

✓ Lesson Check Point

 Directions: Read each target word. Circle the word in the column that has the same vowel "ia," "ie," "io" or "iu" sound(s) as the target word.

Direksyons: Li chak mo objektif. Antoure mo a ki nan kolòn nan ki bay menm son "ia," "ie," "io" oubyen "iu" la (yo) tankou mo objektif la.

fried	a. diet
	b. tried

podium	a. dialing
	b. bacteria

opinion	a. reunion
	b. client

appliance	a. aquarium
	b. reliable

 Directions: Read each target word. Put a check (✓) under the correct column heading.

Direksyons: Li chak mo objektif. Mete yon tchèk (✓) anba antèt kolòn ki kòrèk la.

Target Words	Words have the long "i" sound as in the word <u>dial</u>	Words do not have the long "i" sound
1. fried		
2. podium		
3. opinion		
4. appliance		

Homework

 Name: _____ Date: ___/___/_____ Score: _____

Lesson 9.5

Reading Words with the Final Letter "i"

✓ Lesson Check Point

 Directions: Read each target word. Find the letter "i" and put a check (✓) in the column that identifies its position within the syllable.
Direksyons: Li chak mo objektif. Jwenn lèt "i" a epi mete yon tchèk (✓) nan kolòn nan ki idantifye pozisyon li an nan silab la.

Target Words	"i" is at the end of a one syllable word	"i" is at the end of the first syllable	"i" is at the end of a multi-syllable word
1. I			
2. hi			
3. alib<u>i</u>			
4. dinette			
5. bifocal			

 Directions: Read each target word. Put a check (✓) under the correct column heading.
Direksyons: Li chak mo objektif. Mete yon tchèk (✓) anba antèt kolòn ki kòrèk la.

Target Words	"i" has the /ĭ/ sound as in the word <u>insect</u>	"i" has the /ī/ sound as in the word <u>bike</u>	"i" has the /ə/ sound as in the word <u>pencil</u>	"i" is silent as in the word <u>maid</u>
6. raised				
7. fashion				
8. lipstick				
9. tiger				
10. uniform				

Homework

 Name: _____ Date:___/___/_____ Score: _____

Lesson 9.6

Reading Letter "i" Words with the Schwa Vowel Sound

✓ Lesson Check Point

 Directions: Read each target word. Circle the word in the column that has the same "i" sound as the target word.
Direksyons: Li chak mo objektif. Antoure mo a ki nan kolòn nan ki bay menm son "i" a tankou mo objektif la.

incred**i**ble	a. insect
	b. notify

simpl**i**fy	a. binocular
	b. pink

sim**i**lar	a. ripping
	b. amplify

nostr**i**ls	a. fishing
	b. carnival

 Directions: Read each sentence and underline the letter "i" word that has the schwa vowel /ə/ sound. The anchor word for the letter "i" schwa vowel sound is <u>pencil</u>.
Direksyons: Li chak fraz epi soulinye mo ki genyen lèt "i" a ki bay son schwa /ə/ a. Mo referans pou son schwa lèt "i" a se mo, <u>pencil</u>.

1. The animals in the zoo are excited.

2. Those five children are simply beautiful.

3. The principal approved the school's signs.

4. Irene and her family like to ski in Iceland.

5. The filing cabinets have important documents.

6. Every student is required to wear the school uniform.

Homework

Name: _____ Date: ___/___/_____ Score: _____

Lesson 9.7

Reading Words with the "ir" Letter Combination

Dictionary Skills/ Vocabulary

✓ **Lesson Check Point**

Directions: Read each target word and its definition. Write the letter of the definition on the line of each target word. Use a dictionary or the Internet to check your answers.

Direksyons: Li chak mo objektif ak definisyon yo chak. Ekri lèt la ki koresponn ak definisyon an sou trè chak mo objektif yo. Itilize yon diksyonè oubyen entènèt pou tcheke repons ou yo.

Target Words	Definitions
1. ___ thirst	a. the position before the second
2. ___ squirt	b. having a desire to drink something
3. ___ dirt	c. the upper, brown layer of the earth; garden soil
4. ___ first	d. the use of circular motions to mix or blend something
5. ___ stirred	e. to squeeze liquid out of something

Directions: Read each sentence and write the target word that completes the sentence.

Direksyons: Li chak fraz epi ekri mo objektif ki konplete fraz la kòrèkteman.

6. We planted the seeds deep into the _____.

7. Bertha admires her _____ grade teacher.

8. Iris _____ low-fat milk into her Spanish coffee.

9. I drank a cold glass of water to quench my _____.

10. She will _____ chocolate syrup on her ice cream.

Homework

🕮 Name: _____ Date: ___/___/_____ Score: _____

Lesson 9.8

Reading Letter "i" Words with the Long Vowel "e" Sound

✓ Lesson Check Point

Directions: Read each target word. Circle the word in the column that has the same "i" sound as the target word.

Direksyons: Li chak mo objektif. Antoure mo a ki nan kolòn nan ki bay menm son lèt "i" a tankou mo objektif la.

kiwi	a. pilgrim
	b. deli

Hindi	a. ski
	b. silently

chili	a. giant
	b. maxi

pizza	a. taxi
	b. license

Directions: Read each sentence and underline the letter "i" word that has the long vowel /ē/ sound. Then, write the word on the line. The anchor word, taxi, has a letter "i" that has the long vowel /ē/ sound.

Direksyons: Li chak fraz epi soulinye mo ki gen lèt "i" a ki bay son vwayèl long /ē/ a. Answit, ekri mo a sou trè a. Mo referans, taxi gen yon lèt "i" ladan li ki bay son vwayèl long /ē/.

1. I plan to ride in a yellow taxicab. _____

2. Nick and Jim will join the Marine Corps. _____

3. In the winter, the Rivers family likes to ski. _____

4. The African safari ride costs sixty-six dollars. _____

5. Isaac and Allison ate pepperoni rolls for dinner. _____

6. The chef sprinkled paprika on her stuffed eggs. _____

Homework

Name: _____ Date: ___/___/_____ Score: _____

Lesson 9.9

Reading Words with a Silent Letter "i"

✓ **Lesson Check Point**

Directions: Read the target words in the word box. Write the words that have a silent letter "i" in the first column. Write the words that do not have a silent letter "i" in the second column.

Direksyons: Li mo objektif yo ki nan ti bwat mo a. Ekri mo yo ki genyen lèt "i" ki pa pwononse a nan premye kolòn nan. Ekri mo yo ki pa genyen lèt "i" ki pa pwononse a nan dezyèm kolòn nan.

Target Word Box				
vain	likes	pipe	civil	waist
insects	suits	lines	rails	cruise
inside	instant	tails	dinner	obtained
finding	detailed	gripping	Jamaican	attained

Letter "i" is silent	Letter "i" has a letter "i" sound

Homework

 Name: _____ Date: ___/___/_____ Score: _____

Unit Review - I/i

Reading Words with Vowel "i" Sounds: /ĭ/, /ī/, /ə/ & Silent

✓ **Lesson Check Point**

 Directions: Read each target word. Circle the word in the column that has the same "i" sound as the target word.
Direksyons: Li chak mo objektif. Antoure mo a ki nan kolòn nan ki bay menm son "i" a tankou mo objektif la.

nice	a. item
	b. slim

again	a. ring
	b. bait

sister	a. paid
	b. trip

inform	a. dishes
	b. taxi

 Directions: Read each target word. Put a check (✓) under the correct column heading.
Direksyons: Li chak mo objektif. Mete yon tchèk (✓) anba antèt kolòn ki kòrèk la.

Target Words	"i" has the /ĭ/ sound as in the word <u>insect</u>	"i" has the /ī/ sound as in the word <u>bike</u>	"i" has the /ə/ sound as in the word <u>pencil</u>	"i" is silent as in the word <u>maid</u>
1. nice				
2. again				
3. sister				
4. inform				

Homework

Name: _____ Date: ___/___/_____ Score: _____

The Reading Challenge

Lesson 9.10

Reading Multisyllable Words

✓ Lesson Check Point

Directions: Read and divide each target word into syllables. Write each word and place a hyphen (-) between the syllables in the second column. Write the number of syllables in the third column. Use a dictionary or the Internet to check your answers.

Direksyons: Li epi divize chak mo objektif an silab. Ekri chak mo epi mete yon tirè (-) ant silab yo nan dezyèm kolòn nan. Ekri kantite silab ke yo genyen an nan twazyèm kolòn nan. Itilize yon diksyonè oubyen entènèt pou tcheke repons ou yo.

Target Words	Words Divided into Syllables	Number of Syllables
1. tiger	_____	_____
2. silently	_____	_____
3. outsider	_____	_____
4. relief	_____	_____
5. national	_____	_____
6. wishing	_____	_____
7. compiling	_____	_____
8. regional	_____	_____
9. visionary	_____	_____
10. graciously	_____	_____

Homework

 Name: _____ Date: ___/___/_____ Score: _____

The Reading Challenge

Lesson 9.10

Reading Multisyllable Words

✓ Lesson Check Point

 Directions: Read each target word. Circle the word in the row that is divided correctly into syllables. Use a dictionary or the Internet to check your answers.

Direksyons: Li chak mo objektif. Antoure mo a ki nan ranje a ki divize an silab korèkteman yo. Itilize yon diksyonè oubyen entènèt pou tcheke repons ou yo.

Model

| interesting | a. in-ter-est-ing *(circled)* | b. int-er-est-ing | c. inte-rest-ing |

1. scientific	a. sci-en-tif-ic	b. scien-ti-fic	c. sci-en-ti-fic
2. uniform	a. un-i-form	b. u-ni-form	c. u-nif-orm
3. ingredient	a. in-gre-di-ent	b. in-gre-dient	c. ing-red-i-ent
4. nutrient	a. nu-tri-ent	b. nut-ri-ent	c. nut-rie-nt
5. impatient	a. im-pat-ient	b. im-pa-tient	c. i-mpa-tient
6. tastier	a. tas-ti-er	b. ta-sti-er	c. tast-i-er
7. position	a. po-si-tion	b. pos-it-ion	c. pos-i-tion
8. mediate	a. me-di-ate	b. med-i-ate	c. med-iat-e

Homework

Name: _____ Date: ___/___/_____ Score: _____

Lesson 9.11

Reading and Writing

Proper and Common Nouns and Adjectives

Directions: Read the words in the word box. Put an (X) on the line next to each word that is written incorrectly. Remember that all proper nouns and proper adjectives are capitalized. Use a dictionary or the Internet to check your answers.

Direksyons: Li chak mo yo ki nan bwat mo a. Met yon (X) sou ti trè a ki bò kote mo ki pa kri byen yo. Sonje ke tout non pwòp ak adjektif pwop ekri avèk yon lèt majiskil nan kòmansman yo. Itilize yon diksyonè oubyen entènèt pou tcheke repons ou yo.

Word Box		
___ inca	___ India	___ identify
___ Italy	___ index	___ Industry
___ ireland	___ irrigate	___ Ice cream
___ impressive	___ iberian	___ Illusionist

Directions: Read each unedited sentence and underline the word that is written incorrectly. Write each sentence correctly on the line.

Direksyons: Li chak fraz ki pa edite yo epi soulinye mo ki pa ekri byen an. Ekri chak fraz korèkteman sou liy lan.

Model
New Delhi and Indore are beautiful cities in <u>india</u>.
New Delhi and Indore are beautiful cities in India.

1. My friend, Indira, attends Intel institute.
   _____

2. The Itla family has an interesting indian heritage.
   _____

3. One day, Irwin will Investigate cases in Italy and Indonesia.
   _____

4. Irene wrote a report about the ivory Coast for International Day.
   _____

Homework

Name: _____ Date: ___/___/_____ Score: _____

Lesson 10.1

Reading Words with the Letter J/j

✓ Lesson Check Point

Directions: Read each target word. Find the letter "j" and put a check (✓) in the column that identifies its position: beginning, within or end.

Direksyons: Li chak mo objektif. Jwenn lèt "j" a epi mete yon tchèck (✓) nan kolòn ki idantifye pozisyon li an: nan kòmansman, ladan oubyen nan finisman.

Target Words	Beginning (First Letter)	Within	End (Last Letter)
1. jump			
2. jewel			
3. adjust			
4. rejoice			
5. rejuvenate			

Directions: Read each sentence and underline the words that begin with the letter "j." Write all the underlined words in alphabetical order on the lines below.

Direksyons: Li chak fraz epi soulinye mo ki kòmanse avèk lèt "j" yo. Ekri tout mo ki soulinye yo nan lòd alfabetik sou trè sa yo ki anba.

6. Bob joined the jazz band.

7. Jimmy enjoys eating jellybeans.

8. Mr. Adams has a new job as a janitor.

9. Everyone is joyous at the country jamboree.

10. Gianna's denim jacket has a jaguar on the back.

_____   _____   _____
_____   _____   _____
_____   _____

Unit J
Lesson 10.1

Learn to Read English With Directions In Haitian Creole   Copyrighted Material

Homework

 Name: _____   Date:___/___/_____   Score:_____

The Reading Challenge

Lesson 10.2

Reading Multisyllable Words

✓ **Lesson Check Point**

Directions: Read and divide each target word into syllables. Write each word and place a hyphen (-) between the syllables in the second column. Write the number of syllables in the third column. Use a dictionary or the Internet to check your answers.

Direksyons: Li epi divize chak mo objektif an silab. Ekri chak mo epi mete yon tirè (-) ant silab yo nan dezyèm kolòn nan. Ekri kantite silab ke yo genyen an nan twazyèm kolòn nan. Itilize yon diksyonè oubyen entènèt pou tcheke repons ou yo.

Target Words	Words Divided into Syllables	Number of Syllables
1. jingle	_____	_____
2. joker	_____	_____
3. juror	_____	_____
4. jaguar	_____	_____
5. jersey	_____	_____
6. journey	_____	_____
7. justice	_____	_____
8. jockey	_____	_____
9. jumper	_____	_____
10. jargon	_____	_____

Homework

 Name: _____ Date: ___/___/_____ Score: _____

The Reading Challenge

Lesson 10.2

Reading Multisyllable Words

✓ Lesson Check Point

 Directions: Read each target word. Circle the word in the row that is divided correctly into syllables. Use a dictionary or the Internet to check your answers.

Direksyons: Li chak mo objektif. Antoure mo a ki nan ranje a ki divize an silab korèkteman yo. Itilize yon diksyonè oubyen entènèt pou tcheke repons ou yo.

Model

| janitor | a. ja-ni-tor | b. jan-it-or | c. jan-i-tor (circled) |

| 1. jeweler | a. jew-el-er | b. jewe-le-r | c. je-wel-er |

| 2. jubilee | a. ju-bil-ee | b. jub-i-lee | c. ju-bi-lee |

| 3. joining | a. join-ing | b. jo-in-ing | c. jo-ining |

| 4. jeopardy | a. jeop-ard-y | b. jeo-pard-y | c. jeop-ar-dy |

| 5. journalist | a. jour-na-list | b. journ-a-list | c. jour-nal-ist |

| 6. jovial | a. jov-i-al | b. jo-vi-al | c. jovi-al |

| 7. judicial | a. ju-di-cial | b. jud-i-cial | c. ju-dic-ial |

| 8. jamboree | a. jamb-o-ree | b. jam-bo-ree | c. jam-bor-ee |

Homework

Name: _____ Date:___/___/_____ Score:_____

Lesson 10.3

Reading and Writing

Proper and Common Nouns and Adjectives

Directions: Read the words in the word box. Put an (X) on the line next to each word that is written incorrectly. Remember that all proper nouns and proper adjectives are capitalized. Use a dictionary or the Internet to check your answers.

Direksyons: Li chak mo yo ki nan bwat mo a. Met yon (X) sou ti trè a ki bò kote mo ki pa kri byen yo. Sonje ke tout non pwòp ak adjektif pwop ekri avèk yon lèt majiskil nan kòmansman yo. Itilize yon diksyonè oubyen entènèt pou tcheke repons ou yo.

Word Box		
___ Joke	___ july	___ James
___ june	___ jargon	___ jewel
___ Japan	___ Jungle	___ Jigsaw
___ Jordan	___ jefferson	___ January

Directions: Read each unedited sentence and underline the word that is written incorrectly. Write each sentence correctly on the line.

Direksyons: Li chak fraz ki pa edite yo epi soulinye mo ki pa ekri byen an. Ekri chak fraz korèkteman sou liy lan.

Model
Joey and his family live in New <u>jersey</u>.
<u>Joey and his family live in New Jersey.</u>

1. The Janitor has a good job.

   _____

2. Joseph and james are going to Japan.

   _____

3. In Jamaica, people eat Jerk chicken for dinner.

   _____

4. We are taking a Journey along the Jordan River.

   _____

Homework

Name: _____ Date: ___/___/_____ Score: _____

Lesson 11.1

Reading Words with the Letter K/k

✓ Lesson Check Point

Directions: Read each target word. Find the letter "k" and put a check (✓) in the column that identifies its position: beginning, within or end.
Direksyons: Li chak mo objektif. Jwenn lèt "k" a epi mete yon tchèck (✓) nan kolòn ki idantifye pozisyon li an: nan kòmansman, ladan oubyen nan finisman.

Target Words	Beginning (First Letter)	Within	End (Last Letter)
1. shark			
2. kitchen			
3. ketchup			
4. folktale			
5. comeback			

Directions: Read each sentence and underline the words that begin with the letter "k." Write all the underlined words in alphabetical order on the lines below.
Direksyons: Li chak fraz epi soulinye mo ki kòmanse avèk lèt "k" yo. Ekri tout mo ki soulinye yo nan lòd alfabetik sou trè sa yo ki anba.

6. Kidney beans taste great with ketchup.

7. The three kids are eating in the kitchen.

8. The five kittens are staying in the kennel.

9. Kelvin's kite is flying high above the trees.

10. The powerful kingdom was guarded by knights.

_____   _____   _____

_____   _____   _____

_____   _____

_____

Homework

 Name: _____ Date: ___/___/_____ Score: _____

Lesson 11.2

Reading Words with the Letter "k" and "ck" Letter Combination

✓ **Lesson Check Point**

 Directions: Read each target word. Put a check (✓) in the second column if the target word has one vowel. Put a check (✓) in the third column if the target word has two vowels.

Direksyons: Li chak mo objektif. Mete yon tchèk (✓) nan dezyèm kolòn nan si mo objektif la genyen yon vwayèl. Mete yon tchèk (✓) nan twazyèm kolòn nan si mo objektif la genyen de vwayèl.

Target Words	Words with 1 Vowel	Words with 2 Vowels
1. rack		
2. take		
3. sock		
4. seek		
5. lock		

 Directions: Read each target word in the first column and write the number of vowels within the word in the second column. Read each target word in the third column and write the number of vowels within the word in the fourth column.

Direksyons: Li chak mo objektif ki nan premye kolòn nan, epi ekri kantite vwayèl la ki nan mo a nan dezyèm kolòn nan. Li chak mo objektif ki nan twazyèm kolòn nan, epi ekri kantite vwayèl la ki nan mo a nan katryèm kolòn nan.

Target Words	Number of Vowels	Target Words	Number of Vowels
6. back		bake	
7. pick		pike	
8. stoke		stock	
9. stack		stake	
10. make		Mack	

Name: _____ Date:___/___/_____ Score:_____

Homework

Lesson 11.3

Reading Words with the "kle" Letter Combination

✓ Lesson Check Point

 Directions: Read each target word. Find the "kle" letter combination and put a check (✓) in the column that identifies its position: beginning, within or end.

Direksyons: Li chak mo objektif. Jwenn konbinezon lèt "kle" a epi mete yon tchèk (✓) nan kolòn nan ki idantifye pozisyon li an: nan kòmansman, ladan oubyen nan finisman.

Target Words	Beginning (First 3 Letters)	Within	End (Last 3 Letters)
1. shackle			
2. anklets			
3. wrinkled			
4. unbuckle			
5. kleptomaniac			

 Directions: Read each target word. Put a check (✓) in the "yes" column if the "kle" letter combination has the /k/ + /ə/ + /l/ sounds. Put a check (✓) in the "no" column if the "kle" letter combination does not have the /k/ + /ə/ + /l/ sounds.

Direksyons: Li chak mo objektif. Mete yon tchèk (✓) nan kolòn "yes" an si konbinezon lèt "kle" a bay sons /k/ + /ə/ + /l/. Mete yon tchèk (✓) nan kolòn "no" an si konbinezon lèt "kle" a pa bay sons /k/ + /ə/ + /l/.

Target Words	Yes	No
6. shackle		
7. anklets		
8. wrinkled		
9. unbuckle		
10. kleptomaniac		

Homework

Name: _____ Date: ___/___/_____ Score: _____

Lesson 11.4

Reading Words with a Silent Letter "k"

✓ **Lesson Check Point**

Directions: Read the target words in the word box. Write the words that have a silent letter "k" in the first column. Write the words that do not have a silent letter "k" in the second column.

Direksyons: Li mo objektif yo ki nan ti bwat mo a. Ekri mo yo ki genyen lèt "k" ki pa pwononse a nan premye kolòn nan. Ekri mo yo ki pa genyen lèt "k" ki pa pwononse a nan dezyèm kolòn nan.

Target Word Box				
knife	knits	knots	knew	keys
kneel	knish	leaking	knight	know
keeping	kangaroo	kerosene	market	knack
knowledge	breaking	keyboard	forsake	knuckles

Letter "k" is silent   **Letter "k" has the /k/ sound**

Homework

 Name: _____ Date: ___/___/_____ Score: _____

The Reading Challenge

Lesson 11.5

Reading Multisyllable Words

✓ Lesson Check Point

 Directions: Read and divide each target word into syllables. Write each word and place a hyphen (-) between the syllables in the second column. Write the number of syllables in the third column. Use a dictionary or the Internet to check your answers.

Direksyons: Li epi divize chak mo objektif an silab. Ekri chak mo epi mete yon tirè (-) ant silab yo nan dezyèm kolòn nan. Ekri kantite silab ke yo genyen an nan twazyèm kolòn nan. Itilize yon diksyonè oubyen entènèt pou tcheke repons ou yo.

Target Words	Words Divided into Syllables	Number of Syllables
1. kazoo	_____	_____
2. kidney	_____	_____
3. knocker	_____	_____
4. kosher	_____	_____
5. keycard	_____	_____
6. Kansas	_____	_____
7. kindred	_____	_____
8. kinetic	_____	_____
9. kayak	_____	_____
10. keeping	_____	_____

Homework

Name: _____ Date: ___/___/_____ Score: _____

The Reading Challenge

Lesson 11.5

Reading Multisyllable Words

✓ **Lesson Check Point**

Directions: Read each target word. Circle the word in the row that is divided correctly into syllables. Use a dictionary or the Internet to check your answers.

Direksyons: Li chak mo objektif. Antoure mo a ki nan ranje a ki divize an silab korèkteman yo. Itilize yon diksyonè oubyen entènèt pou tcheke repons ou yo.

Model

| kangaroo | a. kang-a-roo | b. kan-ga-roo | c. kan-gar-oo |

1. kerosene	a. ker-o-sene	b. ker-os-ene	c. ke-ro-sene
2. kneecap	a. knee-cap	b. kn-ee-cap	c. kn-eec-ap
3. Korean	a. K-ore-an	b. Kor-e-an	c. Ko-re-an
4. kneeling	a. kneel-ing	b. knee-ling	c. kne-eling
5. keeper	a. kee-per	b. keep-er	c. ke-eper
6. kinship	a. kinsh-ip	b. ki-nship	c. kin-ship
7. knowing	a. know-ing	b. kno-wing	c. knowi-ng
8. koala	a. ko-al-a	b. k-oa-la	c. ko-a-la

Homework

Name: _____ Date: ___/___/_____ Score: _____

Lesson 11.6

Reading and Writing

Proper and Common Nouns and Adjectives

Directions: Read the words in the word box. Put an (X) on the line next to each word that is written incorrectly. Remember that all proper nouns and proper adjectives are capitalized. Use a dictionary or the Internet to check your answers.

Direksyons: Li chak mo yo ki nan bwat mo a. Met yon (X) sou ti trè a ki bò kote mo ki pa kri byen yo. Sonje ke tout non pwòp ak adjektif pwop ekri avèk yon lèt majiskil nan kòmansman yo. Itilize yon diksyonè oubyen entènèt pou tcheke repons ou yo.

Word Box		
__ korea	__ kuwait	__ Korean
__ kennel	__ Kicking	__ kitchen
__ Kansas	__ Keycard	__ key West
__ ketchup	__ Kwanzaa	__ Kangaroo

Directions: Read each unedited sentence and underline the word that is written incorrectly. Write each sentence correctly on the line.

Direksyons: Li chak fraz ki pa edite yo epi soulinye mo ki pa ekri byen an. Ekri chak fraz korèkteman sou liy lan.

Model
Helen <u>keller</u> was a kind person.
<u>Helen Keller was a kind person.</u>

1. In kuwait, kids like to kick their soccer balls.
   _____

2. The State of kansas is located in America's heartland.
   _____

3. The Kennedy kids enjoy eating klondike ice cream bars.
   _____

4. key West and Key Largo are islands off the coast of Florida.
   _____

Homework

Name: _____ Date: ___/___/_____ Score: _____

Lesson 12.1

Reading Words with the Letter L/l

✓ **Lesson Check Point**

Directions: Read each target word. Find the letter "l" and put a check (✓) in the column that identifies its position: beginning, within or end.

Direksyons: Li chak mo objektif. Jwenn lèt "l" a epi mete yon tchèck (✓) nan kolòn ki idantifye pozisyon li an: nan kòmansman, ladan oubyen nan finisman.

Target Words	Beginning (First Letter)	Within	End (Last Letter)
1. like			
2. curl			
3. bowl			
4. lunch			
5. helper			

Directions: Read each sentence and underline the words that begin with the letter "l." Write all the underlined words in alphabetical order on the lines below.

Direksyons: Li chak fraz epi soulinye mo ki kòmanse avèk lèt "l" yo. Ekri tout mo ki soulinye yo nan lòd alfabetik sou trè sa yo ki anba.

6. I brought my laptop to the library.

7. David applied a handful of lotion to his legs.

8. Everyone knows Abigail loves to write letters.

9. On Friday, the lawyer wrote a legal document.

10. My family and I had liver and lettuce for dinner.

_____   _____   _____
_____   _____   _____
_____   _____   _____
                     _____

Homework

 Name: _____ Date:___/___/_____ Score:_____

Lesson 12.2

Reading Words with the Letter "l" Combinations:
"fl," "pl" & "sl"

Dictionary Skills/ Vocabulary

✓ **Lesson Check Point**

Directions: Read each target word and its definition. Write the target word on the line in front of its meaning. Use a dictionary or the Internet to check your answers.

Direksyons: Li chak mo objektif ak definisyon yo chak. Ekri mo objektif la sou trè ki devan definisyon li an. Itilize yon diksyonè oubyen entènèt pou tcheke repons ou yo.

Target Word Box				
flew	plants	plastic	sleep	slide

1. _____ living things that are grown in soil
2. _____ a flexible man-made material that can be shaped
3. _____ to move in a downward motion on a slippery surface
4. _____ traveled through the air with wings
5. _____ closing eyes and going into a periodic state of rest

Directions: Read each sentence. Underline the word in the parentheses that correctly completes each sentence. Then, write the underlined word on the line.

Direksyons: Li chak fraz. Soulinye mo a ki nan parantèz yo ki konplete chak fraz kòrèkteman. Answit, ekri mo soulinye a sou trè a.

6. At camp, the campers will _____ on bunk beds. (sleep, flew)

7. Pam loves to _____ down the hill with her sled. (plants, slide)

8. Early in the morning, the birds _____ over the pond. (flew, plastic)

9. The _____ in Grandma's garden are colorful. (slide, plants)

10. Paul's comb is made with a strong _____ material. (sleep, plastic)

Homework

Name: _____ Date:___/___/_____ Score:_____

Lesson 12.3

Reading Words with a Silent Letter "l"

✓ **Lesson Check Point**

Directions: Read the target words in the word box. Write the words that have a silent letter "l" in the first column. Write the words that do not have a silent letter "l" in the second column.

Direksyons: Li mo objektif yo ki nan ti bwat mo a. Ekri mo yo ki genyen lèt "l" ki pa pwononse a nan premye kolòn nan. Ekri mo yo ki pa genyen lèt "l" ki pa pwononse a nan dezyèm kolòn nan.

Target Word Box				
love	calf	tail	half	yolk
should	hello	balm	chalk	letter
salmon	ladder	dental	closed	would
Lincoln	telephone	laughs	perfectly	lower

Letter "l" is silent

Letter "l" has the /l/ sound

Homework

 Name: _____ Date: ___/___/_____ Score: _____

The Reading Challenge

Lesson 12.4

Reading Multisyllable Words

✓ **Lesson Check Point**

 Directions: Read and divide each target word into syllables. Write each word and place a hyphen (-) between the syllables in the second column. Write the number of syllables in the third column. Use a dictionary or the Internet to check your answers.

Direksyons: Li epi divize chak mo objektif an silab. Ekri chak mo epi mete yon tirè (-) ant silab yo nan dezyèm kolòn nan. Ekri kantite silab ke yo genyen an nan twazyèm kolòn nan. Itilize yon diksyonè oubyen entènèt pou tcheke repons ou yo.

Target Words	Words Divided into Syllables	Number of Syllables
1. linguistic	_____	_____
2. laughing	_____	_____
3. lighting	_____	_____
4. ligament	_____	_____
5. likely	_____	_____
6. lexicon	_____	_____
7. lavender	_____	_____
8. leftover	_____	_____
9. lasting	_____	_____
10. languish	_____	_____

Homework

Name: _____ Date: ___/___/_____ Score: _____

The Reading Challenge

Lesson 12.4

Reading Multisyllable Words

✓ **Lesson Check Point**

Directions: Read each target word. Circle the word in the row that is divided correctly into syllables. Use a dictionary or the Internet to check your answers.

Direksyons: Li chak mo objektif. Antoure mo a ki nan ranje a ki divize an silab korèkteman yo. Itilize yon diksyonè oubyen entènèt pou tcheke repons ou yo.

Model

liberty	a. li-ber-ty	b. lib-er-ty (circled)	c. lib-ert-y
1. Latino	a. Lat-i-no	b. Lat-in-o	c. La-ti-no
2. leverage	a. le-ver-age	b. lev-e-rage	c. lev-er-age
3. liberate	a. li-ber-ate	b. lib-e-rate	c. lib-er-ate
4. limousine	a. lim-ou-sine	b. li-mou-sine	c. lim-o-usine
5. lyrical	a. lyr-i-cal	b. ly-ri-cal	c. lyr-ic-al
6. lexicon	a. le-xi-con	b. lex-ic-on	c. lex-i-con
7. library	a. lib-rar-y	b. li-brar-y	c. li-bra-ry
8. ligament	a. lig-a-ment	b. li-ga-ment	c. li-gam-ent

Homework

Name: _____ Date:___/___/_____ Score:_____

Lesson 12.5

Reading and Writing

Proper and Common Nouns and Adjectives

Directions: Read the words in the word box. Put an (X) on the line next to each word that is written incorrectly. Remember that all proper nouns and proper adjectives are capitalized. Use a dictionary or the Internet to check your answers.

Direksyons: Li chak mo yo ki nan bwat mo a. Met yon (X) sou ti trè a ki bò kote mo ki pa kri byen yo. Sonje ke tout non pwòp ak adjektif pwop ekri avèk yon lèt majiskil nan kòmansman yo. Itilize yon diksyonè oubyen entènèt pou tcheke repons ou yo.

Word Box		
___ Lagos	___ Libya	___ lima
___ Lunch	___ Lemonade	___ London
___ Laptop	___ living room	___ landlord
___ License	___ Long Island	___ liverpool

Directions: Read each unedited sentence and underline the word that is written incorrectly. Write each sentence correctly on the line.

Direksyons: Li chak fraz ki pa edite yo epi soulinye mo ki pa ekri byen an. Ekri chak fraz korèkteman sou liy lan.

Model
I am studying <u>latin</u> at Lutheran Life Academy.
<u>I am studying Latin at Lutheran Life Academy.</u>

1. My family ate Lunch at Long Beach, New York.

   _____

2. Larry said, "The Largest city in Nigeria is Lagos."

   _____

3. We visited London and liverpool on the same day.

   _____

4. The labrador Peninsula is a large peninsula in Eastern Canada.

   _____

Homework

Name: _____ Date: ___/___/_____ Score: _____

Lesson 13.1

Reading Words with the Letter M/m

✓ **Lesson Check Point**

Directions: Read each target word. Find the letter "m" and put a check (✓) in the column that identifies its position: beginning, within or end.
Direksyons: Li chak mo objektif. Jwenn lèt "m" a epi mete yon tchèck (✓) nan kolòn ki idantifye pozisyon li an: nan kòmansman, ladan oubyen nan finisman.

Target Words	Beginning (First Letter)	Within	End (Last Letter)
1. hermit			
2. mother			
3. summer			
4. romance			
5. upstream			

Directions: Read each sentence and underline the words that begin with the letter "m." Write all the underlined words in alphabetical order on the lines below.
Direksyons: Li chak fraz epi soulinye mo ki kòmanse avèk lèt "m" yo. Ekri tout mo ki soulinye yo nan lòd alfabetik sou trè sa yo ki anba.

6. His sister, Mercy, wrote a great manuscript.

7. Dr. Mingo's class is reading a book about Mexico.

8. The mail carrier placed the letters in the mailbox.

9. Grandma bought mandarin oranges at the market.

10. Our friend, Max, sailed along the great Mississippi River.

_____ _____ _____
_____ _____ _____
_____ _____ _____
               _____

Homework

 Name: _____ Date: ___/___/_____ Score: _____

Lesson 13.2

Reading Words with a Silent Letter "m"

✓ Lesson Check Point

 Directions: Read each target word. Find the letter "m" and put a check (✓) in the column that identifies its position: beginning, within or end.
Direksyons: Li chak mo objektif. Jwenn lèt "m" a epi mete yon tchèck (✓) nan kolòn ki idantifye pozisyon li an: nan kòmansman, ladan oubyen nan finisman.

Target Words	Beginning (First Letter)	Within	End (Last Letter)
1. monkey			
2. immune			
3. symmetry			
4. globalism			
5. mnemonic			

 Directions: Read each target word. Put a check (✓) in the "yes" column if the target word has a silent letter "m." Put a check (✓) in the "no" column if the target word does not have a silent letter "m."
Direksyons: Li chak mo objektif. Mete yon tchèk (✓) nan kolòn "yes" an si mo objektif la genyen yon lèt "m" ki pa pwononse. Mete yon tchèk (✓) nan kolòn "no" an si mo objektif la pa genyen yon lèt "m" ki pa pwononse.

Target Words	Yes	No
6. monkey		
7. immune		
8. symmetry		
9. globalism		
10. mnemonic		

Homework

Name: _____ Date: ___/___/_____ Score: _____

The Reading Challenge

Lesson 13.3

Reading Multisyllable Words

✓ **Lesson Check Point**

Directions: Read and divide each target word into syllables. Write each word and place a hyphen (-) between the syllables in the second column. Write the number of syllables in the third column. Use a dictionary or the Internet to check your answers.

Direksyons: Li epi divize chak mo objektif an silab. Ekri chak mo epi mete yon tirè (-) ant silab yo nan dezyèm kolòn nan. Ekri kantite silab ke yo genyen an nan twazyèm kolòn nan. Itilize yon diksyonè oubyen entènèt pou tcheke repons ou yo.

Target Words	Words Divided into Syllables	Number of Syllables
1. meditate	_____	_____
2. master	_____	_____
3. medium	_____	_____
4. Mexico	_____	_____
5. musical	_____	_____
6. mother	_____	_____
7. mustard	_____	_____
8. mystery	_____	_____
9. membrane	_____	_____
10. multiply	_____	_____

Unit M Lesson 13.3

Homework

 Name: _____ Date: ___/___/_____ Score: _____

The Reading Challenge

Lesson 13.3

Reading Multisyllable Words

✓ Lesson Check Point

 Directions: Read each target word. Circle the word in the row that is divided correctly into syllables. Use a dictionary or the Internet to check your answers.

Direksyons: Li chak mo objektif. Antoure mo a ki nan ranje a ki divize an silab korèkteman yo. Itilize yon diksyonè oubyen entènèt pou tcheke repons ou yo.

Model

| magazine | a. mag-a-zine (circled) | b. ma-ga-zine | c. mag-az-ine |

1. Milwaukee	a. Mil-wa-ukee	b. Mil-wau-kee	c. Mil-wauk-ee
2. monarchy	a. mon-ar-chy	b. mo-nar-chy	c. mon-archy
3. mediate	a. me-di-ate	b. med-i-ate	c. me-dia-te
4. magnetic	a. mag-net-ic	b. mag-ne-tic	c. magn-et-ic
5. Mercury	a. Merc-u-ry	b. Me-rcu-ry	c. Mer-cu-ry
6. mosquito	a. mos-qui-to	b. mo-squi-to	c. mos-quit-o
7. microwave	a. micr-o-wave	b. mic-ro-wave	c. mi-cro-wave
8. memento	a. mem-en-to	b. mem-e-nto	c. me-men-to

Learn to Read English With Directions In Haitian Creole

Homework

Name: _____ Date:___/___/_____ Score:_____

Lesson 13.4

Reading and Writing

Proper and Common Nouns and Adjectives

Directions: Read the words in the word box. Put an (X) on the line next to each word that is written incorrectly. Remember that all proper nouns and proper adjectives are capitalized. Use a dictionary or the Internet to check your answers.

Direksyons: Li chak mo yo ki nan bwat mo a. Met yon (X) sou ti trè a ki bò kote mo ki pa kri byen yo. Sonje ke tout non pwòp ak adjektif pwop ekri avèk yon lèt majiskil nan kòmansman yo. Itilize yon diksyonè oubyen entènèt pou tcheke repons ou yo.

Word Box					
___	miser	___	Mecca	___	Malta
___	muffins	___	manners	___	Master
___	malaysia	___	Millionaire	___	Monarch
___	massachusetts	___	manchester	___	Mexico

Directions: Read each unedited sentence and underline the word that is written incorrectly. Write each sentence correctly on the line.

Direksyons: Li chak fraz ki pa edite yo epi soulinye mo ki pa ekri byen an. Ekri chak fraz korèkteman sou liy lan.

Model
My son, Mark, is going to attend MIT in <u>massachusetts</u>.
<u>My son, Mark, is going to attend MIT in Massachusetts.</u>

1. Miss Miller will Marry Mr. McShine next month.

_____

2. My teacher, mr. Mann, lives in Martha's Vineyard.

_____

3. Every morning, my friend, molly, eats multi-grain cereal.

_____

4. In the morning, Matthew loves to listen to mozart's music.

_____

Homework

Name: _____ **Date:** ___/___/_____ **Score:** _____

Lesson 14.1

Reading Words with the Letter N/n

✓ **Lesson Check Point**

Directions: Read each target word. Find the letter "n" and put a check (✓) in the column that identifies its position: beginning, within or end.
Direksyons: Li chak mo objektif. Jwenn lèt "n" a epi mete yon tchèck (✓) nan kolòn ki idantifye pozisyon li an: nan kòmansman, ladan oubyen nan finisman.

Target Words	Beginning (First Letter)	Within	End (Last Letter)
1. freshen			
2. noodle			
3. number			
4. transfer			
5. linguistic			

Directions: Read each sentence and underline the words that begin with the letter "n." Write all the underlined words in alphabetical order on the lines below.
Direksyons: Li chak fraz epi soulinye mo ki kòmanse avèk lèt "n" yo. Ekri tout mo ki soulinye yo nan lòd alfabetik sou trè sa yo ki anba.

6. Jack wrote a note in his blue notebook.

7. Andrew narrated the play entitled, "Our Nation."

8. My grandmother is nibbling on nachos and cheese.

9. Newton wrote the numerator above the denominator.

10. Native Americans navigated their canoes along the Mississippi River.

_____   _____   _____
_____   _____   _____
_____   _____   _____
                _____

Unit N Lesson 14.1

Learn to Read English With Directions In Haitian Creole

Homework

Name: _____ Date:___/___/_____ Score:_____

Lesson 14.2

Reading Words with the "ng" Letter Combination

✓ Lesson Check Point

Directions: Read each target word. Circle the word in the column that has the same "ng" sound(s) as the target word.

Direksyons: Li chak mo objektif. Antoure mo a ki nan kolòn nan ki bay menm son "ng" la (yo) tankou mo objektif la.

engulf	a. manger
	b. engage

mango	a. linguist
	b. change

hanger	a. ranger
	b. younger

challenger	a. arranging
	b. angle

Directions: Read each target word. Put a check (✓) under the correct column heading.

Direksyons: Li chak mo objektif. Mete yon tchèk (✓) anba antèt kolòn ki kòrèk la.

Target Words	"ng" has the /n/ + /g/ sounds as in the word ingrain	"ng" has the /n/ + /j/ sounds as in the word ginger	"ng" has the /ng/ sound as in the word bang	"ng" has the /ng/ + /g/ sounds as in the word congress
1. engulf				
2. mango				
3. hanger				
4. challenger				

Homework

 Name: _____ Date: ___/___/_____ Score: _____

Lesson 14.3

Reading Words with a Silent Letter "n"

✓ Lesson Check Point

 Directions: Read the target words in the word box. Write the words that have a silent letter "n" in the first column. Write the words that do not have a silent letter "n" in the second column.

Direksyons: Li mo objektif yo ki nan ti bwat mo a. Ekri mo yo ki genyen lèt "n" ki pa pwononse a nan premye kolòn nan. Ekri mo yo ki pa genyen lèt "n" ki pa pwononse a nan dezyèm kolòn nan.

Target Word Box				
inner	needle	hymn	annex	solemn
frozen	bundle	handle	network	expanse
cannon	columns	landmark	chimneys	autumn
condemn	dominate	cinnamon	comments	column

Letter "n" is silent   Letter "n" has the /n/ sound

Homework

Name: _____ Date: ___/___/_____ Score: _____

The Reading Challenge

Lesson 14.4

Reading Multisyllable Words

✓ Lesson Check Point

Directions: Read and divide each target word into syllables. Write each word and place a hyphen (-) between the syllables in the second column. Write the number of syllables in the third column. Use a dictionary or the Internet to check your answers.

Direksyons: Li epi divize chak mo objektif an silab. Ekri chak mo epi mete yon tirè (-) ant silab yo nan dezyèm kolòn nan. Ekri kantite silab ke yo genyen an nan twazyèm kolòn nan. Itilize yon diksyonè oubyen entènèt pou tcheke repons ou yo.

Target Words	Words Divided into Syllables	Number of Syllables
1. nucleus	_____	_____
2. nobleman	_____	_____
3. nightly	_____	_____
4. nebula	_____	_____
5. navel	_____	_____
6. needless	_____	_____
7. ninety	_____	_____
8. noodle	_____	_____
9. negative	_____	_____
10. nervously	_____	_____

Homework

 Name: _____ Date: ___/___/_____ Score: _____

The Reading Challenge

Lesson 14.4

Reading Multisyllable Words

✓ Lesson Check Point

 Directions: Read each target word. Circle the word in the row that is divided correctly into syllables. Use a dictionary or the Internet to check your answers.

Direksyons: Li chak mo objektif. Antoure mo a ki nan ranje a ki divize an silab korèkteman yo. Itilize yon diksyonè oubyen entènèt pou tcheke repons ou yo.

Model

| napkin | a. na-pkin | b. napk-in | c. nap-kin (circled) |

1. nephew	a. neph-ew	b. ne-phew	c. nep-hew
2. nature	a. nat-ure	b. na-ture	c. natu-re
3. nursery	a. nurse-r-y	b. nurs-er-y	c. nur-ser-y
4. nominee	a. nom-i-nee	b. no-mi-nee	c. no-min-ee
5. nitrogen	a. nit-ro-gen	b. ni-tro-gen	c. nit-rog-en
6. Nevada	a. Nev-ad-a	b. Ne-va-da	c. Ne-vad-a
7. negative	a. ne-ga-tive	b. neg-a-tive	c. ne-gat-ive
8. nectarine	a. nec-ta-rine	b. nect-a-rine	c. nec-tar-ine

Homework

Name: _____ Date: ___/___/_____ Score: _____

Lesson 14.5

Reading and Writing

Proper and Common Nouns and Adjectives

Directions: Read the words in the word box. Put an (X) on the line next to each word that is written incorrectly. Remember that all proper nouns and proper adjectives are capitalized. Use a dictionary or the Internet to check your answers.

Direksyons: Li chak mo yo ki nan bwat mo a. Met yon (X) sou ti trè a ki bò kote mo ki pa kri byen yo. Sonje ke tout non pwòp ak adjektif pwop ekri avèk yon lèt majiskil nan kòmansman yo. Itilize yon diksyonè oubyen entènèt pou tcheke repons ou yo.

Word Box		
___ needy	___ nectar	___ negative
___ Nepal	___ Nibble	___ Newscast
___ new York	___ newark	___ New Mexico
___ niagara Falls	___ Neglect	___ New Amsterdam

Directions: Read each unedited sentence and underline the word that is written incorrectly. Write each sentence correctly on the line.

Direksyons: Li chak fraz ki pa edite yo epi soulinye mo ki pa ekri byen an. Ekri chak fraz korèkteman sou liy lan.

Model
Nick and Nancy live in the <u>netherlands</u>.
<u>Nick and Nancy live in the Netherlands.</u>

1. I bought my gold Necklace in Nigeria.

   _____

2. New York State is next to new Jersey.

   _____

3. The Newspaper article is about Nicaragua.

   _____

4. My Nephew, Nat, navigated his boat along the Nile River.

   _____

Unit N Lesson 14.5

Homework

 Name: _____ Date: ___/___/_____ Score: _____

Lesson 15.1

Reading Words with the Letter O/o

✓ Lesson Check Point

 Directions: Read each target word. Find the letter "o" and put a check (✓) in the column that identifies its position: beginning, within or end.
Direksyons: Li chak mo objektif. Jwenn lèt "o" a epi mete yon tchèck (✓) nan kolòn ki idantifye pozisyon li an: nan kòmansman, ladan oubyen nan finisman.

Target Words	Beginning (First Letter)	Within	End (Last Letter)
1. office			
2. house			
3. turbo			
4. object			
5. going			

 Directions: Read each target word. Read the words in the row and circle the word that has a different vowel "o" sound.
Direksyons: Li chak mo objektif. Li mo yo ki nan ranje a epi antoure mo a ki bay yon son vwayèl "o" ki diferan an.

Target Words				
6. most	boat	poke	cope	mob
7. doing	going	who	to	move
8. colder	bone	no	dot	poet
9. chosen	boxes	ago	float	hose
10. popping	knock	roll	lost	sock

Homework

 Name: _____ Date: ___/___/_____ Score: _____

Lesson 15.2

Reading Words with the Short Vowel "o" Sound

✓ **Lesson Check Point**

 Directions: Read the words in the four boxes. Circle two words with the short vowel /ŏ/ or /ô/ sound. The anchor word for the short vowel /ŏ/ and /ô/ sounds is <u>frog</u>.

Direksyons: Li mo yo ki nan kat ti bwat yo. Antoure de mo ki genyen son vwayèl kout /ŏ/ oubyen /ô/ a. Mo referans pou son vwayèl kout /ŏ/ ak /ô/ a se mo, <u>frog</u>.

cone	boast	poem	jock	knock	cold
snob	mock	boat	hog	bolt	blotch

open	soft	toll	frost	lot	almost
floss	old	soap	stock	fold	hog

 Directions: Read the words in the four boxes. Circle two words that rhyme. Rhyming words have the same ending sound, such as <u>hot</u> and <u>not</u>.

Direksyons: Li mo yo ki nan kat ti bwat yo. Antoure de mo ki rime. De mo oubyen plizyè mo ki rime genyen menm son nan finisman yo, tankou <u>hot</u> ak <u>not</u>.

dot	pot	yolk	clock	most	open
cold	cargo	yo-yo	block	pop	top

log	so	box	fox	doc	joke
fog	over	scold	token	mold	wok

Homework

Name: _____ Date: ___/___/_____ Score: _____

Lesson 15.2

Reading & Writing Words with the Short Vowel "o" Sound

✓ **Lesson Check Point**

Directions: Read each sentence and underline three words with the short vowel /ŏ/ or /ô/ sound. Then, write the underlined words on the lines below. The anchor word for the short vowel /ŏ/ and /ô/ sounds is <u>frog</u>.

Direksyons: Li chak fraz epi soulinye twa mo ki genyen son vwayèl kout /ŏ/ oubyen /ô/ a. Answit, ekri mo soulinye yo sou trè sa yo ki anba. Mo referans pou son vwayèl kout /ŏ/ ak /ô/ a se mo, <u>frog</u>.

Model

Everyone saw the <u>frog</u> <u>hop</u> close to the <u>rock</u>.

   frog   hop   rock
_____   _____   _____

1. Bob will jog around one block.

_____   _____   _____

2. Owen dropped the hot pot by the oven.

_____   _____   _____

3. My boss crossed the street and bought codfish.

_____   _____   _____

4. Odessa tossed the oversized frog back into the pond.

_____   _____   _____

5. Tom and Ricardo have three animals: an ox, a cat and a hog.

_____   _____   _____

Learn to Read English With Directions In Haitian Creole

Homework

 Name: _____   Date:___/___/_____   Score:_____

Lesson 15.3

Reading Words with the Long Vowel "o" Sound

✓ **Lesson Check Point**

 Directions: Read the words in the four boxes. Circle two words with the long vowel /ō/ sound. The anchor word for the long vowel /ō/ sound is <u>open</u>.

Direksyons: Li mo yo ki nan kat ti bwat yo. Antoure de mo ki genyen son vwayèl long /ō/ a. Mo referans pou son vwayèl long /ō/ a se mo, <u>open</u>.

note	stop
plot	foam

flop	loaf
soft	vote

blond	roam
shock	lobe

gloss	gloat
robe	doll

lock	stock
doe	goat

floss	nose
over	slot

 Directions: Read the words in the four boxes. Circle two words that rhyme. Rhyming words have the same ending sound, such as <u>hope</u> and <u>soap</u>.

Direksyons: Li mo yo ki nan kat ti bwat yo. Antoure de mo ki rime. De mo oubyen plizyè mo ki rime genyen menm son nan finisman yo, tankou <u>hope</u> ak <u>soap</u>.

chop	troll
toast	bowl

bond	dome
float	throat

long	coal
mock	goal

soak	poke
hose	moss

rope	most
load	rode

hose	rose
cope	dock

Homework

Name: _____ Date: ___/___/_____ Score: _____

Lesson 15.3

Reading & Writing Words with the Long Vowel "o" Sound

✓ Lesson Check Point

Directions: Read each sentence and underline three words with the long vowel /ō/ sound. Then, write the underlined words on the lines below. The anchor word for the long vowel /ō/ sound is <u>open</u>.

Direksyons: Li mo yo ki nan kat ti bwat yo. Antoure de mo ki genyen son vwayèl long /ō/ a. Mo referans pou son vwayèl long /ō/ a se mo, <u>open</u>.

Model

We will <u>go</u> to the <u>rodeo</u> and <u>limbo</u> competitions for fun.

     go   rodeo   limbo

1. The motel's lunch combo has two donuts for dessert.

   _____   _____   _____

2. The outstanding critic said, "Carlo's company logo is so-so."

   _____   _____   _____

3. The new apartment condo is going to become available in October.

   _____   _____   _____

4. The disc jockey will play disco music as we go under the limbo bar.

   _____   _____   _____

5. I read a poem about nomads who traveled along the Atlantic Ocean.

   _____   _____   _____

Learn to Read English With Directions In Haitian Creole

Homework

Name: _____ Date:___/___/_____ Score: _____

Review Lessons 15.2 & 15.3

Reading Short Vowel and Long Vowel Words

Directions: Read the target words in the word box. In the first column, write the words that have the short vowel /ŏ/ or /ô/ sound, as in the word <u>frog</u>. In the second column, write the words that have the long vowel /ō/ sound, as in the word <u>open</u>.

Direksyons: Li mo objektif yo ki nan bwat mo a. Nan premye kolòn nan, ekri mo yo ki bay son vwayèl kout /ŏ/ oubyen /ô/ a, tankou li ye nan mo <u>frog</u> la. Nan dezyèm kolòn nan, ekri mo yo ki bay son vwayèl long /ō/ a, tankou li ye nan mo <u>open</u> la.

Target Word Box				
close	mom	solar	poster	oval
almost	colder	ocean	boxers	patrol
conflict	hotter	jogging	proceed	doctor
dropping	swollen	stopped	mopping	potting

Letter "o" has the /ŏ/ or /ô/ sound as in the word <u>frog</u>

Letter "o" has the /ō/ sound as in the word <u>open</u>

_____   _____
_____   _____
_____   _____
_____   _____
_____   _____
_____   _____
_____   _____
_____   _____

Homework

 Name: _____ Date: ___/___/_____ Score: _____

Lesson 15.4

Reading Words with Letter "o" Vowel Pairs

✓ Lesson Check Point

 Directions: Read each target word. Circle the word in the column that has the same vowel "oa," "oe," "oo" or "ou" sound(s) as the target word.

Direksyons: Li chak mo objektif. Antoure mo a ki nan kolòn nan ki bay menm son vwayèl "oa," "oe," "oo" oubyen "ou" la (yo) tankou mo objektif la.

scout	a. goalie
	b. flounder

moan	a. aloe
	b. pounds

toast	a. lagoon
	b. banjoes

oboe	a. roast
	b. typhoon

 Directions: Read each target word. Put a check (✓) under the correct column heading.

Direksyons: Li chak mo objektif. Mete yon tchèk (✓) anba antèt kolòn ki kòrèk la.

Target Words	Words have the long "o" sound as in the word <u>coat</u>	Words do not have the long "o" sound
1. scout		
2. moan		
3. toast		
4. oboe		

Homework

 Name: _____ Date: ___/___/_____ Score: _____

Lesson 15.5

Reading Words with the Final Letter "o"

✓ **Lesson Check Point**

 Directions: Read each target word. Find the letter "o" and put a check (✓) in the column that identifies its position within the syllable.
Direksyons: Li chak mo objektif. Jwenn lèt "o" a epi mete yon tchèck (✓) nan kolòn nan ki idantifye pozisyon li an nan silab la.

Target Words	"o" is at the end of a one syllable word	"o" is at the end of the first syllable	"o" is at the end of a multi-syllable word
1. go			
2. ghetto			
3. bravo			
4. grocer			
5. hydro			

 Directions: Read each target word. Put a check (✓) under the correct column heading.
Direksyons: Li chak mo objektif. Mete yon tchèk (✓) anba antèt kolòn ki kòrèk la.

Target Words	"o" has the /ŏ/ sound as in the word frog	"o" has the /ō/ sound as in the word go	"o" has the /ə/ sound as in the word carrot	"o" is silent as in the word people
6. hotel				
7. pocket				
8. leopards				
9. complete				
10. wisdom				

Unit O Lesson 15.5

Homework

Name: _____ Date:___/___/_____ Score: _____

Lesson 15.6

Reading Letter "o" Words with the Schwa Vowel Sound

✓ Lesson Check Point

Directions: Read each target word. Circle the word in the column that has the same "o" sound as the target word.

Direksyons: Li chak mo objektif. Antoure mo a ki nan kolòn nan ki bay menm son "o" a tankou mo objektif la.

dozen	a. other
	b. opening

actor	a. parrot
	b. books

oppose	a. docks
	b. together

gallop	a. occur
	b. oceans

Directions: Read each sentence and underline the letter "o" word that has the schwa vowel /ə/ sound or short vowel /ŭ/ sound. The anchor word for the letter "o" schwa vowel /ə/ sound is carrot and the letter "o" short vowel /ŭ/ sound is dove.

Direksyons: Li chak fraz epi soulinye mo ki genyen lèt "o" a ki bay son schwa /ə/ oubyen son /ŭ/ a. Mo referans pou son schwa /ə/ lèt "o" a se carrot epi son lèt "o" /ŭ/ kout la se dove.

1. My brother opened two large, orange boxes.

2. Nothing was written in Oscar's new notebooks.

3. Mr. and Mrs. Lopez are going to the Ivory Coast.

4. In the afternoon, Orin drank cold coconut water.

5. My nephew is enrolled in an interesting history class.

6. Early in the morning, the pilot flew over South Africa.

Homework

 Name: _____ Date:___/___/_____ Score: _____

Lesson 15.7

Reading Words with Vowel "o" Sounds: /ŏ/, /ō/ & /o͞o/

✓ **Lesson Check Point**

Directions: Read each target word. Put a check (✓) under the correct column heading.

Direksyons: Li chak mo objektif. Mete yon tchèk (✓) anba antèt kolòn ki kòrèk la.

Target Words	"o" has the /ŏ/ sound as in the word <u>frog</u>	"o" has the /ō/ sound as in the word <u>go</u>	"o" has the /o͞o/ sound as in the word <u>to</u>
1. total			
2. doing			
3. proven			
4. holiday			
5. dollars			

Directions: Read each sentence and underline the word that has a letter "o" that has the vowel /o͞o/ sound, as in the word <u>too</u>.

Direksyons: Li chak fraz epi soulinye mo a ki genyen let "o" a ki bay son /o͞o/ an, tankou li ye nan mo <u>too</u> la.

6. Do we have an appointment?

7. Don will return home at two o'clock.

8. Ron skillfully proved his answer was correct.

9. I did not lose any money in the stock market.

10. Mrs. Oscar said, "Everyone must move their books."

Homework

 Name: _____ Date: ___/___/_____ Score: _____

Lesson 15.8

Reading Words with the "or" Letter Combination

✓ **Lesson Check Point**

 Directions: Read each target word. Circle the word in the column that has the same "o" + "r" sounds as the target word.
Direksyons: Li chak mo objektif. Antoure mo a ki nan kolòn nan ki bay menm son "o" + "r" yo tankou mo objektif la.

core	a. corn
	b. corrupt

border	a. normal
	b. corral

memory	a. forest
	b. doctor

spectator	a. conductor
	b. boring

 Directions: Read each target word. Put a check (✓) under the correct column heading.
Direksyons: Li chak mo objektif. Mete yon tchèk (✓) anba antèt kolòn ki kòrèk la.

Target Words	"or" has the /ô/ + /r/ sounds as in the word <u>door</u>	"or" has the /ə/ + /r/ sounds as in the word <u>doctor</u>
1. core		
2. border		
3. memory		
4. spectator		

Homework

Name: _____ Date: ___/___/_____ Score: _____

Lesson 15.8

Reading Words with the "or" Letter Combination

Dictionary Skills/ Vocabulary

✓ **Lesson Check Point**

Directions: Read each target word and its definition. Write the target word on the line in front of its meaning. Use a dictionary or the Internet to check your answers.

Direksyons: Li chak mo objektif ak definisyon yo chak. Ekri mo objektif la sou trè ki devan definisyon li an. Itilize yon diksyonè oubyen entènèt pou tcheke repons ou yo.

Target Word Box				
shortest	corn	horse	poor	sport

1. _____ yellow or white grain
2. _____ a large four-legged animal
3. _____ measurement that is least in a series
4. _____ a physical activity and/or game
5. _____ a state of not having money for basic

Directions: Read each sentence and write the target word that correctly completes the sentence.

Direksyons: Li chak fraz epi ekri mo objektif ki konplete fraz la kòrèkteman.

6. Tom's favorite _____ is baseball.

7. The _____ woman is applying for a job.

8. The _____ is eating a pile of hay by the barn.

9. Horace is the _____ boy in Mr. James' class.

10. The farmer has healthy stalks of _____ on his farm.

Homework

 Name: _____ Date:___/___/_____ Score:_____

Lesson 15.9

Reading Words with a Silent Letter "o"

✓ Lesson Check Point

 Directions: Read the target words in the word box. Write the words that have a silent letter "o" in the first column. Write the words that do not have a silent letter "o" in the second column.

Direksyons: Li mo objektif yo ki nan ti bwat mo a. Ekri mo yo ki genyen lèt "o" ki pa pwononse a nan premye kolòn nan. Ekri mo yo ki pa genyen lèt "o" ki pa pwononse a nan dezyèm kolòn nan.

Target Word Box				
total	rocks	orders	leopard	zero
leopards	Leonard	mouse	popular	people
subpoena	opening	Phoenix	brother	hoping
Phoenician	jeopardy	subpoenas	someone	jeopardize

Letter "o" is silent   Letter "o" has a letter "o" sound

Unit O
Lesson 15.9

Learn to Read English With Directions In Haitian Creole   155   Copyrighted Material

Homework

Name: _____ Date: ___/___/_____ Score: _____

Unit Review - O/o

Reading Words with Vowel "o" Sounds: /ŏ/, /ō/, /ə/ & Silent

✓ **Lesson Check Point**

Directions: Read each target word. Circle the word in the column that has the same "o" sound as the target word.

Direksyons: Li chak mo objektif. Antoure mo a ki nan kolòn nan ki bay menm son "o" a tankou mo objektif la.

motel	a. poster
	b. monkey

optical	a. rocking
	b. doing

observe	a. retrospect
	b. opening

subpoena	a. marigold
	b. leopard

Directions: Read each target word. Put a check (✓) under the correct column heading.

Direksyons: Li chak mo objektif. Mete yon tchèk (✓) anba antèt kolòn ki kòrèk la.

Target Words	"o" has the /ŏ/ sound as in the word **frog**	"o" has the /ō/ sound as in the word **go**	"o" has the /ə/ sound as in the word **carrot**	"o" is silent as in the word **people**
1. motel				
2. optical				
3. observe				
4. subpoena				

Learn to Read English With Directions In Haitian Creole

Homework

 Name: _____ Date: ___/___/_____ Score: _____

The Reading Challenge

Lesson 15.10

Reading Multisyllable Words

✓ **Lesson Check Point**

 Directions: Read and divide each target word into syllables. Write each word and place a hyphen (-) between the syllables in the second column. Write the number of syllables in the third column. Use a dictionary or the Internet to check your answers.

Direksyons: Li epi divize chak mo objektif an silab. Ekri chak mo epi mete yon tirè (-) ant silab yo nan dezyèm kolòn nan. Ekri kantite silab ke yo genyen an nan twazyèm kolòn nan. Itilize yon diksyonè oubyen entènèt pou tcheke repons ou yo.

Target Words	Words Divided into Syllables	Number of Syllables
1. localize		
2. total		
3. remote		
4. poetry		
5. noble		
6. devoting		
7. pony		
8. morning		
9. moisture		
10. pointless		

Learn to Read English With Directions In Haitian Creole

Homework

 Name: _____ Date: ___/___/_____ Score: _____

The Reading Challenge

Lesson 15.10

Reading Multisyllable Words

✓ **Lesson Check Point**

 Directions: Read each target word. Circle the word in the row that is divided correctly into syllables. Use a dictionary or the Internet to check your answers.

Direksyons: Li chak mo objektif. Antoure mo a ki nan ranje a ki divize an silab korèkteman yo. Itilize yon diksyonè oubyen entènèt pou tcheke repons ou yo.

Model

| proposal | a. prop-o-sal | b. pro-po-sal | c. pro-pos-al |

1. calculator	a. cal-cul-ator	b. calc-ul-ator	c. cal-cu-la-tor
2. Yoruba	a. Yo-ru-ba	b. Yor-u-ba	c. Yor-ub-a
3. reservoir	a. re-ser-voir	b. res-er-voir	c. res-e-rvoir
4. monitor	a. mon-it-or	b. mon-i-tor	c. mo-nit-or
5. avocado	a. av-o-ca-do	b. av-oca-do	c. a-voc-a-do
6. creditor	a. cre-dit-or	b. cred-it-or	c. cred-i-tor
7. diploma	a. dip-lo-ma	b. di-plo-ma	c. di-plom-a
8. marigold	a. ma-ri-gold	b. mar-i-gold	c. ma-rig-old

Homework

Name: _____ Date: ___/___/_____ Score: _____

Lesson 15.11

Reading and Writing

Proper and Common Nouns and Adjectives

Directions: Read the words in the word box. Put an (X) on the line next to each word that is written incorrectly. Remember that all proper nouns and proper adjectives are capitalized. Use a dictionary or the Internet to check your answers.

Direksyons: Li chak mo yo ki nan bwat mo a. Met yon (X) sou ti trè a ki bò kote mo ki pa kri byen yo. Sonje ke tout non pwòp ak adjektif pwop ekri avèk yon lèt majiskil nan kòmansman yo. Itilize yon diksyonè oubyen entènèt pou tcheke repons ou yo.

Word Box		
___ orion	___ Ohio	___ optical
___ Oxford	___ occupant	___ Omnivore
___ october	___ Octopus	___ Ornament
___ observable	___ oval Office	___ Ottoman Empire

Directions: Read each unedited sentence and underline the word that is written incorrectly. Write each sentence correctly on the line.

Direksyons: Li chak fraz ki pa edite yo epi soulinye mo ki pa ekri byen an. Ekri chak fraz korèkteman sou liy lan.

Model
At <u>One</u> o'clock, the Owens family went to Onega Bay.
<u>At one o'clock, the Owens family went to Onega Bay.</u>

1. Mr. and Mrs. Oscar bought a house by the Ocean.

   _____

2. Odessa is reading about the origin of the olympics.

   _____

3. The professors at oxford are studying the ozone layer.

   _____

4. our cruise ship, Odyssey, sailed across the Atlantic Ocean.

   _____

Homework

Name: _____ Date: ___/___/_____ Score: _____

Lesson 16.1

Reading Words with the Letter P/p

✓ **Lesson Check Point**

Directions: Read each target word. Find the letter "p" and put a check (✓) in the column that identifies its position: beginning, within or end.
Direksyons: Li chak mo objektif. Jwenn lèt "p" a epi mete yon tchèck (✓) nan kolòn ki idantifye pozisyon li an: nan kòmansman, ladan oubyen nan finisman.

Target Words	Beginning (First Letter)	Within	End (Last Letter)
1. grip			
2. pilot			
3. plain			
4. octopus			
5. complain			

Directions: Read each sentence and underline the words that begin with the letter "p." Write all the underlined words in alphabetical order on the lines below.
Direksyons: Li chak fraz epi soulinye mo ki kòmanse avèk lèt "p" yo. Ekri tout mo ki soulinye yo nan lòd alfabetik sou trè sa yo ki anba.

6. The Perez family is from Peru.

7. I work part-time at a perfume company.

8. The pharmacy is located in Houston Plaza.

9. Jenny has a pencil and five pens in her bag.

10. Dr. Andrew gave me a private physical examination.

_____ _____ _____
_____ _____ _____
_____

Homework

 Name: _____ Date: ___/___/_____ Score: _____

Lesson 16.2

Reading Words with the "ph" Letter Combination

✓ Lesson Check Point

 Directions: Read each target word. Circle the word in the column that has the same "ph" sound(s) as the target word.

Direksyons: Li chak mo objektif. Antoure mo a ki nan kolòn nan ki bay menm son "ph" la (yo) tankou mo objektif la.

| dolphin | a. physical |
| | b. shepherd |

| esophagus | a. photography |
| | b. upheaval |

| haphazard | a. physics |
| | b. upholster |

| physician | a. phrase |
| | b. uphold |

 Directions: Read each target word. Put a check (✓) under the correct column heading.

Dircksyons: Li chak mo objektif. Mete yon tchèk (✓) anba antèt kolòn ki kòrèk la.

Target Words	"ph" has the /f/ sound as in the word <u>phone</u>	"ph" has the /p/ +/h/ sounds as in the word <u>uphill</u>
1. dolphin		
2. esophagus		
3. haphazard		
4. physician		

Homework

Name: _____ Date: ___/___/_____ Score: _____

Lesson 16.3

Reading Words with the "pr" Letter Combination

Dictionary Skills/ Vocabulary

✓ **Lesson Check Point**

Directions: Read each target word and its definition. Write the letter of the definition on the line of each target word. Use a dictionary or the Internet to check your answers.

Direksyons: Li chak mo objektif ak definisyon yo chak. Ekri lèt la ki koresponn ak definisyon an sou trè chak mo objektif yo. Itilize yon diksyonè oubyen entènèt pou tcheke repons ou yo.

Target Words	Definitions
1. __ print	a. the son of a king
2. __ profit	b. money earned from the sale of products
3. __ prince	c. to do something repeatedly in order to improve
4. __ practice	d. state of a woman carrying a baby within her womb
5. __ pregnant	e. to produce an image or text on a surface

Directions: Read each sentence and write the target word that correctly completes the sentence.
Direksyons: Li chak fraz epi ekri mo objektif ki konplete fraz la kòrèkteman.

6. Alex has to _____ his violin every day.

7. My teacher, Mrs. Primis, is six months _____.

8. I will _____ a picture of an artist on my cover page.

9. The king is preparing the _____ to become a great ruler.

10. The business owner is planning to make a _____ this year.

Homework

Name: _____ Date: ___/___/_____ Score: _____

Lesson 16.4

Reading Words with the "pl" Letter Combination

Dictionary Skills/ Vocabulary

✓ Lesson Check Point

Directions: Read each target word and its definition. Write the target word on the line in front of its meaning. Use a dictionary or the Internet to check your answers.

Direksyons: Li chak mo objektif ak definisyon yo chak. Ekri mo objektif la sou trè ki devan definisyon li an. Itilize yon diksyonè oubyen entènèt pou tcheke repons ou yo.

Target Word Box				
planet	play	pliers	plaza	pleaded

1. _____ a metal or durable plastic tool
2. _____ the act of doing something fun
3. _____ to have appealed earnestly
4. _____ a small shopping center within a community
5. _____ sphere shaped, celestial object within the solar

Directions: Read each sentence. Underline the word in the parentheses that correctly completes each sentence. Then, write the underlined word on the line.

Direksyons: Li chak fraz. Soulinye mo a ki nan parantèz yo ki konplete chak fraz kòrèkteman. Answit, ekri mo soulinye a sou trè a.

6. Earth is the third _____ from the sun. (planet, pleaded)

7. The children will _____ baseball on Saturday. (plaza, play)

8. Paul needs a pair of _____ to fix the bench. (planet, pliers)

9. Peter's pastry shop is in the new shopping _____. (plaza, play)

10. At court, the plaintiff _____ with the judge. (pleaded, pliers)

Homework

 Name: _____ Date:___/___/_____ Score: _____

Lesson 16.4

Reading Words with the "ple" Letter Combination

✓ Lesson Check Point

 Directions: Read each target word. Find the "ple" letter combination and put a check (✓) in the column that identifies its position: beginning, within or end.

Direksyons: Li chak mo objektif. Jwenn konbinezon lèt "ple" a epi mete yon tchèk (✓) nan kolòn nan ki idantifye pozisyon li an: nan kòmansman, ladan oubyen nan finisman.

Target Words	Beginning (First 3 Letters)	Within	End (Last 3 Letters)
1. dimple			
2. example			
3. pleasant			
4. principle			
5. incomplete			

 Directions: Read each target word. Put a check (✓) in the "yes" column if the "ple" letter combination has the /p/ + /ə/ + /l/ sounds. Put a check (✓) in the "no" column if the "ple" letter combination does not have the /p/ + /ə/ + /l/ sounds.

Direksyons: Li chak mo objektif. Mete yon tchèk (✓) nan kolòn "yes" an si konbinezon let "ple" a bay sons /p/ + /ə/ + /l/. Mete yon tchèk (✓) nan kolòn "no" an si konbinezon let "ple" a pa bay sons /p/ + /ə/ + /l/.

Target Words	Yes	No
6. dimple		
7. example		
8. pleasant		
9. principle		
10. incomplete		

Homework

 Name: _____ Date: ___/___/_____ Score: _____

Lesson 16.5

Reading Words with a Silent Letter "p"

✓ Lesson Check Point

   Directions: Read the target words in the word box. Write the words that have a silent letter "p" in the first column. Write the words that do not have a silent letter "p" in the second column.

Direksyons: Li mo objektif yo ki nan ti bwat mo a. Ekri mo yo ki genyen lèt "p" ki pa pwononse a nan premye kolòn nan. Ekri mo yo ki pa genyen lèt "p" ki pa pwononse a nan dezyèm kolòn nan.

Target Word Box				
trips	coup	receipt	rump	jumps
lamp	pseudo	happen	prove	bishop
cupboard	approve	opposite	hamper	pepper
pamphlet	raspberry	trappings	complete	presume

Letter "p" is silent

Letter "p" has the /p/ sound

Homework

Name: _____ Date: ___/___/_____ Score: _____

The Reading Challenge

Lesson 16.6

Reading Multisyllable Words

✓ Lesson Check Point

Directions: Read and divide each target word into syllables. Write each word and place a hyphen (-) between the syllables in the second column. Write the number of syllables in the third column. Use a dictionary or the Internet to check your answers.

Direksyons: Li epi divize chak mo objektif an silab. Ekri chak mo epi mete yon tirè (-) ant silab yo nan dezyèm kolòn nan. Ekri kantite silab ke yo genyen an nan twazyèm kolòn nan. Itilize yon diksyonè oubyen entènèt pou tcheke repons ou yo.

Target Words	Words Divided into Syllables	Number of Syllables
1. painting		
2. paragraph		
3. pinwheel		
4. provoking		
5. precedent		
6. player		
7. pipeline		
8. peninsula		
9. pyramid		
10. program		

Homework

 Name: _____ Date: ___/___/_____ Score: _____

The Reading Challenge

Lesson 16.6

Reading Multisyllable Words

✓ Lesson Check Point

 Directions: Read each target word. Circle the word in the row that is divided correctly into syllables. Use a dictionary or the Internet to check your answers.

Direksyons: Li chak mo objektif. Antoure mo a ki nan ranje a ki divize an silab korèkteman yo. Itilize yon diksyonè oubyen entènèt pou tcheke repons ou yo.

Model

| paragraph | a. par-a-graph ⬭ | b. pa-ra-graph | c. par-ag-raph |

| 1. policy | a. po-li-cy | b. pol-i-cy | c. polic-y |

| 2. popular | a. pop-u-lar | b. po-pu-lar | c. po-pul-ar |

| 3. Pacific | a. Pac-i-fic | b. Pa-cif-ic | c. Pa-ci-fic |

| 4. piano | a. pia-n-o | b. pi-an-o | c. pi-a-no |

| 5. pajamas | a. paj-a-mas | b. pa-jam-as | c. pa-ja-mas |

| 6. president | a. pre-sid-ent | b. pres-i-dent | c. pres-id-ent |

| 7. physical | a. phys-i-cal | b. phy-si-cal | c. ph-ysic-al |

| 8. politics | a. po-lit-ics | b. po-li-tics | c. pol-i-tics |

Homework

Name: _____ Date:___/___/_____ Score:_____

Lesson 16.7

Reading and Writing

Proper and Common Nouns and Adjectives

Directions: Read the words in the word box. Put an (X) on the line next to each word that is written incorrectly. Remember that all proper nouns and proper adjectives are capitalized. Use a dictionary or the Internet to check your answers.

Direksyons: Li chak mo yo ki nan bwat mo a. Met yon (X) sou ti trè a ki bò kote mo ki pa kri byen yo. Sonje ke tout non pwòp ak adjektif pwop ekri avèk yon lèt majiskil nan kòmansman yo. Itilize yon diksyonè oubyen entènèt pou tcheke repons ou yo.

Word Box		
___ panda	___ parrot	___ patient
___ partner	___ Person	___ Peacock
___ Parakeet	___ portland	___ portugal
___ Paraguay	___ Paralegal	___ Panama

Directions: Read each unedited sentence and underline the word that is written incorrectly. Write each sentence correctly on the line.

Direksyons: Li chak fraz ki pa edite yo epi soulinye mo ki pa ekri byen an. Ekri chak fraz korèkteman sou liy lan.

Model
The poem, "puddles," was written by Patrick Parker.
The poem, "Puddles," was written by Patrick Parker.

1. The Pouter pigeons flew to Paramount plaza.

   _____

2. The Pilot will land the plane in the Philippines.

   _____

3. The Passengers are on their way to Poland, Oregon.

   _____

4. The Paterson police officers are trained to protect the People.

   _____

Homework

Name: _____ Date: ___/___/_____ Score: _____

Lesson 17.1

Reading Words with the Letter Q/q

✓ Lesson Check Point

Directions: Read each target word. Find the letter "q" and put a check (✓) in the column that identifies its position: beginning, within or end.
Direksyons: Li chak mo objektif. Jwenn lèt "q" a epi mete yon tchèck (✓) nan kolòn ki idantifye pozisyon li an: nan kòmansman, ladan oubyen nan finisman.

Target Words	Beginning (First Letter)	Within	End (Last Letter)
1. conquer			
2. question			
3. quadruplet			
4. disqualified			
5. consequence			

Directions: Read each sentence and underline the words that begin with the letter "q." Write all the underlined words in alphabetical order on the lines below.
Direksyons: Li chak fraz epi soulinye mo ki kòmanse avèk lèt "q" yo. Ekri tout mo ki soulinye yo nan lòd alfabetik sou trè sa yo ki anba.

6. Janice plans to quit her job at the quilting mill.

7. Queenisha and Christopher quibbled over an issue.

8. Recently, the profits at Quantum Inc. have quadrupled.

9. Quincy is a quarterback on the high school's football team.

10. My mother made a beautiful queen-size quilt for her bed.

_____   _____   _____
_____   _____   _____
_____   _____   _____
                 _____

Learn to Read English With Directions In Haitian Creole   169   Copyrighted Material

Homework

 Name: _____ Date: ___/___/_____ Score: _____

Lesson 17.2

Reading Words with the Letter "q" and "qu" Letter Combination

✓ **Lesson Check Point**

 Directions: Read each target word. Circle the word in the column that has the same "q" or "qu" sound(s) as the target word.

Direksyons: Li chak mo objektif. Antoure mo a ki nan kolòn nan ki bay menm son "q" oubyen "qu" a (yo) tankou mo objektif la.

| antique | a. quietly |
| | b. Albuquerque |

| quicken | a. acquire |
| | b. conquer |

| quarters | a. equator |
| | b. qindarka |

| boutique | a. question |
| | b. mosque |

 Directions: Read each target word. Put a check (✓) under the correct column heading.

Direksyons: Li chak mo objektif. Mete yon tchèk (✓) anba antèt kolòn ki kòrèk la.

Target Words	"qu" has the /k/ sound as in the word plaque	"qu" has the /k/ + /w/ sounds as in the word queen
1. antique		
2. quicken		
3. quarters		
4. boutique		

Homework

 Name: _____ Date:___/___/_____ Score: _____

Lesson 17.2

Reading Words with the "qu" Letter Combination

✓ Lesson Check Point

 Directions: Read each target word. Circle the word in the column that has the same "qu" sound(s) as the target word.
Direksyons: Li chak mo objektif. Antoure mo a ki nan kolòn nan ki bay menm son "qu" a (yo) tankou mo objektif la.

lacquer	a. requirement
	b. racquet

squirrel	a. inquisitive
	b. boutique

inquiring	a. lacquer
	b. requests

consequence	a. opaque
	b. squarely

 Directions: Read each target word. Put a check (✓) under the correct column heading.
Direksyons: Li chak mo objektif. Mete yon tchèk (✓) anba antèt kolòn ki kòrèk la.

Target Words	"qu" has the /k/ + /w/ sounds as in the word <u>queen</u>	"qu" has the /k/ sound as in the word <u>plaque</u>	"qu" is silent as in the word <u>racquet</u>
1. lacquer			
2. squirrel			
3. inquiring			
4. consequence			

Homework

Name: _____ Date: ___/___/_____ Score: _____

The Reading Challenge

Lesson 17.3

Reading Multisyllable Words

 Lesson Check Point

 Directions: Read and divide each target word into syllables. Write each word and place a hyphen (-) between the syllables in the second column. Write the number of syllables in the third column. Use a dictionary or the Internet to check your answers.

Direksyons: Li epi divize chak mo objektif an silab. Ekri chak mo epi mete yon tirè (-) ant silab yo nan dezyèm kolòn nan. Ekri kantite silab ke yo genyen an nan twazyèm kolòn nan. Itilize yon diksyonè oubyen entènèt pou tcheke repons ou yo.

Target Words	Words Divided into Syllables	Number of Syllables
1. quirky	_____	_____
2. quicksand	_____	_____
3. quilted	_____	_____
4. questioning	_____	_____
5. queasy	_____	_____
6. quality	_____	_____
7. qualitative	_____	_____
8. quarterly	_____	_____
9. qualification	_____	_____
10. quickening	_____	_____

Homework

 Name: _____ Date: ___/___/_____ Score: _____

The Reading Challenge

Lesson 17.3

Reading Multisyllable Words

✓ Lesson Check Point

Directions: Read each target word. Circle the word in the row that is divided correctly into syllables. Use a dictionary or the Internet to check your answers.

Direksyons: Li chak mo objektif. Antoure mo a ki nan ranje a ki divize an silab korèkteman yo. Itilize yon diksyonè oubyen entènèt pou tcheke repons ou yo.

Model

| quarter | a. quart-er | b. quar-ter | c. qu-arter |

| 1. quarantine | a. quar-an-tine | b. qua-rant-ine | c. qua-ran-tine |

| 2. quadruplet | a. qua-drup-let | b. quad-rup-let | c. quad-rupl-et |

| 3. qualified | a. qua-lif-ied | b. qua-li-fied | c. qual-i-fied |

| 4. quicken | a. quick-en | b. qui-cken | c. quic-ken |

| 5. quivering | a. qui-veri-ng | b. quiv-er-ing | c. qui-ver-ing |

| 6. quotation | a. quot-a-tion | b. quo-ta-tion | c. quot-at-ion |

| 7. quotient | a. quo-tient | b. quot-ient | c. qu-otient |

| 8. quotable | a. quo-tab-le | b. quo-ta-ble | c. quot-a-ble |

Homework

Name: _____ Date: ___/___/_____ Score: _____

Lesson 17.4

Reading and Writing

Proper and Common Nouns and Adjectives

Directions: Read the words in the word box. Put an (X) on the line next to each word that is written incorrectly. Remember that all proper nouns and proper adjectives are capitalized. Use a dictionary or the Internet to check your answers.

Direksyons: Li chak mo yo ki nan bwat mo a. Met yon (X) sou ti trè a ki bò kote mo ki pa kri byen yo. Sonje ke tout non pwòp ak adjektif pwop ekri avèk yon lèt majiskil nan kòmansman yo. Itilize yon diksyonè oubyen entènèt pou tcheke repons ou yo.

Word Box		
___ quarterly	___ Quaker	___ qatar
___ Quotient	___ Questions	___ queen
___ quarantine	___ Mrs. quincy	___ quickly
___ Mr. Quinn	___ queen's Park	___ Quiver

Directions: Read each unedited sentence and underline the word that is written incorrectly. Write each sentence correctly on the line.

Direksyons: Li chak fraz ki pa edite yo epi soulinye mo ki pa ekri byen an. Ekri chak fraz korèkteman sou liy lan.

Model

The <u>queen</u> of England was very quiet.
<u>The Queen of England was very quiet.</u>

1. Quinn said, "Yemen and qatar are located on the Arabian Peninsula."
   _____

2. Dr. quinta practices medicine at Queens General Hospital.
   _____

3. Mr. Q is qualified for the position at quantum Incorporated.
   _____

4. Pam's Quadruplets are named Queen, Queenie, Quincy and Quinsy.
   _____

Homework

Name: _____ Date: ___/___/_____ Score: _____

Lesson 18.1

Reading Words with the Letter R/r

✓ Lesson Check Point

Directions: Read each target word. Find the letter "r" and put a check (✓) in the column that identifies its position: beginning, within or end.
Direksyons: Li chak mo objektif. Jwenn lèt "r" a epi mete yon tchèck (✓) nan kolòn ki idantifye pozisyon li an: nan kòmansman, ladan oubyen nan finisman.

Target Words	Beginning (First Letter)	Within	End (Last Letter)
1. finger			
2. radius			
3. carpet			
4. dollar			
5. graduation			

Directions: Read each sentence and underline the words that begin with the letter "r." Write all the underlined words in alphabetical order on the lines below.
Direksyons: Li chak fraz epi soulinye mo ki kòmanse avèk lèt "r" yo. Ekri tout mo ki soulinye yo nan lòd alfabetik sou trè sa yo ki anba.

6. The runners are training for the Riverside Marathon.

7. Gary received a green rocket ship from his favorite aunt.

8. We are returning from a revitalizing tour of the Amazon.

9. Lily and her friends ate chicken and rice at the restaurant.

10. Molly read four nonfiction books about dogs and raccoons.

_____   _____   _____
_____   _____   _____
_____   _____   _____
                   _____

Homework

Name: _____ Date: ___/___/_____ Score: _____

Lesson 18.2

Reading Words with the Letter "r" Combinations:
"br," "cr," "dr," "fr," "gr," "pr" and "tr"

✓ **Lesson Check Point**

Directions: Read the target words in the word box. Identify the words with the following letter combinations: "br," "cr," "dr," "fr," "gr," "pr" and "tr." Write the target word on the line that correctly completes each sentence.

Direksyons: Li chak mo objektif yo ki nan bwat mo a. Idantifye mo yo ki gen konbinezon lèt: "br," "cr," "dr," "fr," "gr," "pr" ak "tr" yo. Ekri mo objektif la sou liy nan ki konplete korèkteman fraz la.

Target Word Box			
groom	brown	truck	dress
cream || frozen || president	
train	cross-examined || cry	

1. Francis is eating fresh fruit with vanilla _____.

2. The bride and _____ are standing on a bridge.

3. Frank said, "The block of ice is _____ solid."

4. The _____ driver is driving along the highway.

5. Brenda is wearing a pretty _____ to the prom.

6. Yesterday, Brad was elected senior class _____.

7. The colors of the crayons are red, blue and _____.

8. The lawyer effectively _____ the character witness.

9. All babies _____ when they experience hunger.

10. Gare du Lyon is a magnificent _____ station in France.

Learn to Read English With Directions In Haitian Creole   Copyrighted Material

Homework

 Name: _____ Date: ___/___/_____ Score: _____

The Reading Challenge

Lesson 18.3

Reading Multisyllable Words

✓ **Lesson Check Point**

Directions: Read and divide each target word into syllables. Write each word and place a hyphen (-) between the syllables in the second column. Write the number of syllables in the third column. Use a dictionary or the Internet to check your answers.

Direksyons: Li epi divize chak mo objektif an silab. Ekri chak mo epi mete yon tirè (-) ant silab yo nan dezyèm kolòn nan. Ekri kantite silab ke yo genyen an nan twazyèm kolòn nan. Itilize yon diksyonè oubyen entènèt pou tcheke repons ou yo.

Target Words	Words Divided into Syllables	Number of Syllables
1. rocket	_____	_____
2. rarely	_____	_____
3. recalling	_____	_____
4. ratify	_____	_____
5. recap	_____	_____
6. ravine	_____	_____
7. receiver	_____	_____
8. redeeming	_____	_____
9. raisin	_____	_____
10. robotics	_____	_____

Homework

Name: _____ Date: ___/___/_____ Score: _____

The Reading Challenge

Lesson 18.3

Reading Multisyllable Words

✓ **Lesson Check Point**

Directions: Read each target word. Circle the word in the row that is divided correctly into syllables. Use a dictionary or the Internet to check your answers.

Direksyons: Li chak mo objektif. Antoure mo a ki nan ranje a ki divize an silab korèkteman yo. Itilize yon diksyonè oubyen entènèt pou tcheke repons ou yo.

Model

| runaway | a. ru-na-way | b. run-a-way | c. run-aw-ay |

| 1. recapture | a. re-cap-ture | b. re-capt-ure | c. rec-ap-ture |

| 2. romantic | a. rom-an-tic | b. ro-mant-ic | c. ro-man-tic |

| 3. rigorous | a. rig-o-rous | b. ri-gor-ous | c. rig-or-ous |

| 4. refugee | a. re-fu-gee | b. ref-u-gee | c. ref-ug-ee |

| 5. ridicule | a. rid-i-cule | b. ri-dic-ule | c. ri-di-cule |

| 6. royalty | a. ro-yal-ty | b. roy-al-ty | c. roy-a-lty |

| 7. reversal | a. re-ver-sal | b. rev-er-sal | c. re-vers-al |

| 8. recliner | a. recl-i-ner | b. re-clin-er | c. rec-li-ner |

Homework

Name: _____ Date: ___/___/_____ Score: _____

Lesson 18.4

Reading and Writing

Proper and Common Nouns and Adjectives

Directions: Read the words in the word box. Put an (X) on the line next to each word that is written incorrectly. Remember that all proper nouns and proper adjectives are capitalized. Use a dictionary or the Internet to check your answers.

Direksyons: Li chak mo yo ki nan bwat mo a. Met yon (X) sou ti trè a ki bò kote mo ki pa kri byen yo. Sonje ke tout non pwòp ak adjektif pwop ekri avèk yon lèt majiskil nan kòmansman yo. Itilize yon diksyonè oubyen entènèt pou tcheke repons ou yo.

Word Box					
__	Ranger	__	RSVP	__	Raffle
__	reunion	__	royalty	__	realtor
__	Raccoon	__	roman Empire	__	ruthenia
__	rio Grande	__	Rhodes scholar	__	riverside

Directions: Read each unedited sentence and underline the word that is written incorrectly. Write each sentence correctly on the line.

Direksyons: Li chak fraz ki pa edite yo epi soulinye mo ki pa ekri byen an. Ekri chak fraz korèkteman sou liy lan.

Model
We saw two <u>Retired</u> racehorses at Richardson Ranch.
<u>We saw two retired racehorses at Richardson Ranch.</u>

1. Roya is Reading her favorite play, "Romeo and Juliet!"

   _____

2. My friend, Rose, bought a nice ring in rio de Janeiro, Brazil.

   _____

3. Mr. Raymond is studying russian at Russia's best university.

   _____

4. rita learned that the Nile River provides rich soil for agriculture.

   _____

Homework

Name: _____   Date: ___/___/_____   Score: _____

Lesson 19.1

Reading Words with the Letter S/s

✓ **Lesson Check Point**

Directions: Read each target word. Find the letter "s" and put a check (✓) in the column that identifies its position: beginning, within or end.
Direksyons: Li chak mo objektif. Jwenn lèt "s" a epi mete yon tchèck (✓) nan kolòn ki idantifye pozisyon li an: nan kòmansman, ladan oubyen nan finisman.

Target Words	Beginning (First Letter)	Within	End (Last Letter)
1. single			
2. seminar			
3. constant			
4. brothers			
5. cheeseburger			

Directions: Read each sentence and underline the words that begin with the letter "s." Write all the underlined words in alphabetical order on the lines below.
Direksyons: Li chak fraz epi soulinye mo ki kòmanse avèk lèt "s" yo. Ekri tout mo ki soulinye yo nan lòd alfabetik sou trè sa yo ki anba.

6. You cannot cut a sandwich with scissors.

7. Joy wrote four sentences about sailboats.

8. At college, I am studying computer science.

9. Everyone is saving money for the school trip.

10. We are scheduled to go shopping at one o'clock.

_____   _____   _____
_____   _____   _____
               _____

Homework

 Name: _____ Date: ___/___/_____ Score: _____

Lesson 19.1

Reading Words with the Letter S/s

✓ Lesson Check Point

 Directions: Read each target word. Circle the word in the column that has the same "s" sound as the target word.
Direksyons: Li chak mo objektif. Antoure mo a ki nan kolòn nan ki bay menm son "s" a tankou mo objektif la.

daisy	a. twins
	b. sauce

tissue	a. wins
	b. sugary

version	a. leisure
	b. impose

sandwich	a. classmate
	b. divisible

 Directions: Read each target word. Put a check (✓) under the correct column heading.
Direksyons: Li chak mo objektif. Mete yon tchèk (✓) anba antèt kolòn ki kòrèk la.

Target Words	"s" has the /s/ sound as in the word sun	"s" has the /sh/ sound as in the word sugar	"s" has the /z/ sound as in the word his	"s" has the /zh/ sound as in the word vision
1. daisy				
2. tissue				
3. version				
4. sandwich				

Learn to Read English With Directions In Haitian Creole

Homework

Name: _____ Date: ___/___/_____ Score: _____

Lesson 19.2

Reading Words with the "sion," "sial" & "scious" Suffixes

✓ Lesson Check Point

Directions: Read each target word. Circle the word in the column that has the same "sion," "sial" or "scious" sound as the target word.

Direksyons: Li chak mo objektif. Antoure mo a ki nan kolòn nan ki bay menm son "sion", "sial" oubyen "scious" yo tankou mo objektif la.

decision	a. version
	b. controversial

discussion	a. collision
	b. expression

submission	a. division
	b. compassion

unconscious	a. consensus
	b. preconscious

Directions: Read each target word. Put a check (✓) under the correct column heading.

Direksyons: Li chak mo objektif. Mete yon tchèk (✓) anba antèt kolòn ki kòrèk la.

Target Words	"sion" has the /sh/ +/ə/+/n/ sounds as in the word <u>passion</u>	"sion" has the /zh/ +/ə/+/n/ sounds as in the word <u>vision</u>	"scious" has the /sh/ +/ə/+/s/ sounds as in the word <u>conscious</u>
1. decision			
2. discussion			
3. submission			
4. unconscious			

Homework

  Name: _____ Date: ___/___/_____ Score: _____

Lesson 19.3

Reading Words with the "sch" Letter Combination

✓ Lesson Check Point

  Directions: Read each target word. Circle the word in the column that has the same "sch" sound(s) as the target word.
Direksyons: Li chak mo objektif. Antoure mo a ki nan kolòn nan ki bay menm son "sch" la (yo) tankou mo objektif la.

| schlep | a. school |
| | b. schmear |

| schism | a. schlep |
| | b. schema |

| scholar | a. schilling |
| | b. school |

| schooner | a. schmooze |
| | b. schematic |

  Directions: Read each target word. Put a check (✓) under the correct column heading.
Direksyons: Li chak mo objektif. Mete yon tchèk (✓) anba antèt kolòn ki kòrèk la.

Target Words	"sch" has the /s/ + /k/ sounds as in the word <u>school</u>	"sch" has the /sh/ sound as in the word <u>schilling</u>
1. schlep		
2. schism		
3. scholar		
4. schooner		

Learn to Read English With Directions In Haitian Creole

Homework

Name: _____ Date: ___/___/_____ Score: _____

Lesson 19.4

Reading Words with the "scr," "shr," "spr" & "str" Letter Combinations

Dictionary Skills/ Vocabulary

✓ **Lesson Check Point**

Directions: Read each target word and its definition. Write the letter of the definition on the line of each target word. Use a dictionary or the Internet to check your answers.

Direksyons: Li chak mo objektif ak definisyon yo chak. Ekri lèt la ki koresponn ak definisyon an sou trè chak mo objektif yo. Itilize yon diksyonè oubyen entènèt pou tcheke repons ou yo.

Target Words	Definitions
1. __ script	a. written words of a play
2. __ sprained	b. an emotional state of being worried
3. __ stressed	c. to have raised shoulders up and down
4. __ shrugged	d. to have used a small amount of something
5. __ scrimped	e. to have had a physical injury to a body part

Directions: Read each sentence. Underline the word in the parentheses that correctly completes each sentence. Then, write the underlined word on the line.

Direksyons: Li chak fraz. Soulinye mo a ki nan parantèz yo ki konplete chak fraz kòrèkteman. Answit, ekri mo soulinye a sou trè a.

6. I _____ and saved money to buy supplies. (scrimped, shrugged)

7. I am learning to write a _____ in my English class. (shrugged, script)

8. Jamal is _____ about taking his examinations. (stressed, script)

9. I _____ my ankle during the ball game. (sprained, stressed)

10. He _____ his shoulders in response to the questions. (scrimped, shrugged)

Homework

Name: _____ Date: ___/___/_____ Score: _____

Lesson 19.5

Reading Words with the "sl" & "sle" Letter Combinations

Dictionary Skills/ Vocabulary

✓ Lesson Check Point

Directions: Read each target word and its definition. Write the target word on the line in front of its meaning. Use a dictionary or the Internet to check your answers.

Direksyons: Li chak mo objektif ak definisyon yo chak. Ekri mo objektif la sou trè ki devan definisyon li an. Itilize yon diksyonè oubyen entènèt pou tcheke repons ou yo.

Target Word Box				
slanting	slimy	slippers	slow	slurps

1. _____ backless footwear
2. _____ not moving quickly
3. _____ something that feels sticky or slippery
4. _____ making noise while drinking a beverage
5. _____ the position of an object leaning in one

Directions: Read each sentence. Underline the word in the parentheses that correctly completes each sentence. Then, write the underlined word on the line.

Direksyons: Li chak fraz. Soulinye mo a ki nan parantèz yo ki konplete chak fraz kòrèkteman. Answit, ekri mo soulinye a sou trè a.

6. The new driver drove in the _____ lane. (slow, slimy)

7. Samantha _____ her soda loudly. (slurps, slippers)

8. The _____ fish slipped out of my hands. (slanting, slimy)

9. Mrs. Smith wears her _____ in the kitchen. (slurps, slippers)

10. The people in the painting are _____ to the right. (slanting, slow)

Homework

 Name: _____ Date: ___/___/_____ Score: _____

Lesson 19.5

Reading Words with the "sle" Letter Combination

✓ Lesson Check Point

Directions: Read each target word. Find the "sle" letter combination and put a check (✓) in the column that identifies its position: beginning, within or end.

Direksyons: Li chak mo objektif. Jwenn konbinezon lèt "sle" a epi mete yon tchèk (✓) nan kolòn nan ki idantifye pozisyon li an: nan kòmansman, ladan oubyen nan finisman.

Target Words	Beginning (First 3 Letters)	Within	End (Last 3 Letters)
1. sled			
2. hassle			
3. slender			
4. measles			
5. sleeping			

Directions: Read each target word. Put a check (✓) in the "yes" column if the "sle" letter combination has the /s/ + /ə/ + /l/ or /z/ + /ə/ + /l/ sounds. Put a check (✓) in the "no" column if the "sle" letter combination does not have the /s/ + /ə/ + /l/ or /z/ + /ə/ + /l/ sounds.

Direksyons: Li chak mo objektif. Mete yon tchèk (✓) nan kolòn "yes" an si konbinezon lèt "sle" a bay sons /s/ + /ə/ + /l/ oubyen /z/ + /ə/ + /l/. Mete yon tchèk (✓) nan kolòn "no" an si konbinezon lèt "sle" a pa bay sons /s/ + /ə/ + /l/ oubyen /z/ + /ə/ + /l/.

Target Words	Yes	No
6. sled		
7. hassle		
8. slender		
9. measles		
10. sleeping		

Homework

Name: _____ Date: ___/___/_____ Score: _____

Lesson 19.6

Reading Words with the "sm" Letter Combination

✓ Lesson Check Point

Directions: Read each target word. Circle the word in the column that has the same "sm" sounds as the target word.

Direksyons: Li chak mo objektif. Antoure mo a ki nan kolòn nan ki bay menm son "sm" la (yo) tankou mo objektif la.

| activism | a. cosmopolitan |
| | b. capitalism |

| cytoplasm | a. absenteeism |
| | b. cosmonauts |

| bridesmaid | a. vandalism |
| | b. newsman |

| newsmonger | a. extremism |
| | b. mesmerized |

Directions: Read each target word. Put a check (✓) under the correct column heading.

Direksyons: Li chak mo objektif. Mete yon tchèk (✓) anba antèt kolòn ki kòrèk la.

Target Words	"sm" has the /s/ + /m/ sounds as in the word smell	"sm" has the /z/ + /m/ sounds as in the word cosmic	"sm" has the /z/ + /ə/ + /m/ sounds as in the word autism
1. activism			
2. cytoplasm			
3. bridesmaid			
4. newsmonger			

Homework

Name: _____ Date: ___/___/_____ Score: _____

Lesson 19.7

Reading Words with the "ss" Letter Combination

✓ **Lesson Check Point**

Directions: Read each target word. Circle the word in the column that has the same "ss" sound(s) as the target word.

Direksyons: Li chak mo objektif. Antoure mo a ki nan kolòn nan ki bay menm son "ss" la (yo) tankou mo objektif la.

| Missouri | a. misstep |
| | b. dissolve |

| misstated | a. misspelled |
| | b. mission |

| aggression | a. concussion |
| | b. disservice |

| mission | a. tissues |
| | b. dissatisfy |

Directions: Read each target word. Put a check (✓) under the correct column heading.

Direksyons: Li chak mo objektif. Mete yon tchèk (✓) anba antèt kolòn ki kòrèk la.

Target Words	"ss" has the /sh/ sound as in the word <u>tissue</u>	"ss" has the /s/ + /s/ sounds as in the word <u>misspell</u>	"ss" has the /z/ sound as in the word <u>dissolve</u>
1. Missouri			
2. misstated			
3. aggression			
4. mission			

Homework

Name: _____ Date: ___/___/_____ Score: _____

Lesson 19.8

Reading Words with a Silent Letter "s"

✓ **Lesson Check Point**

Directions: Read the target words in the word box. Write the words that have a silent letter "s" in the first column. Write the words that do not have a silent letter "s" in the second column.

Direksyons: Li mo objektif yo ki nan ti bwat mo a. Ekri mo yo ki genyen lèt "s" ki pa pwononse a nan premye kolòn nan. Ekri mo yo ki pa genyen lèt "s" ki pa pwononse a nan dezyèm kolòn nan.

Target Word Box				
obese	isles	mass	aisle	guess
results	nests	assist	pupils	lesson
island	screen	debris	forsake	stories
Arkansas	humans	exposes	coconuts	blossom

Letter "s" is silent	Letter "s" has the /s/, /z/ or /sh/ sound

Learn to Read English With Directions In Haitian Creole

Homework

 Name: _____ Date: ___/___/_____ Score: _____

The Reading Challenge

Lesson 19.9

Reading Multisyllable Words

✓ Lesson Check Point

 Directions: Read and divide each target word into syllables. Write each word and place a hyphen (-) between the syllables in the second column. Write the number of syllables in the third column. Use a dictionary or the Internet to check your answers.

Direksyons: Li epi divize chak mo objektif an silab. Ekri chak mo epi mete yon tirè (-) ant silab yo nan dezyèm kolòn nan. Ekri kantite silab ke yo genyen an nan twazyèm kolòn nan. Itilize yon diksyonè oubyen entènèt pou tcheke repons ou yo.

Target Words	Words Divided into Syllables	Number of Syllables
1. sentiment		
2. silver		
3. shipment		
4. seventh		
5. soda		
6. sneaker		
7. shamrock		
8. secondly		
9. scheduling		
10. sewing		

Homework

 Name: _____ Date:___/___/_____ Score:_____

The Reading Challenge

Lesson 19.9

Reading Multisyllable Words

✓ Lesson Check Point

 Directions: Read each target word. Circle the word in the row that is divided correctly into syllables. Use a dictionary or the Internet to check your answers.

Direksyons: Li chak mo objektif. Antoure mo a ki nan ranje a ki divize an silab korèkteman yo. Itilize yon diksyonè oubyen entènèt pou tcheke repons ou yo.

Model

| Saturday | a. Sa-tur-day | b. Sat-ur-day | c. Sa-turd-ay |

1. sectional	a. sec-tion-al	b. sect-ion-al	c. se-ction-al
2. solution	a. so-lut-ion	b. sol-ut-ion	c. so-lu-tion
3. situate	a. si-tuat-e	b. sit-ua-te	c. sit-u-ate
4. slavery	a. sla-ver-y	b. slav-er-y	c. sla-ve-ry
5. sisterhood	a. sis-ter-hood	b. si-ster-hood	c. sis-terh-ood
6. sodium	a. sod-i-um	b. so-diu-m	c. so-di-um
7. scorpion	a. scor-p-ion	b. scor-pi-on	c. sco-rpi-on
8. survival	a. sur-viv-al	b. sur-vi-val	c. surv-i-val

Homework

Name: _____ Date: ___/___/_____ Score: _____

Lesson 19.10

Reading and Writing

Proper and Common Nouns and Adjectives

Directions: Read the words in the word box. Put an (X) on the line next to each word that is written incorrectly. Remember that all proper nouns and proper adjectives are capitalized. Use a dictionary or the Internet to check your answers.

Direksyons: Li chak mo yo ki nan bwat mo a. Met yon (X) sou ti trè a ki bò kote mo ki pa kri byen yo. Sonje ke tout non pwòp ak adjektif pwop ekri avèk yon lèt majiskil nan kòmansman yo. Itilize yon diksyonè oubyen entènèt pou tcheke repons ou yo.

Word Box		
___ Senegal	___ senior	___ sidney
___ seaweed	___ Shelter	___ Seminar
___ Shipyard	___ Saturday	___ saudi Arabia
___ Shepherd	___ Sahara Desert	___ Sierra Leone

Directions: Read each unedited sentence and underline the word that is written incorrectly. Write each sentence correctly on the line.

Direksyons: Li chak fraz ki pa edite yo epi soulinye mo ki pa ekri byen an. Ekri chak fraz korèkteman sou liy lan.

Model
<u>sandy</u> is going to Salt Lake City on Sunday.
Sandy is going to Salt Lake City on Sunday.

1. The students cannot sit in silence for Six minutes.

   _____

2. On saturday, Senator Smith made a sensational speech.

   _____

3. The short story entitled, "Seven siblings" has a shocking plot.

   _____

4. Sidney Elementary School is scheduled to open in september.

   _____

Homework

 Name: _____ Date: ___/___/_____ Score: _____

Lesson 20.1

Reading Words with the Letter T/t

✓ Lesson Check Point

 Directions: Read each target word. Find the letter "t" and put a check (✓) in the column that identifies its position: beginning, within or end.
Direksyons: Li chak mo objektif. Jwenn lèt "t" a epi mete yon tchèck (✓) nan kolòn ki idantifye pozisyon li an: nan kòmansman, ladan oubyen nan finisman.

Target Words	Beginning (First Letter)	Within	End (Last Letter)
1. poet			
2. rocket			
3. liberty			
4. thunder			
5. mustard			

 Directions: Read each sentence and underline the words that begin with the letter "t." Write all the underlined words in alphabetical order on the lines below.
Direksyons: Li chak fraz epi soulinye mo yo ki kòmanse avèk lèt "t" a. Ekri tout mo ki souliye yo nan lòd alfabetik sou trè sa yo ki anba.

6. I taped four pages in my textbook.

7. Patrick said, "Tortillas are very tasty."

8. Gina's telephone is tan and dark brown.

9. On Saturday, we will watch television together.

10. My second grade teacher read a book about tigers.

_____   _____   _____
_____   _____   _____
_____   _____   _____
                _____

Learn to Read English With Directions In Haitian Creole

Homework

Name: _____   Date: ___/___/_____   Score: _____

Lesson 20.2

Reading Words with the "thm" Letter Combination

✓ **Lesson Check Point**

Directions: Read each target word. Circle the word in the column that has the same "thm" sound(s) as the target word.

Direksyons: Li chak mo objektif. Antoure mo a ki nan kolòn nan ki bay menm son "thm" la (yo) tankou mo objektif la.

birthmark	a. asthmatic
	b. bathmat

isthmian	a. asthma
	b. Pathmark

algorithm	a. rhythm
	b. isthmus

biorhythm	a. birthmarks
	b. antilogarithm

Directions: Read each target word. Put a check (✓) under the correct column heading.

Direksyons: Li chak mo objektif. Mete yon tchèk (✓) anba antèt kolòn ki kòrèk la.

Target Words	"thm" has the /th/ + /ə/ + /m/ sounds as in the word **rhythm**	"thm" has the /th/ + /m/ sounds as in the word **bathmat**	"thm" silent "th" + /m/ sound as in the word **asthma**
1. birthmark			
2. isthmian			
3. algorithm			
4. biorhythm			

Homework

Name: _____ Date: ___/___/_____ Score: _____

Lesson 20.3

Reading Words with the "tion," "tial" & "tious" Suffixes

✓ Lesson Check Point

Directions: Read each target word. Circle the word in the column that has the same "tion," "tial" or "tious" sound as the target word.

Direksyons: Li chak mo objektif. Antoure mo a ki nan kolòn nan ki bay menm son "tion", "tial" oubyen "tious" yo tankou mo objektif la.

| sequential | a. deferential |
| | b. traditional |

| fractional | a. partial |
| | b. attention |

| additional | a. extinction |
| | b. cautiously |

| bumptious | a. federation |
| | b. conscientious |

Directions: Read each target word. Put a check (✓) under the correct column heading.

Direksyons: Li chak mo objektif. Mete yon tchèk (✓) anba antèt kolòn ki kòrèk la.

Target Words	"tion" has the /sh/ +/ə/+/n/ sounds as in the word <u>education</u>	"tial" has the /sh/ +/ə/+/l/ sounds as in the word <u>partial</u>	"tious" has the /sh/ +/ə/+/s/ sounds as in the word <u>ambitious</u>
1. sequential			
2. fractional			
3. additional			
4. bumptious			

Learn to Read English With Directions In Haitian Creole

Homework

Name: _____ Date: ___/___/_____ Score: _____

Lesson 20.4

Reading Words with the "tr" Letter Combination

Dictionary Skills/ Vocabulary

✓ **Lesson Check Point**

Directions: Read each target word and its definition. Write the letter of the definition on the line of each target word. Use a dictionary or the Internet to check your answers.

Direksyons: Li chak mo objektif ak definisyon yo chak. Ekri lèt la ki koresponn ak definisyon an sou trè chak mo objektif yo. Itilize yon diksyonè oubyen entènèt pou tcheke repons ou yo.

Target Words	Definitions
1. __ tree	a. a path in a wooden area
2. __ trap	b. a device used to catch things
3. __ trail	c. to take a trip from one place to another
4. __ travel	d. the betrayal of one's country by helping its enemies
5. __ treason	e. woody plant with a thick trunk

Directions: Read each sentence. Underline the word in the parentheses that correctly completes each sentence. Then, write the underlined word on the line.

Direksyons: Li chak fraz. Soulinye mo a ki nan parantèz yo ki konplete chak fraz kòrèkteman. Answit, ekri mo soulinye a sou trè a.

6. The mouse was caught in the _____. (trap, travel)

7. I sat under a shady _____ in the park. (tree, treason)

8. The traitor was arrested for high _____. (treason, trap)

9. The toddlers are riding their tricycles along the _____. (tree, trail)

10. Today, Troy is scheduled to _____ to Tennessee. (trail, travel)

Homework

 Name: _____   Date: ___/___/_____   Score: _____

Lesson 20.5

Reading Words with the "tle" Letter Combination

✓ Lesson Check Point

 Directions: Read each target word. Find the "tle" letter combination and put a check (✓) in the column that identifies its position: beginning, within or end.

Direksyons: Li chak mo objektif. Jwenn konbinezon lèt "tle" a epi mete yon tchèk (✓) nan kolòn nan ki idantifye pozisyon li an: nan kòmansman, ladan oubyen nan finisman.

Target Words	Beginning (First 3 Letters)	Within	End (Last 3 Letters)
1. beetle			
2. rattle			
3. bootleg			
4. limitless			
5. effortless			

 Directions: Read each target word. Put a check (✓) in the "yes" column if the "tle" letter combination has the /t/ + /ə/ + /l/ sounds. Put a check (✓) in the "no" column if the "tle" letter combination does not have the /t/ + /ə/ + /l/ sounds.

Direksyons: Li chak mo objektif. Mete yon tchèk (✓) nan kolòn "yes" an si konbinezon let "tle" a bay sons /t/ + /ə/ + /l/. Mete yon tchèk (✓) nan kolòn "no" an si konbinezon let "tle" a pa bay sons /t/ + /ə/ + /l/.

Target Words	Yes	No
6. beetle		
7. rattle		
8. bootleg		
9. limitless		
10. effortless		

Homework

 Name: _____   Date: ___/___/_____   Score: _____

Lesson 20.6

Reading Words with the Letter "t" Sounds

✓ **Lesson Check Point**

 Directions: Read each target word. Circle the word in the column that has the same "t" sound as the target word.

Direksyons: Li chak mo objektif. Antoure mo a ki nan kolòn nan ki bay menm son "t" a tankou mo objektif la.

| actor | a. fracture |
| | b. connective |

| fixture | a. expect |
| | b. feature |

| indicted | a. factor |
| | b. actuary |

| righteous | a. thunder |
| | b. obituary |

 Directions: Read each target word. Put a check (✓) under the correct column heading.

Direksyons: Li chak mo objektif. Mete yon tchèk (✓) anba antèt kolòn ki kòrèk la.

Target Words	"t" has the /t/ sound as in the word <u>multiply</u>	"t" has the /ch/ sound as in the word <u>picture</u>	"t" has the /sh/ sound as in the word <u>position</u>
1. actor			
2. fixture			
3. indicted			
4. righteous			

Homework

 Name: _____   Date: ___/___/_____   Score: _____

Lesson 20.7

Reading Words with a Silent Letter "t"

✓ Lesson Check Point

 Directions: Read the target words in the word box. Write the words that have a silent letter "t" in the first column. Write the words that do not have a silent letter "t" in the second column.

Direksyons: Li mo objektif yo ki nan ti bwat mo a. Ekri mo yo ki genyen lèt "t" ki pa pwononse a nan premye kolòn nan. Ekri mo yo ki pa genyen lèt "t" ki pa pwononse a nan dezyèm kolòn nan.

Target Word Box				
hasten	fault	contract	ballet	digit
educate	debut	buffet	soften	litter
chapter	fainting	fasten	trouble	timely
rapport	tsunami	attach	generate	dustpan

Letter "t" is silent	Letter "t" has the /t/ sound

Homework

 Name: _____ Date: ___/___/_____ Score: _____

The Reading Challenge

Lesson 20.8

Reading Multisyllable Words

✓ **Lesson Check Point**

 Directions: Read and divide each target word into syllables. Write each word and place a hyphen (-) between the syllables in the second column. Write the number of syllables in the third column. Use a dictionary or the Internet to check your answers.

Direksyons: Li epi divize chak mo objektif an silab. Ekri chak mo epi mete yon tirè (-) ant silab yo nan dezyèm kolòn nan. Ekri kantite silab ke yo genyen an nan twazyèm kolòn nan. Itilize yon diksyonè oubyen entènèt pou tcheke repons ou yo.

Target Words	Words Divided into Syllables	Number of Syllables
1. treatment	_____	_____
2. tutorial	_____	_____
3. tenderly	_____	_____
4. today	_____	_____
5. tiger	_____	_____
6. thicken	_____	_____
7. treadmill	_____	_____
8. twentieth	_____	_____
9. themselves	_____	_____
10. transported	_____	_____

Homework

 Name: _____ Date: ___/___/_____ Score: _____

The Reading Challenge

Lesson 20.8

Reading Multisyllable Words

✓ **Lesson Check Point**

 Directions: Read each target word. Circle the word in the row that is divided correctly into syllables. Use a dictionary or the Internet to check your answers.

Direksyons: Li chak mo objektif. Antoure mo a ki nan ranje a ki divize an silab korèkteman yo. Itilize yon diksyonè oubyen entènèt pou tcheke repons ou yo.

Model

| telephone | a. te-lep-hone | b. tel-e-phone | c. te-le-phone |

| 1. typify | a. typ-i-fy | b. ty-pi-fy | c. typ-if-y |

| 2. tropical | a. tro-pi-cal | b. tro-pic-al | c. trop-i-cal |

| 3. thematic | a. them-at-ic | b. the-m-atic | c. the-mat-ic |

| 4. tendency | a. ten-denc-y | b. ten-den-cy | c. tend-en-cy |

| 5. treasury | a. treas-u-ry | b. treas-ur-y | c. trea-sur-y |

| 6. tragedy | a. trag-e-dy | b. tra-ged-y | c. trag-ed-y |

| 7. together | a. tog-et-her | b. to-geth-er | c. to-get-her |

| 8. tricycle | a. tri-cy-cle | b. tri-cyc-le | c. tric-yc-le |

Homework

Name: _____ Date: ___/___/_____ Score: _____

Lesson 20.9

Reading and Writing

Proper and Common Nouns and Adjectives

Directions: Read the words in the word box. Put an (X) on the line next to each word that is written incorrectly. Remember that all proper nouns and proper adjectives are capitalized. Use a dictionary or the Internet to check your answers.

Direksyons: Li chak mo yo ki nan bwat mo a. Met yon (X) sou ti trè a ki bò kote mo ki pa kri byen yo. Sonje ke tout non pwòp ak adjektif pwop ekri avèk yon lèt majiskil nan kòmansman yo. Itilize yon diksyonè oubyen entènèt pou tcheke repons ou yo.

Word Box					
___	thirst	___	Tibet	___	teapot
___	Tutor	___	triplet	___	Tornado
___	tampa	___	texture	___	Trickster
___	tuesday	___	Tomorrow	___	Tennessee

Directions: Read each unedited sentence and underline the word that is written incorrectly. Write each sentence correctly on the line.

Direksyons: Li chak fraz ki pa edite yo epi soulinye mo ki pa ekri byen an. Ekri chak fraz korèkteman sou liy lan.

Model
On <u>thursday</u>, a tornado destroyed my hometown.
<u>On Thursday, a tornado destroyed my hometown.</u>

1. The Taxicab driver drives all over Trenton, Tennessee.
   _____

2. the Texas tourism office is located in Town Hall.
   _____

3. I quenched my thirst with green tea from thailand.
   _____

4. My English Textbook has a passage about the City of Troy.
   _____

Homework

 Name: _____ Date:___/___/_____ Score:_____

Lesson 21.1

Reading Words with the Letter U/u

✓ **Lesson Check Point**

 Directions: Read each target word. Find the letter "u" and put a check (✓) in the column that identifies its position: beginning, within or end.
Direksyons: Li chak mo objektif. Jwenn lèt "u" a epi mete yon tchèck (✓) nan kolòn ki idantifye pozisyon li an: nan kòmansman, ladan oubyen nan finisman.

Target Words	Beginning (First Letter)	Within	End (Last Letter)
1. Peru			
2. south			
3. refuge			
4. umbrella			
5. university			

 Directions: Read each target word. Read the words in the row and circle the word that has a different vowel "u" sound.
Direksyons: Li chak mo objektif. Li mo yo ki nan ranje a epi antoure mo a ki bay yon son vwayèl "u" ki diferan an.

Target Words				
6. glum	bug	pub	dual	rug
7. dunk	sup	hug	puff	fluke
8. lung	puck	rule	jug	dug
9. hunch	hub	plug	flume	mug
10. umbrella	club	buns	hunting	quiet

Learn to Read English With Directions In Haitian Creole

Homework

Name: _____ Date: ___/___/_____ Score: _____

Lesson 21.2

Reading Words with the Short Vowel "u" Sound

✓ **Lesson Check Point**

Directions: Read the words in the four boxes. Circle two words with the short vowel /ŭ/ sound. The anchor word for the short vowel /ŭ/ sound is <u>up</u>.

Direksyons: Li mo yo ki nan kat ti bwat yo. Antoure de mo ki genyen son vwayèl kout /ŭ/ a. Mo referans pou son vwayèl kout /ŭ/ a se mo, <u>up</u>.

gulp	duke
huge	stump

skull	chunk
mule	brute

munch	tofu
blush	cube

flush	tube
skunk	fluke

hung	fuss
blue	rude

guard	true
slush	hump

Directions: Read the words in the four boxes. Circle two words that rhyme. Rhyming words have the same ending sound, such as <u>just</u> and <u>must</u>.

Direksyons: Li mo yo ki nan kat ti bwat yo. Antoure de mo ki rime. De mo oubyen plizyè mo ki rime genyen menm son nan finisman yo, tankou <u>just</u> ak <u>must</u>.

rub	tub
guess	guide

dusk	quite
tusk	duo

jump	muse
buy	pump

cue	gruel
rung	sung

run	bruise
burn	sun

hutch	Dutch
prune	hue

Homework

Name: _____ Date: ___/___/_____ Score: _____

Lesson 21.2

Reading & Writing Words with the Short Vowel "u" Sound

✓ **Lesson Check Point**

Directions: Read each sentence and underline three words with the short vowel /ŭ/ sound. Then, write the underlined words on the lines below. The anchor word for the short vowel /ŭ/ sound is <u>up</u>.

Direksyons: Li chak fraz epi soulinye twa mo ki genyen son vwayèl kout /ŭ/ a. Answit, ekri mo soulinye yo sou trè sa yo ki anba. Mo referans pou son vwayèl kout /ŭ/a se mo, <u>up</u>.

Model

Ulysses, the <u>drummer</u>, <u>jumps</u> when he plays the <u>drums</u>.

    drummer   jumps   drums
   _____   _____   _____

1. At lunchtime, Sue said, "Do not run in the hut!"

   _____   _____   _____

2. The baby cubs used to jump on the tree stumps.

   _____   _____   _____

3. The truck driver had a huge lunch at the clubhouse.

   _____   _____   _____

4. The cute bugs look like they are having fun in the mud.

   _____   _____   _____

5. Bruce's new album is entitled, "Running in the Hot Summer Sun."

   _____   _____   _____

Learn to Read English With Directions In Haitian Creole   Copyrighted Material

Homework

 Name: _____ Date: ___/___/_____ Score: _____

Lesson 21.3

Reading Words with the Long Vowel "u" Sound

✓ **Lesson Check Point**

 Directions: Read the words in the four boxes. Circle two words with the long vowel /y$\overline{oo}$/ or /$\overline{oo}$/ sound. The anchor word for the long vowel /y$\overline{oo}$/ and /$\overline{oo}$/ sounds is <u>tube</u>.

Direksyons: Li mo yo ki nan kat ti bwat yo. Antoure de mo ki genyen son vwayèl long /y$\overline{oo}$/ oubyen / $\overline{oo}$/ a. Mo referans pou son vwayèl long /y$\overline{oo}$/ ak / $\overline{oo}$ /es la palabra, <u>tube</u>.

tribute	dune
hump	puff

much	used
rusty	defuse

produce	nullify
hunch	exclude

intrude	rung
huge	plumber

pollute	jaguar
guitar	spruce

liquid	guess
dual	visual

 Directions: Read the words in the four boxes. Circle two words that rhyme. Rhyming words have the same ending sound, such as <u>rule</u> and <u>mule</u>.

Direksyons: Li mo yo ki nan kat ti bwat yo. Antoure de mo ki rime. De mo oubyen plizyè mo ki rime genyen menm son nan finisman yo, tankou <u>rule</u> ak <u>mule</u>.

rung	tube
cube	hush

hung	true
issue	blushing

hunter	truck
tissue	argue

husky	duke
bumper	fluke

dusty	lunch
cute	brute

slum	blue
brush	cue

Homework

Name: _____ Date: ___/___/_____ Score: _____

Lesson 21.3

Reading & Writing Words with the Long Vowel "u" Sound

✓ **Lesson Check Point**

Directions: Read each sentence and underline three words with the long vowel /yo͞o/ or /o͞o/ sound. Then, write the underlined words on the lines below. The anchor word for the long vowel /yo͞o/ and /o͞o/ sounds is tube.

Direksyons: Li chak fraz epi soulinye twa mo ki genyen son vwayèl long /yo͞o/ oubyen /o͞o/ yo. Answit, ekri mo soulinye yo sou trè sa yo ki anba. Mo referans pou son vwayèl long /yo͞o/ ak /o͞o/ es la palabra, tube.

Model

<u>Bruce</u> is going to play the <u>tuba</u> and drums in <u>Uganda</u>.

    Bruce   tuba   Uganda
   _____   _____   _____

1. The students are studying about producers and consumers.

   _____   _____   _____

2. The truants did not graduate because of their acts of truancy.

   _____   _____   _____

3. The students living on Hunter Avenue will graduate in August.

   _____   _____   _____

4. In June, I will take a fun-filled vacation to Peru and Yugoslavia.

   _____   _____   _____

5. In July, the drummer argued about our contractual agreement.

   _____   _____   _____

Learn to Read English With Directions In Haitian Creole   Copyrighted Material

Homework

Name: _____ Date: ___/___/_____ Score: _____

Review Lessons 21.2 & 21.3

Reading Short Vowel and Long Vowel Words

Directions: Read the target words in the word box. In the first column, write the words that have the short vowel /ŭ/ sound, as in the word <u>up</u>. In the second column, write the words that have the long vowel /yoō/ or /oō/ sound, as in the word <u>tube</u>.

Direksyons: Li mo yoobjektif yo ki nan bwat mo a. Nan premye kolòn nan, ekri mo ki bay son vwayèl kout /ŭ/ yo, tankou li ye nan mo <u>up</u> la. Nan dezyèm kolòn nan, ekri mo ki bay son vwayèl long /yoō/ oubyen /oō/, yo, tankou li ye nan mo <u>tube</u> la.

Target Word Box				
husky	true	lunch	argue	salute
Dutch	rusty	visual	drunk	chunky
confuse	reduce	flushing	strung	annual
pollute	execute	blushing	graduate	brushing

Letter "u" has the /ŭ/ sound as in the word <u>up</u>

Letter "u" has the /yoō/ or /oō/ sound as in the word <u>tube</u>

Homework

 Name: _____ Date: ___/___/_____ Score: _____

Lesson 21.4

Reading Words with Letter "u" Vowel Pairs

✓ **Lesson Check Point**

 Directions: Read each target word. Circle the word in the column that has the same vowel "ua," "ue" or "ui" sound(s) as the target word.

Direksyons: Li chak mo objektif. Antoure mo a ki nan kolòn nan ki bay menm son vwayèl "ua," "ue" oubyen "ui" la (yo) tankou mo objektif la.

venue	a. Joshua
	b. argue

clues	a. juicer
	b. conceptual

nuisance	a. bruise
	b. perpetual

visual	a. blue
	b. usual

 Directions: Read each target word. Put a check (✓) under the correct column heading.

Direksyons: Li chak mo objektif. Mete yon tchèk (✓) anba antèt kolòn ki kòrèk la.

Target Words	Words have the long "u" sound as in the word blue	Words do not have the long "u" sound
1. due		
2. suite		
3. factual		
4. continue		

Homework

 Name: _____ Date: ___/___/_____ Score: _____

Lesson 21.5

Reading Words with the Final Letter "u"

✓ **Lesson Check Point**

 Directions: Read each target word. Find the letter "u" and put a check (✓) in the column that identifies its position within the syllable.
Direksyons: Li chak mo objektif. Jwenn lèt "u" a epi mete yon tchèck (✓) nan kolòn nan ki idantifye pozisyon li an nan silab la.

Target Words	"u" is at the end of a one syllable word	"u" is at the end of the first syllable	"u" is at the end of a multi-syllable word
1. flu			
2. Peru			
3. menu			
4. humor			
5. tubercle			

 Directions: Read each target word. Put a check (✓) under the correct column heading.
Direksyons: Li chak mo objektif. Mete yon tchèk (✓) anba antèt kolòn ki kòrèk la.

Target Words	"u" has the /ŭ/ sound as in the word <u>tub</u>	"u" has the /yoo/ sound as in the word <u>tube</u>	"u" has the /ə/ sound as in the word <u>circus</u>	"u" is silent as in the word <u>build</u>
6. argue				
7. built				
8. sunny				
9. particular				
10. vaguely				

Homework

 Name: _____ Date:___/___/_____ Score:_____

Lesson 21.6

Reading Letter "u" Words with the Schwa Vowel Sound

✓ Lesson Check Point

 Directions: Read each target word. Circle the word in the column that has the same "u" sound as the target word.
Direksyons: Li chak mo objektif. Antoure mo a ki nan kolòn nan ki bay menm son "u" a tankou mo objektif la.

Saturday	a. campus
	b. upstairs

autumn	a. pitiful
	b. umbrella

focus	a. curve
	b. litmus

support	a. busted
	b. circus

 Directions: Read each sentence and underline the letter "u" word that has the schwa vowel /ə/ sound. The anchor word for the letter "u" schwa vowel sound is <u>campus</u>.
Direksyons: Li chak fraz epi soulinye mo ki genyen lèt "u" a ki bay son schwa /ə/. Mo referans pou son schwa lèt "u" a se mo, <u>campus</u>.

1. Porcupines are mammals with a coat of sharp quills.

2. Eugene is having difficulty completing his assignment.

3. My students are learning to subtract two-digit numbers.

4. Today, the faculty members received their course outline.

5. On Sunday, my uncle drank a medium glass of plum juice.

6. At the circus, the students looked up and saw the acrobats.

Homework

Name: _____ Date:___/___/_____ Score:_____

Lesson 21.7

Reading Words with the "ur" Letter Combination

Dictionary Skills/ Vocabulary

✓ **Lesson Check Point**

Directions: Read each target word and its definition. Write the letter of the definition on the line of each target word. Use a dictionary or the Internet to check your answers.

Direksyons: Li chak mo objektif ak definisyon yo chak. Ekri lèt la ki koresponn ak definisyon an sou trè chak mo objektif yo. Itilize yon diksyonè oubyen entènèt pou tcheke repons ou yo.

Target Words	Definitions
1. __ curly	a. someone who steals things
2. __ curtain	b. description of something twisted into coils
3. __ burglar	c. fabric that hangs by a window
4. __ hurricane	d. to have designed a place with furniture
5. __ furnished	e. a cyclone with strong winds and heavy rain

Directions: Read each sentence and write the target word on the line that correctly completes the sentence.

Direksyons: Li chak fraz epi ekri mo objektif ki konplete fraz la kòrèkteman.

6. Susan tied the gifts with red _____ ribbons.

7. The tropical storm was upgraded to a _____.

8. The living room _____ is designed to block the sun.

9. The _____ was arrested for robbing the jewelry store.

10. David _____ his apartment with expensive antiques.

Homework

◘ Name: _____ Date: ___/___/_____ Score: _____

Lesson 21.8

Reading Words with a Silent Letter "u"

✓ **Lesson Check Point**

Directions: Read the target words in the word box. Write the words that have a silent letter "u" in the first column. Write the words that do not have a silent letter "u" in the second column.

Direksyons: Li mo objektif yo ki nan ti bwat mo a. Ekri mo yo ki genyen lèt "u" ki pa pwononse a nan premye kolòn nan. Ekri mo yo ki pa genyen lèt "u" ki pa pwononse anan dezyèm kolòn nan.

Target Word Box				
Peru	buildings	butcher	disguise	league
guilty	numerous	laughter	rubbing	intrigue
biscuits	pudding	puppy	perfume	musical
salute	vogue	summer	guess	Guinea

Letter "u" is silent | **Letter "u" has a letter "u" sound**

Homework

Name: _____ Date: ___/___/_____ Score: _____

Unit Review - U/u

Reading Words with Vowel "u" Sounds: /ŭ/, /o͞o/, /ə/ & Silent

✓ **Lesson Check Point**

Directions: Read each target word. Circle the word in the column that has the same "u" sound as the target word.

Direksyons: Li chak mo objektif. Antoure mo a ki nan kolòn nan ki bay menm son vwayèl "u" atankou mo objektif la.

ruler	a. frugal
	b. struck

laugh	a. shoulder
	b. argument

support	a. crumble
	b. industry

drummer	a. clubs
	b. beauty

Directions: Read each target word. Put a check (✓) under the correct column heading.

Direksyons: Li chak mo objektif. Mete yon tchèk (✓) anba antèt kolòn ki kòrèk la.

Target Words	"u" has the /ŭ/ sound as in the word **tub**	"u" has the /o͞o/ sound as in the word **tube**	"u" has the /ə/ sound as in the word **circus**	"u" is silent as in the word **build**
1. ruler				
2. laugh				
3. support				
4. drummer				

Homework

 Name: _____ Date: ___/___/_____ Score: _____

The Reading Challenge

Lesson 21.9

Reading Multisyllable Words

✓ Lesson Check Point

 Directions: Read and divide each target word into syllables. Write each word and place a hyphen (-) between the syllables in the second column. Write the number of syllables in the third column. Use a dictionary or the Internet to check your answers.

Direksyons: Li epi divize chak mo objektif an silab. Ekri chak mo epi mete yon tirè (-) ant silab yo nan dezyèm kolòn nan. Ekri kantite silab ke yo genyen an nan twazyèm kolòn nan. Itilize yon diksyonè oubyen entènèt pou tcheke repons ou yo.

Target Words	Words Divided into Syllables	Number of Syllables
1. jumpers	_____	_____
2. cushion	_____	_____
3. brushing	_____	_____
4. fullest	_____	_____
5. eluding	_____	_____
6. butcher	_____	_____
7. volume	_____	_____
8. defusing	_____	_____
9. customer	_____	_____
10. arguing	_____	_____

Homework

Name: _____ Date:___/___/_____ Score:_____

The Reading Challenge

Lesson 21.9

Reading Multisyllable Words

✓ **Lesson Check Point**

Directions: Read each target word. Circle the word in the row that is divided correctly into syllables. Use a dictionary or the Internet to check your answers.

Direksyons: Li chak mo objektif. Antoure mo a ki nan ranje a ki divize an silab korèkteman yo. Itilize yon diksyonè oubyen entènèt pou tcheke repons ou yo.

Model

| visualize | a. vis-ua-lize | b. vi-su-al-ize | c. vis-u-a-lize |

(b. vi-su-al-ize is circled)

| 1. execute | a. ex-e-cute | b. ex-ec-ute | c. e-xec-ute |

| 2. absolute | a. ab-so-lute | b. abs-o-lute | c. ab-sol-ute |

| 3. punctual | a. pun-ctu-al | b. punc-tu-al | c. pu-nctu-al |

| 4. resuming | a. res-u-ming | b. re-sum-ing | c. re-sumi-ng |

| 5. included | a. incl-u-ded | b. in-clud-ed | c. inc-lud-ed |

| 6. refusing | a. ref-u-sing | b. re-fus-ing | c. ref-us-ing |

| 7. gradual | a. grad-ual | b. gra-du-al | c. grad-u-al |

| 8. consuming | a. con-sum-ing | b. cons-u-ming | c. con-su-ming |

Homework

Name: _____ Date: ___/___/_____ Score: _____

Lesson 21.10

Reading and Writing

Proper and Common Nouns and Adjectives

Directions: Read the words in the word box. Put an (X) on the line next to each word that is written incorrectly. Remember that all proper nouns and proper adjectives are capitalized. Use a dictionary or the Internet to check your answers.

Direksyons: Li chak mo yo ki nan bwat mo a. Met yon (X) sou ti trè a ki bò kote mo ki pa kri byen yo. Sonje ke tout non pwòp ak adjektif pwop ekri avèk yon lèt majiskil nan kòmansman yo. Itilize yon diksyonè oubyen entènèt pou tcheke repons ou yo.

Word Box		
__ utah	__ usually	__ USA
__ Uproar	__ ural River	__ Ugliest
__ UNICEF	__ ursa Minor	__ upgrade
__ United Kingdom	__ Uzbekistan	__ Utterance

Directions: Read each unedited sentence and underline the word that is written incorrectly. Write each sentence correctly on the line.

Direksyons: Li chak fraz ki pa edite yo epi soulinye mo ki pa ekri byen an. Ekri chak fraz korèkteman sou liy lan.

Model
Mrs. Ubangi usually has union meetings at a local University.
Mrs. Ubangi usually has union meetings at a local university.

1. Last year, university students hiked Up the Ural Mountains.
   _____

2. The UNICEF volunteers are helping Underprivileged children.
   _____

3. Mr. Udell enjoys reading Unusual books about UFO sightings.
   _____

4. The students from uzbekistan are on our university's honor roll.
   _____

Homework

Name: _____ Date: ___/___/_____ Score: _____

Lesson 22.1

Reading Words with the Letter V/v

✓ Lesson Check Point

Directions: Read each target word. Find the letter "v" and put a check (✓) in the column that identifies its position: beginning, within or end.
Direksyons: Li chak mo objektif. Jwenn lèt "v" a epi mete yon tchèck (✓) nan kolòn ki idantifye pozisyon li an: nan kòmansman, ladan oubyen nan finisman.

Target Words	Beginning (First Letter)	Within	End (Last Letter)
1. travail			
2. savings			
3. Vikings			
4. volcanic			
5. Yugoslav			

Directions: Read each sentence and underline the words that begin with the letter "v." Write all the underlined words in alphabetical order on the lines below.
Direksyons: Li chak fraz epi soulinye mo ki kòmanse avèk lèt "v" yo. Ekri tout mo ki soulinye yo nan lòd alfabetik sou trè sa yo ki anba.

6. My visor blocks the vivid rays of the sun.

7. Our new vitamins taste like vanilla cream.

8. I used the computer to enter a virtual volcano.

9. During the tour, I had a clear view of Victoria Falls.

10. The villagers voted for an entirely new government.

_____   _____   _____
_____   _____   _____
_____   _____   _____
               _____

Homework

 Name: _____ Date:___/___/_____ Score: _____

The Reading Challenge

Lesson 22.2

Reading Multisyllable Words

✓ Lesson Check Point

 Directions: Read and divide each target word into syllables. Write each word and place a hyphen (-) between the syllables in the second column. Write the number of syllables in the third column. Use a dictionary or the Internet to check your answers.

Direksyons: Li epi divize chak mo objektif an silab. Ekri chak mo epi mete yon tirè (-) ant silab yo nan dezyèm kolòn nan. Ekri kantite silab ke yo genyen an nan twazyèm kolòn nan. Itilize yon diksyonè oubyen entènèt pou tcheke repons ou yo.

Target Words	Words Divided into Syllables	Number of Syllables
1. veto	_____	_____
2. voiceless	_____	_____
3. vaulting	_____	_____
4. version	_____	_____
5. video	_____	_____
6. vascular	_____	_____
7. vividly	_____	_____
8. versus	_____	_____
9. viruses	_____	_____
10. vigorous	_____	_____

Unit V
Lesson 22.2

Homework

 Name: _____ Date: ___/___/_____ Score: _____

The Reading Challenge

Lesson 22.2

Reading Multisyllable Words

✓ **Lesson Check Point**

 Directions: Read each target word. Circle the word in the row that is divided correctly into syllables. Use a dictionary or the Internet to check your answers.

Direksyons: Li chak mo objektif. Antoure mo a ki nan ranje a ki divize an silab korèkteman yo. Itilize yon diksyonè oubyen entènèt pou tcheke repons ou yo.

Model

| volcano | a. vo-lcan-o | b. vol-can-o | c. vol-ca-no |

| 1. violin | a. vi-ol-in | b. vi-o-lin | c. vio-li-n |

| 2. verbalize | a. ver-bali-ze | b. verb-al-ize | c. ver-bal-ize |

| 3. vanity | a. van-i-ty | b. va-ni-ty | c. van-it-y |

| 4. vocable | a. vo-cab-le | b. vo-c-able | c. vo-ca-ble |

| 5. virtual | a. virt-u-al | b. vir-tu-al | c. vir-tua-l |

| 6. venison | a. ve-nis-on | b. ven-i-son | c. ven-is-on |

| 7. Vietnam | a. Vi-et-nam | b. Vie-t-nam | c. Vi-etna-m |

| 8. vestibule | a. ves-ti-bule | b. ves-tib-ule | c. vest-i-bule |

Homework

Lesson 22.3

Reading and Writing

Proper and Common Nouns and Adjectives

Directions: Read the words in the word box. Put an (X) on the line next to each word that is written incorrectly. Remember that all proper nouns and proper adjectives are capitalized. Use a dictionary or the Internet to check your answers.

Direksyons: Li chak mo yo ki nan bwat mo a. Met yon (X) sou ti trè a ki bò kote mo ki pa kri byen yo. Sonje ke tout non pwòp ak adjektif pwop ekri avèk yon lèt majiskil nan kòmansman yo. Itilize yon diksyonè oubyen entènèt pou tcheke repons ou yo.

Word Box					
—	version	__	venus	__	vertex
—	vocal cord	__	venice	__	Vessel
__	victoria Falls	__	virginia	__	vocabulary
—	Volcano Island	__	Vanessa	__	valentine's Day

Directions: Read each unedited sentence and underline the word that is written incorrectly. Write each sentence correctly on the line.

Direksyons: Li chak fraz ki pa edite yo epi soulinye mo ki pa ekri byen an. Ekri chak fraz korèkteman sou liy lan.

Model
In the fall, the leaves in <u>vermont</u> have vibrant colors.
<u>In the fall, the leaves in Vermont have vibrant colors.</u>

1. The vikings made many treacherous ocean voyages.

   _____

2. vinny received five African violet plants on Valentine's Day.

   _____

3. We are scheduled to play four Volleyball games in Virginia.

   _____

4. In November, I plan to Vacation in the British Virgin Islands.

   _____

Homework

Name: _____ Date: ___/___/_____ Score: _____

Lesson 23.1

Reading Words with the Letter W/w

✓ **Lesson Check Point**

Directions: Read each target word. Find the letter "w" and put a check (✓) in the column that identifies its position: beginning, within or end.
Direksyons: Li chak mo objektif. Jwenn lèt "w" a epi mete yon tchèck (✓) nan kolòn ki idantifye pozisyon li an: nan kòmansman, ladan oubyen nan finisman.

Target Words	Beginning (First Letter)	Within	End (Last Letter)
1. answer			
2. washing			
3. somehow			
4. tomorrow			
5. crossword			

Directions: Read each sentence and underline the words that begin with the letter "w." Write all the underlined words in alphabetical order on the lines below.
Direksyons: Li chak fraz epi soulinye mo ki kòmanse avèk lèt "w" yo. Ekri tout mo ki soulinye yo nan lòd alfabetik sou trè sa yo ki anba.

6. I ate white fish and rice at Adrienne's wedding.

7. The man in the wheelchair is a wealthy businessman.

8. My college professor is writing a wonderful new book.

9. Joanne bought her hair extensions at Western Wig Store.

10. During the summer, Brenda likes to walk in the wilderness.

_____ _____ _____

_____ _____ _____

_____ _____ _____

_____

Homework

 Name: _____ Date: ___/___/_____ Score: _____

Lesson 23.2

Reading Words with a Vowel before the Letter "w"

✓ Lesson Check Point

 Directions: Read each target word. Circle the word in the column that has the same "aw," "ew" or "ow" sound as the target word.
Direksyons: Li chak mo objektif. Antoure mo a ki nan kolòn nan ki bay menm son vwayèl "aw," "ew" oubyen "ow" la (yo) tankou mo objektif la.

nephew	a. sewn
	b. renewal

flawless	a. awareness
	b. pawn

plowing	a. widow
	b. crowds

tomorrow	a. sew
	b. crew

 Directions: Read each target word. Put a check (✓) under the correct column heading.
Direksyons: Li chak mo objektif. Mete yon tchèk (✓) anba antèt kolòn ki kòrèk la.

Target Words	Underlined letters have /o͞o/ sound as in the word <u>few</u>	Underlined letters have /ȯ/ sound as in the word <u>law</u>	Underlined letters have /ō/ sound as in the word <u>sew</u>	Underlined letters have /ou/ sound as in the word <u>cow</u>
1. neph<u>ew</u>				
2. fl<u>aw</u>less				
3. pl<u>ow</u>ing				
4. tomorr<u>ow</u>				

Homework

Name: _____ Date: ___/___/_____ Score: _____

Lesson 23.3

Reading Words with a Silent "w" and "wr" Letter Combination

Dictionary Skills/ Vocabulary

✓ **Lesson Check Point**

Directions: Read each target word and its definition. Write the letter of the definition on the line of each target word. Use a dictionary or the Internet to check your answers.

Direksyons: Li chak mo objektif ak definisyon yo chak. Ekri lèt la ki koresponn ak definisyon an sou trè chak mo objektif yo. Itilize yon diksyonè oubyen entènèt pou tcheke repons ou yo.

Target Words	Definitions
1. __ wrote	a. in an incorrect manner
2. __ wreck	b. to destroy or damage something
3. __ wrench	c. a tool used to tighten or loosen an object
4. __ wrongly	d. a material used to wrap something
5. __ wrapping	e. to have communicated by forming letters on paper

Directions: Read each sentence. Underline the word in the parentheses that correctly completes each sentence. Then, write the underlined word on the line.

Direksyons: Li chak fraz. Soulinye mo a in an parantèz yo ki konplete chak fraz kòrèkteman. Answit, ekri mo soulinye a sou trè a.

6. Wanda _____ a long business letter. (wrecked, wrote)

7. The storm _____ the fishing fleet. (wrecked, wrongly)

8. Wendell was _____ accused of a crime. (wrapping, wrongly)

9. I used a hammer and a _____ to fix the chair. (wrote, wrench)

10. Remove the plastic _____ before eating the sandwich. (wrapping, wrench)

Homework

Name: _____ Date: ___/___/_____ Score: _____

Lesson 23.3

Reading Words with a Silent Letter "w"

✓ **Lesson Check Point**

Directions: Read the target words in the word box. Write the words that have a silent letter "w" in the first column. Write the words that do not have a silent letter "w" in the second column.

Direksyons: Li mo objektif yo in an ti bwat mo a. Ekri mo yo ki genyen lèt "w" ki pa pwononse a nan premye kolòn nan. Ekri mo yo ki pa genyen lèt "w" ki pa pwononse anan dezyèm kolòn nan.

Target Word Box				
wrong	two	pillow	writes	wrap
answer	wrench	earwax	writings	widow
backward	wrinkle	freeway	earthworm	winter
driftwood	doorway	dwindle	Wednesday	firewood

Letter "w" is silent   **Letter "w" has the /w/ sound**

_____ _____
_____ _____
_____ _____
_____ _____
_____ _____
_____ _____
_____ _____
_____ _____

Homework

Name: _____   Date:___/___/_____   Score:_____

The Reading Challenge

Lesson 23.4

Reading Multisyllable Words

✓ **Lesson Check Point**

Directions: Read and divide each target word into syllables. Write each word and place a hyphen (-) between the syllables in the second column. Write the number of syllables in the third column. Use a dictionary or the Internet to check your answers.

Direksyons: Li epi divize chak mo objektif an silab. Ekri chak mo epi mete yon tirè (-) ant silab yo nan dezyèm kolòn nan. Ekri kantite silab ke yo genyen an nan twazyèm kolòn nan. Itilize yon diksyonè oubyen entènèt pou tcheke repons ou yo.

Target Words	Words Divided into Syllables	Number of Syllables
1. winterize	_____	_____
2. worldly	_____	_____
3. windy	_____	_____
4. weather	_____	_____
5. watchman	_____	_____
6. wetland	_____	_____
7. walnut	_____	_____
8. wrinkle	_____	_____
9. welcoming	_____	_____
10. window	_____	_____

Homework

 Name: _____ Date: ___/___/_____ Score: _____

The Reading Challenge

Lesson 23.4

Reading Multisyllable Words

✓ **Lesson Check Point**

 Directions: Read each target word. Circle the word in the row that is divided correctly into syllables. Use a dictionary or the Internet to check your answers.

Direksyons: Li chak mo objektif. Antoure mo a ki nan ranje a ki divize an silab korèkteman yo. Itilize yon diksyonè oubyen entènèt pou tcheke repons ou yo.

Model

| wonderful | a. wo-nder-ful | b. won-der-ful | c. won-derf-ul |

| 1. waterfall | a. wa-ter-fall | b. wat-er-fall | c. wa-terf-all |

| 2. weathering | a. wea-ther-ing | b. weath-e-ring | c. weath-er-ing |

| 3. wolverine | a. wol-ver-ine | b. wol-ve-rine | c. wolv-er-ine |

| 4. westernize | a. we-stern-ize | b. west-ern-ize | c. west-er-nize |

| 5. whatever | a. wha-tev-er | b. whate-v-er | c. what-ev-er |

| 6. webpage | a. web-page | b. web-pa-ge | c. we-bpa-ge |

| 7. washable | a. wa-sha-ble | b. wa-shab-le | c. wash-a-ble |

| 8. westerly | a. wes-ter-ly | b. west-er-ly | c. we-ster-ly |

Homework

Name: _____ Date: ___/___/_____ Score: _____

Lesson 23.5

Reading and Writing

Proper and Common Nouns and Adjectives

Directions: Read the words in the word box. Put an (X) on the line next to each word that is written incorrectly. Remember that all proper nouns and proper adjectives are capitalized. Use a dictionary or the Internet to check your answers.

Direksyons: Li chak mo yo ki nan bwat mo a. Met yon (X) sou ti trè a ki bò kote mo ki pa kri byen yo. Sonje ke tout non pwòp ak adjektif pwop ekri avèk yon lèt majiskil nan kòmansman yo. Itilize yon diksyonè oubyen entènèt pou tcheke repons ou yo.

Word Box					
___	witness	___	woman	___	Weasel
___	Wetland	___	wakayama	___	wellness
___	Workout	___	wednesday	___	Waterbury
___	woodcutter	___	West Indian	___	Waterfront

Directions: Read each unedited sentence and underline the word that is written incorrectly. Write each sentence correctly on the line.

Direksyons: Li chak fraz ki pa edite yo epi soulinye mo ki pa ekri byen an. Ekri chak fraz korèkteman sou liy lan.

Model

We walked along the winding path that led to the <u>Waterfalls</u>.
<u>We walked along the winding path that led to the waterfalls.</u>

1. A factory in wisconsin made Wendell's wristwatch.

   _____

2. In the West Indies, I ate delicious fish with White sauce.

   _____

3. wendy said, "South America is in the Western Hemisphere."

   _____

4. In my opinion, Woody woodpecker is a wonderful character.

   _____

Homework

☺ Name: _____ Date:___/___/_____ Score:_____

Lesson 24.1

Reading Words with the Letter X/x

✓ **Lesson Check Point**

Directions: Read each target word. Find the letter "x" and put a check (✓) in the column that identifies its position: beginning, within or end.
Direksyons : Li chak mo objektif. Jwenn lèt "x" a epi mete yon tchèck (✓) nan kolòn ki idantifye pozisyon li an: nan kòmansman, ladan oubyen nan finisman.

Target Words	Beginning (First Letter)	Within	End (Last Letter)
1. annex			
2. fixate			
3. explore			
4. complex			
5. xylophone			

Directions: Read each sentence and underline the words that begin with the letter "x." Write all the underlined words in alphabetical order on the lines below.
Direksyons: Li chak fraz epi soulinye mo ki kòmanse avèk lèt "x" yo. Ekri tout mo ki soulinye in an lòd alfabetik sou trè in a ki anba.

6. Xander attends xylophone lessons every Tuesday.

7. During my vacation to China, I will visit Xian and Xining.

8. I am reading the biographies of Malcolm X and Francis Xavier.

9. Dr. Xerxes used the surgical instrument, xyster, to scrape bones.

10. X-linked refers to a trait controlled by genes on the X-chromosome.

_____   _____   _____
_____   _____   _____
_____   _____   _____
            _____

Homework

 Name: _____ Date: ___/___/_____ Score: _____

Lesson 24.1

Reading Words with the Letter X/x

✓ Lesson Check Point

 Directions: Read each target word. Circle the word in the column that has the same "x" sound(s) as the target word.
Direksyons: Li chak mo objektif. Antoure mo a ki nan kolòn nan ki bay menm son "x" yo tankou mo objektif la.

xylem	a. exhaustive
	b. xeric

Xerxes	a. anxious
	b. Xerox

excellent	a. galaxy
	b. exact

exhilarate	a. existence
	b. explicit

 Directions: Read each target word. Put a check (✓) under the correct column heading.
Direksyons: Li chak mo objektif. Mete yon tchèk (✓) anba antèt kolòn ki kòrèk la.

Target Words	"x" has the /k/ + /s/ sounds as in the word <u>box</u>	"x" has the /z/ sound as in the word <u>xylophone</u>	"x" has the /g/ + /z/ sounds as in the word <u>exhibit</u>	"x" has the /k/ + /sh/ sounds as in the word <u>anxious</u>
1. xylem				
2. Xerxes I				
3. excellent				
4. exhilarate				

Homework

 Name: _____ Date:___/___/_____ Score:_____

The Reading Challenge

Lesson 24.2

Reading Multisyllable Words

✓ Lesson Check Point

 Directions: Read and divide each target word into syllables. Write each word and place a hyphen (-) between the syllables in the second column. Write the number of syllables in the third column. Use a dictionary or the Internet to check your answers.

Direksyons: Li epi divize chak mo objektif an silab. Ekri chak mo epi mete yon tirè (-) ant silab yo nan dezyèm kolòn nan. Ekri kantite silab ke yo genyen an nan twazyèm kolòn nan. Itilize yon diksyonè oubyen entènèt pou tcheke repons ou yo.

Target Words	Words Divided into Syllables	Number of Syllables
1. xylophone	_____	_____
2. oxide	_____	_____
3. fixture	_____	_____
4. extracting	_____	_____
5. example	_____	_____
6. oxygen	_____	_____
7. textile	_____	_____
8. waxing	_____	_____
9. taxation	_____	_____
10. exercise	_____	_____

Homework

 Name: _____ Date:___/___/_____ Score:_____

The Reading Challenge

Lesson 24.2

Reading Multisyllable Words

✓ Lesson Check Point

 Directions: Read each target word. Circle the word in the row that is divided correctly into syllables. Use a dictionary or the Internet to check your answers.
Direksyons: Li chak mo objektif. Antoure mo a ki nan ranje a ki divize an silab korèkteman yo. Itilize yon diksyonè oubyen entènèt pou tcheke repons ou yo.

Model

| oxidized | a. ox-i-dized (circled) | b. oxi-d-ized | c. o-xi-dized |

1. extremely	a. ex-tremel-y	b. ex-tre-mely	c. ex-treme-ly
2. deoxidize	a. de-oxi-dize	b. de-ox-i-dize	c. deo-xi-dize
3. exactly	a. ex-act-ly	b. e-xact-ly	c. ex-a-ctly
4. xenoliths	a. xen-o-liths	b. xe-noli-ths	c. xe-nolit-hs
5. expanding	a. exp-an-ding	b. ex-pand-ing	c. exp-and-ing
6. vexation	a. vex-at-ion	b. vex-a-tion	c. ve-xat-ion
7. xerophytes	a. xer-o-phytes	b. xe-rophy-tes	c. xero-phytes
8. oxygen	a. oxy-g-en	b. o-xyg-en	c. ox-y-gen

Homework

Name: _____ Date: ___/___/_____ Score: _____

Lesson 24.3

Reading and Writing

Proper and Common Nouns and Adjectives

Directions: Read the words in the word box. Put an (X) on the line next to each word that is written incorrectly. Remember that all proper nouns and proper adjectives are capitalized. Use a dictionary or the Internet to check your answers.

Direksyons: Li chak mo yo ki nan bwat mo a. Met yon (X) sou ti trè a ki bò kote mo ki pa kri byen yo. Sonje ke tout non pwòp ak adjektif pwop ekri avèk yon lèt majiskil nan kòmansman yo. Itilize yon diksyonè oubyen entènèt pou tcheke repons ou yo.

Word Box		
__ xuzhou	__ xebec	__ Xenon
__ xylocaine	__ xylems	__ Xavier
__ xylophone	__ xanthus	__ xerxes I
__ Xylography	__ Xenophobia	__ xenophobes

Directions: Read each unedited sentence and underline the word that is written incorrectly. Write each sentence correctly on the line.

Direksyons: Li chak fraz ki pa edite yo epi soulinye mo ki pa ekri byen an. Ekri chak fraz korèkteman sou liy lan.

Model
Xia said, "The population of xankandi is 33,000 people."
Xia said, "The population of Xankandi is 33,000 people."

1. xian's mother bought her a new xylophone.
   _____

2. The greatest King of Persia was King xerxes I.
   _____

3. I am convinced that Xylocaine numbs the pain.
   _____

4. Dr. Xavier was gentle as he scraped his patient's bones with a Xyster.
   _____

Homework

Name: _____ Date:___/___/_____ Score:_____

Lesson 25.1

Reading Words with the Letter Y/y

✓ **Lesson Check Point**

Directions: Read each target word. Find the letter "y" and put a check (✓) in the column that identifies its position: beginning, within or end.
Direksyons : Li chak mo objektif. Jwenn lèt "y" a epi mete yon tchèck (✓) nan kolòn ki idantifye pozisyon li an: nan kòmansman, ladan oubyen nan finisman.

Target Words	Beginning (First Letter)	Within	End (Last Letter)
1. yogurt			
2. money			
3. slippery			
4. keyboard			
5. yearning			

Directions: Read each sentence and underline the words that begin with the letter "y." Write all the underlined words in alphabetical order on the lines below.
Direksyons: Li chak fraz epi soulinye mo ki kòmanse avèk lèt "y" yo. Ekri tout mo ki soulinye in an lòd alfabetik sou trè in a ki anba.

6. The yellow yogurt has an artificial lemon flavor.

7. Our yogi practices yoga at least three times a day.

8. The young people are staying at the local youth hostel.

9. Kathy bought a bright orange yo-yo for her younger sister.

10. Yesterday, I drew the y-axis and the x-axis on graph paper.

_____   _____   _____
_____   _____   _____
_____   _____   _____
_____

Homework

 Name: _____ Date: ___/___/_____ Score: _____

Lesson 25.1

Reading Words with the Letter Y/y

✓ **Lesson Check Point**

 Directions: Read each target word. Circle the word in the row that has a different "y" sound than the target word.
Direksyons: Li chak mo objektif. Antoure mo a in an ranje a ki bay yon son vwayèl "y" ki diferan an.

Target Words				
1. yahoo	you'll	youth	baby	yours
2. Egypt	typical	symbol	hymn	yesterday
3. magnify	typing	money	goodbye	styling
4. analysis	catalyst	rhyming	calypso	bicycle
5. Wednesday	younger	prayer	honey	highway

 Directions: Read the words in the four boxes. Circle two words that have the same "y" sound.
Direksyons: Li mo yo in an kat kat ti bwat yo. Antoure de mo ki bay menm son "y" yo.

baby	style
yours	eyeballs

type	thyme
today	mystery

Kenya	May
yield	typing

candy	gym
analyze	rhyme

symptom	paralyze
yucky	hypnosis

young	yogurt
goodbye	bicycles

Homework

 Name: _____   Date:___/___/_____   Score:_____

Lesson 25.2

Reading Words with a Vowel before the Letter "y"

✓ Lesson Check Point

 Directions: Read each target word. Circle the word in the column that has the same "y" sound as the target word.
Li chak mo objektif. Antoure mo a ki nan kolòn nan ki bay menm son "y" la tankou mo objektif la.

oyster	a. voyagers
	b. money

buyers	a. guys
	b. soliloquy

papaya	a. today
	b. yielding

monkey	a. youngest
	b. playing

 Directions: Read each target word. Put a check (✓) under the correct column heading.
Direksyons: Li chak mo objektif. Mete yon tchèk (✓) anba antèt kolòn ki kòrèk la.

Target Words	"y" has the /y/ sound as in the word yes	"oy" has the /oi/ sound as in the word boy	"y" has the /ɪ/ sound as in the word by	"y" is silent as in the word day
1. oyster				
2. buyers				
3. papaya				
4. monkey				

Homework

 Name: _____ Date:___/___/_____ Score: _____

Lesson 25.3

Reading Words with the "cy" Letter Combination

✓ **Lesson Check Point**

 Directions: Read each target word. Find the "cy" letter combination and put a check (✓) in the column to identify its position in the word: beginning, within or end.

Direksyons : Li chak mo objektif. Jwenn konbinezon lèt "cy" laepi mete yon tchèk (✓) nan kolòn nan ki idantifye pozisyon li an : nan kòmansman, ladan oubyen nan finisman.

Target Words	Beginning (First 2 Letters)	Within	End (Last 2 Letters)
1. cycling			
2. cynical			
3. regency			
4. democracy			
5. encyclopedia			

 Directions: Read each target word. Put a check (✓) under the correct column heading.

Direksyons: Li chak mo objektif. Mete yon tchèk (✓) anba antèt kolòn ki kòrèk la.

Target Words	"cy" has the /s/ + /ĭ/ sounds as in the word <u>cylinder</u>	"cy" has the /s/ + /ī/ sounds as in the word <u>cycle</u>	"cy" has the /s/ + /ē/ sounds as in the word <u>agency</u>
6. cycling			
7. cynical			
8. regency			
9. democracy			
10. encyclopedia			

Homework

 Name: _____ Date: ___/___/_____ Score: _____

Lesson 25.4

Reading Words with the Final Letter "y"

✓ **Lesson Check Point**

 Directions: Read each target word. Find the letter "y" and put a check (✓) in the column that identifies its position within the word.

Direksyons: Li chak mo objektif. Jwenn lèt "y" la epi mete yon tchèck (✓) nan kolòn nan ki idantifye pozisyon li an nan mo a.

Target Words	"y" is at the end of a one syllable word	"y" is at the end of the first syllable	"y" is at the end of a multi-syllable word
1. guy			
2. testify			
3. hybrid			
4. comply			
5. mommy			

 Directions: Read each target word. Put a check (✓) under the correct column heading.

Direksyons: Li chak mo objektif. Mete yon tchèk (✓) anba antèt kolòn ki kòrèk la.

Target Words	"y" has the /ē/ sound as in the word <u>agency</u>	"y" has the /ī/ sound as in the word <u>flying</u>
6. guy		
7. testify		
8. hybrid		
9. comply		
10. mommy		

Unit Y
Lesson 25.4

Homework

 Name: _____ Date:___/___/_____ Score: _____

Lesson 25.5

Reading Words with the "yr" Letter Combination

✓ **Lesson Check Point**

 Directions: Read each target word. Circle the word in the column that has the same "yr" sounds as the target word.
Direksyons: Li chak mo objektif. Antoure mo a ki nan kolòn nan ki bay menm son "yr" yo tankou mo objektif la.

Tyrol	a. myrtle
	b. syringe

papyrus	a. playroom
	b. Byron

pyramidal	a. lyrical
	b. lyre

pyrotechnics	a. gyrate
	b. tyrannous

 Directions: Read each target word. Put a check (✓) under the correct column heading.
Direksyons: Li chak mo objektif. Mete yon tchèk (✓) anba antèt kolòn ki kòrèk la.

Target Words	"yr" has the /û/ + /r/ sounds as in the word myrtle	"yr" has the /ĭ/ + /r/ sounds as in the word pyramid	"yr" has the /ī/ + /r/ sounds as in the word gyro	"yr" has the /ə/ + /r/ sounds as in the word martyr
1. Tyrol				
2. papyrus				
3. pyramidal				
4. pyrotechnics				

Homework

 Name: _____ Date: ___/___/_____ Score: _____

Lesson 25.6

Reading Letter "y" Words with the Schwa Vowel Sound

✓ **Lesson Check Point**

 Directions: Read each target word. Circle the word in the column that has the same "y" sound as the target word.

Direksyons: Li chak mo objektif. Antoure mo a ki nan kolòn nan ki bay menm son "y" la tankou mo objektif la.

vinyl	a. briefly
	b. polymer

beryl	a. mandatory
	b. Pennsylvania

polyvinyl	a. Polynesia
	b. instantly

Tyrrhenian Sea	a. Polynesian
	b. pyrometer

 Directions: Read each target word. Put a check (✓) under the correct column heading.

Direksyons: Li chak mo objektif. Mete yon tchèk (✓) anba antèt kolòn ki kòrèk la.

Target Words	"y" has the /ə/ sound as in the word <u>syringe</u>	"y" does not have the /ə/ sound
1. vinyl		
2. beryl		
3. polyvinyl		
4. Tyrrhenian Sea		

Homework

Name: _____ Date: ___/___/_____ Score: _____

Lesson 25.7

Reading Words with a Silent Letter "y"

✓ **Lesson Check Point**

Directions: Read the target words in the word box. Write the words that have a silent letter "y" in the first column. Write the words that do not have a silent letter "y" in the second column.

Direksyons: Li mo objektif yo ki nan ti bwat mo a. Ekri mo yo ki genyen lèt "y" ki pa pwononse a nan premye kolòn nan. Ekri mo yo ki pa genyen lèt "y" ki pa pwononse anan dezyèm kolòn nan.

Target Word Box				
gray	day	yes	sway	essay
yellow	steady	clay	young	Yankee
yardage	needy	prey	journey	academy
Tuesday	honey	yearbook	yardstick	Thursday

Letter "y" is silent

Letter "y" has the /y/ or /ē/ sound

Learn to Read English With Directions In Haitian Creole

Unit Y Lesson 25.7

Homework

 Name: _____ Date: ___/___/_____ Score: _____

The Reading Challenge

Lesson 25.8

Reading Multisyllable Words

✓ **Lesson Check Point**

Directions: Read and divide each target word into syllables. Write each word and place a hyphen (-) between the syllables in the second column. Write the number of syllables in the third column. Use a dictionary or the Internet to check your answers.

Direksyons: Li epi divize chak mo objektif an silab. Ekri chak mo epi mete yon tirè (-) ant silab yo nan dezyèm kolòn nan. Ekri kantite silab ke yo genyen an nan twazyèm kolòn nan. Itilize yon diksyonè oubyen entènèt pou tcheke repons ou yo.

Target Words	Words Divided into Syllables	Number of Syllables
1. yachting	_____	_____
2. youngsters	_____	_____
3. Yuletide	_____	_____
4. yahoo	_____	_____
5. yielding	_____	_____
6. youthful	_____	_____
7. yardstick	_____	_____
8. yelping	_____	_____
9. yearly	_____	_____
10. yardage	_____	_____

Homework

 Name: _____ Date: ___/___/_____ Score: _____

The Reading Challenge

Lesson 25.8

Reading Multisyllable Words

✓ **Lesson Check Point**

 Directions: Read each target word. Circle the word in the row that is divided correctly into syllables. Use a dictionary or the Internet to check your answers.

Direksyons: Li chak mo objektif. Antoure mo a ki nan ranje a ki divize an silab korèkteman yo. Itilize yon diksyonè oubyen entènèt pou tcheke repons ou yo.

Model

| yesterday | a. ye-ster-day | b. yest-er-day | c. yes-ter-day |

1. Yoruba	a. Yor-u-ba	b. Yo-ru-ba	c. Yo-rub-a
2. Yugoslav	a. Yug-o-slav	b. Yu-go-slav	c. Yu-gos-lav
3. yearly	a. year-ly	b. ye-ar-ly	c. yearl-y
4. yodeler	a. yo-del-er	b. yod-e-ler	c. yod-el-er
5. yielding	a. yie-ldi-ng	b. yield-ing	c. yie-lding
6. yonder	a. yond-er	b. yon-der	c. yo-nder
7. yourself	a. yo-ur-self	b. your-self	c. you-rse-lf
8. yoking	a. yo-king	b. yok-ing	c. yoki-ng

Homework

Name: _____ Date: ___/___/_____ Score: _____

Lesson 25.9

Reading and Writing

Proper and Common Nouns and Adjectives

Directions: Read the words in the word box. Put an (X) on the line next to each word that is written incorrectly. Remember that all proper nouns and proper adjectives are capitalized. Use a dictionary or the Internet to check your answers.

Direksyons: Li chak mo yo ki nan bwat mo a. Met yon (X) sou ti trè a ki bò kote mo ki pa kri byen yo. Sonje ke tout non pwòp ak adjektif pwop ekri avèk yon lèt majiskil nan kòmansman yo. Itilize yon diksyonè oubyen entènèt pou tcheke repons ou yo.

Word Box		
___ Yeast	___ Yoga	___ yeshiva
___ Youth	___ yugoslavia	___ yucatan
___ Yiddish	___ Yokohama	___ Yearbook
___ Yellow River	___ Yogyakarta	___ Yinchuan

Directions: Read each unedited sentence and underline the word that is written incorrectly. Write each sentence correctly on the line.

Direksyons: Li chak fraz ki pa edite yo epi soulinye mo ki pa ekri byen an. Ekri chak fraz korèkteman sou liy lan.

Model
Is the New York <u>yankees</u> your favorite baseball team?
<u>Is the New York Yankees your favorite baseball team?</u>

1. I scheduled two Yoga classes at Yorktown Gym.

   _____

2. Mr. yelp painted his house in Yorktown sunshine yellow.

   _____

3. The Yearbook pictures were taken at Yosemite National Park.

   _____

4. All the young people in my class have new, brightly colored Yo-yos.

   _____

Homework

Name: _____ Date: ___/___/_____ Score: _____

Lesson 26.1

Reading Words with the Letter Z/z

✓ **Lesson Check Point**

Directions: Read each target word. Find the letter "z" and put a check (✓) in the column that identifies its position: beginning, within or end.
Direksyons: Li chak mo objektif. Jwenn lèt "z" a epi mete yon tchèck (✓) nan kolòn ki idantifye pozisyon li an: nan kòmansman, ladan oubyen nan finisman.

Target Words	Beginning (First Letter)	Within	End (Last Letter)
1. waltz			
2. quartz			
3. Zambia			
4. realized			
5. organized			

Directions: Read each sentence and underline the words that begin with the letter "z." Write all the underlined words in alphabetical order on the lines below.
Direksyons: Li chak fraz epi soulinye mo ki kòmanse avèk lèt "z" yo. Ekri tout mo ki soulinye yo nan lòd alfabetik sou trè sa yo ki anba.

6. The zookeeper's car is in the no parking zone.

7. The zipper on Jenny's zebra print coat is broken.

8. One day, Mr. and Mrs. Zangara will visit Zambia.

9. The interns at the zoo are enrolled in the zoology program.

10. Zeezee said, "Zululand is steeped in ancient history and tradition."

_____ _____ _____
_____ _____ _____
_____ _____ _____
_____

Homework

 Name: _____ Date: ___/___/_____ Score: _____

Lesson 26.1

Reading Words with the Letter Z/z

✓ Lesson Check Point

 Directions: Read each target word. Circle the word in the column that has the same "z" sound as the target word.
Direksyons: Li chak mo objektif. Antoure mo a ki nan kolòn nan ki bay menm son "z" la tankou mo objektif la.

| ritzy | a. lizard |
| | b. Biarritz |

| zebras | a. chutzpah |
| | b. capitalizes |

| zippers | a. squeezes |
| | b. quetzal |

| influenza | a. freezes |
| | b. Lutz |

 Directions: Read each target word. Put a check (✓) under the correct column heading.
Direksyons: Li chak mo objektif. Mete yon tchèk (✓) anba antèt kolòn ki kòrèk la.

Target Words	"z" has the /z/ sound as in the word <u>zipper</u>	"z" has the /s/ sound as in the word <u>quartz</u>
1. ritzy		
2. zebras		
3. zippers		
4. influenza		

Homework

 Name: _____ Date:___/___/_____ Score: _____

Lesson 26.2

Reading Words with a Silent Letter "z"

✓ Lesson Check Point

 Directions: Read the target words in the word box. Write the words that have a silent letter "z" in the first column. Write the words that do not have a silent letter "z" in the second column.

Direksyons: Li mo objektif yo ki nan ti bwat mo a. Ekri mo yo ki genyen lèt "z" ki pa pwononse a nan premye kolòn nan. Ekri mo yo ki pa genyen lèt "z" ki pa pwononse anan dezyèm kolòn nan.

Target Word Box				
lazy	sizzle	grizzly	fizzled	blazed
drizzle	dazzle	hazel	puzzles	sizzling
buzzing	emphasize	lizard	influenza	magnetize
amazement	burglarize	nuzzle	computerize	intermezzo

Letter "z" is silent

Letter "z" has the /z/ or /s/ sound

Unit Z
Lesson 26.2

Learn to Read English With Directions In Haitian Creole   247   Copyrighted Material

Homework

Name: _____ Date: ___/___/_____ Score: _____

The Reading Challenge

Lesson 26.3

Reading Multisyllable Words

✓ **Lesson Check Point**

Directions: Read and divide each target word into syllables. Write each word and place a hyphen (-) between the syllables in the second column. Write the number of syllables in the third column. Use a dictionary or the Internet to check your answers.

Direksyons: Li epi divize chak mo objektif an silab. Ekri chak mo epi mete yon tirè (-) ant silab yo nan dezyèm kolòn nan. Ekri kantite silab ke yo genyen an nan twazyèm kolòn nan. Itilize yon diksyonè oubyen entènèt pou tcheke repons ou yo.

Target Words	Words Divided into Syllables	Number of Syllables
1. zygote	_____	_____
2. zealots	_____	_____
3. zirconium	_____	_____
4. zenith	_____	_____
5. zero	_____	_____
6. zestful	_____	_____
7. Zambia	_____	_____
8. Zanzibar	_____	_____
9. zinger	_____	_____
10. zodiac	_____	_____

Homework

 Name: _____ Date:___/___/_____ Score:_____

The Reading Challenge

Lesson 26.3

Reading Multisyllable Words

✓ Lesson Check Point

 Directions: Read each target word. Circle the word in the row that is divided correctly into syllables. Use a dictionary or the Internet to check your answers.

Direksyons: Li chak mo objektif. Antoure mo a ki nan ranje a ki divize an silab korèkteman yo. Itilize yon diksyonè oubyen entènèt pou tcheke repons ou yo.

Model

| zoology | a. zo-ol-o-gy | b. zoo-lo-gy | c. zool-o-gy |

(a. zo-ol-o-gy is circled)

| 1. zestful | a. ze-stful | b. zes-tful | c. zest-ful |

| 2. Zambian | a. Zam-bi-an | b. Zam-b-ian | c. Zamb-ian |

| 3. Zanzibar | a. Za-nzib-ar | b. Zan-zi-bar | c. Zanz-i-bar |

| 4. Zealand | a. Ze-aland | b. Zeal-and | c. Zea-land |

| 5. zealous | a. zeal-ous | b. zea-lous | c. zeal-ou-s |

| 6. zebra | a. ze-bra | b. zeb-ra | c. ze-br-a |

| 7. zygote | a. zygo-te | b. zyg-ote | c. zy-gote |

| 8. zymurgy | a. zy-mur-gy | b. zym-u-rgy | c. zy-mu-rgy |

Unit Z
Lesson 26.3

Learn to Read English With Directions In Haitian Creole

Homework

Name: _____ Date: ___/___/_____ Score: _____

Lesson 26.4

Reading and Writing

Proper and Common Nouns and Adjectives

Directions: Read the words in the word box. Put an (X) on the line next to each word that is written incorrectly. Remember that all proper nouns and proper adjectives are capitalized. Use a dictionary or the Internet to check your answers.

Direksyons: Li chak mo yo ki nan bwat mo a. Met yon (X) sou ti trè a ki bò kote mo ki pa kri byen yo. Sonje ke tout non pwòp ak adjektif pwop ekri avèk yon lèt majiskil nan kòmansman yo. Itilize yon diksyonè oubyen entènèt pou tcheke repons ou yo.

Word Box		
___ zenith	___ zonal	___ Zealot
___ zucchini	___ Zoology	___ zealous
___ zambezi	___ zululand	___ Zippers
___ Zaragoza	___ zero hour	___ Zebra

Directions: Read each unedited sentence and underline the word that is written incorrectly. Write each sentence correctly on the line.

Direksyons: Li chak fraz ki pa edite yo epi soulinye mo ki pa ekri byen an. Ekri chak fraz korèkteman sou liy lan.

Model
The steep path zigzags through the <u>zagros</u> Mountains.
The steep path zigzags through the Zagros Mountains.

1. Yesterday, I saw three large Zebras at the San Diego Zoo.
   _____

2. On Friday, the bright sun in zimbabwe rose towards its zenith.
   _____

3. Zola said, "zanzibar is located off the east coast of Africa."
   _____

4. The zambezi River flows from Zambia into the Mozambique Channel.
   _____

Name: _____ Date: ___/___/_____ Score: _____

Homework

Appendix 1.0

Introduction of the Letter A/a

✓ Lesson Check Point

 Directions: Circle the correct letter "a" pair: uppercase and lowercase letters.
Direksyons: Antoure lèt ki kòrèk "a" pè: lèt majiskil ak lèt miniskil.

    Ea   Ae   Ao   Aa   aZ

 Directions: The uppercase letter "A" is in the first column. Look at the four letters in the row and circle the lowercase letter that matches the uppercase letter "A."
Direksyons: Lèt majiskil "A" se nan premye kolòn nan. Gade kat lèt ki nan ranje a epi antoure lèt miniskil ki koresponn ak lèt majiskil "A".

A	g	a	e	o
A	u	e	i	a
A	a	o	y	e
A	e	c	a	q

 Directions: The lowercase letter "a" is in the first column. Look at the four letters in the row and circle the uppercase letter that matches the lowercase letter "a."
Direksyons: Lèt miniskil "a" se nan premye kolòn nan. Gade kat lèt ki nan ranje a epi antoure lèt majiskil ki koresponn ak lèt miniskil "a".

a	C	A	E	R
a	X	D	G	A
a	A	G	D	S
a	O	C	A	W

Homework

 Name: _____ Date: ___/___/_____ Score: _____

Appendix 2.0

Introduction of the Letter B/b

✓ Lesson Check Point

 Directions: Circle the correct letter "b" pair: uppercase and lowercase letters.
Direksyons: Antoure lèt ki kòrèk "b" pè: lèt majiskil ak lèt miniskil.

fB   Bq   bB   bD   Pb

 Directions: The uppercase letter "B" is in the first column. Look at the four letters in the row and circle the lowercase letter that matches the uppercase letter "B."
Direksyons: Lèt majiskil "B" se nan premye kolòn nan. Gade kat lèt ki nan ranje a epi antoure lèt miniskil ki koresponn ak lèt majiskil "B".

B	p	q	b	d
B	f	d	h	b
B	m	b	f	h
B	k	d	b	l

 Directions: The lowercase letter "b" is in the first column. Look at the four letters in the row and circle the uppercase letter that matches the lowercase letter "b."
Direksyons: Lèt miniskil "b" nan premye kolòn nan. Gade kat lèt ki nan ranje a epi antoure lèt majiskil ki koresponn ak lèt miniskil "b".

b	B	M	F	H
b	P	H	B	G
b	M	B	V	N
b	X	T	B	J

Homework

Name: _____ Date: ___/___/_____ Score: _____

Appendix 2.0

Letter Recognition B/b

Uppercase and Lowercase Letter

✓ **Lesson Check Point**

Directions: Read each target word. Read the words in the row and circle the word that begins with a different letter.

Direksyons: Li chak mo sib. Li mo ki nan ranje a epi antoure mo ki kòmanse ak yon lèt diferan.

Target Words				
1. buffet	boss	danger	bottle	biscuit
2. brain	basket	blank	pads	bride
3. brick	behave	beef	big	demand
4. butter	dent	bank	black	bill
5. brass	blade	bin	bell	queen

Directions: Read the words in the four boxes. Circle two words that start with the uppercase and lowercase letter "b."

Direksyons: Li mo ki nan kat kare yo. Ansèkle de mo ki kòmanse ak lèt majiskil ak lèt miniskil "b".

Boy	Toy
boy	Soy

Ball	hall
Hall	ball

Book	Hook
book	Took

Had	had
bad	Bad

Bank	Tank
bank	tank

Bread	head
bread	Head

Homework

 Name: _____ Date: ___/___/_____ Score: _____

Appendix 3.0

Introduction of the Letter C/c

✓ Lesson Check Point

 Directions: Circle the correct letter "c" pair: uppercase and lowercase letters.
Direksyons: Antoure lèt ki kòrèk "c" pè: lèt majiskil ak lèt miniskil.

    Cf   Cc   Kc   cD   Co

 Directions: The uppercase letter "C" is in the first column. Look at the four letters in the row and circle the lowercase letter that matches the uppercase letter "C."
Direksyons: Lèt majiskil "C" se nan premye kolòn nan. Gade kat lèt ki nan ranje a epi antoure lèt miniskil ki koresponn ak lèt majiskil "C".

C	c	g	h	k
C	s	c	u	j
C	n	p	d	c
C	c	v	s	o

 Directions: The lowercase letter "c" is in the first column. Look at the four letters in the row and circle the uppercase letter that matches the lowercase letter "c."
Direksyons: Lèt miniskil "c" nan premye kolòn nan. Gade kat lèt ki nan ranje a epi antoure lèt majiskil ki koresponn ak lèt miniskil "c".

c	K	G	C	O
c	H	J	D	C
c	Q	G	C	V
c	C	B	Q	G

Homework

Name: _____ Date: ___/___/_____ Score: _____

Appendix 3.0

Letter Recognition C/c

Uppercase and Lowercase Letter

✓ **Lesson Check Point**

Directions: Read each target word. Read the words in the row and circle the word that begins with a different letter.

Direksyons: Li chak mo sib. Li mo ki nan ranje a epi antoure mo ki kòmanse ak yon lèt diferan.

Target Words				
1. cart	cry	oblong	curtain	city
2. choice	calculate	queen	cutter	cycle
3. cherish	ankle	chill	comb	cup
4. calcium	Goat	circle	choke	caption
5. convert	cherish	career	cell	boss

Directions: Read the words in the four boxes. Circle two words that start with the uppercase and lowercase letter "c."

Direksyons: Li mo ki nan kat kare yo. Ansèkle de mo ki kòmanse ak lèt majiskil ak lèt miniskil "c".

Case	base	Open	Cream	Castle	vase
Quiet	camp	cargo	pool	keep	coat

cream	Chase	jump	cash	old	orange
box	grapes	Child	food	cold	Crib

Learn To Read English With Directions In Haitian Creole

Homework

 Name: _____ Date: ___/___/_____ Score: _____

Appendix 4.0

Introduction of the Letter D/d

✓ **Lesson Check Point**

 Directions: Circle the correct letter "d" pair: uppercase and lowercase letters.
Direksyons: Fè yon wonn pè lèt kòrèk "d": lèt majiskil ak lèt miniskil.

Db   Fd   Dd   Od   Gd

 Directions: The uppercase letter "D" is in the first column. Look at the four letters in the row and circle the lowercase letter that matches the uppercase letter "D."
Direksyons: Lèt majiskil "D" se nan premye kolòn nan. Gade kat lèt ki nan ranje a epi ansèkle lèt miniskil ki koresponn ak lèt majiskil "D".

D	b	f	h	d
D	j	d	p	t
D	h	n	d	b
D	p	b	d	k

 Directions: The lowercase letter "d" is in the first column. Look at the four letters in the row and circle the uppercase letter that matches the lowercase letter "d."
Direksyons: Lèt miniskil "d" nan premye kolòn nan. Gade kat lèt ki nan ranje a epi antoure lèt majiskil ki koresponn ak lèt miniskil "d".

d	H	D	B	K
d	P	J	D	B
d	D	B	E	R
d	S	K	B	D

Homework

Name: _____ Date: ___/___/_____ Score: _____

Appendix 4.0

Letter Recognition D/d

Uppercase and Lowercase Letter

✓ Lesson Check Point

Directions: Read each target word. Read the words in the row and circle the word that begins with a different letter.

Direksyons: Li chak mo sib. Li mo ki nan ranje a epi antoure mo ki kòmanse ak yon lèt diferan.

Target Words				
1. dog	dive	dress	dew	both
2. due	deal	place	date	draw
3. dole	ditch	dome	bread	dwarf
4. depth	drop	dish	prize	deck
5. drain	quite	doze	dream	dodge

Directions: Read the words in the four boxes. Circle two words that start with the uppercase and lowercase letter "d."

Direksyons: Li mo ki nan kat kare yo. Ansèkle de mo ki kòmanse ak lèt majiskil ak lèt miniskil "d".

top	Dance
dear	ball

drum	Open
Pop	Deck

dry	Queen
Deer	Prince

friend	Due
Ox	drink

Box	Dress
dodge	boat

Old	Pie
Dad	doubt

Learn To Read English With Directions In Haitian Creole   257   Copyrighted Material

Homework

 Name: _____ Date: ___/___/_____ Score: _____

Appendix 5.0

Introduction of the Letter E/e

✓ **Lesson Check Point**

 Directions: Circle the correct letter "e" pair: uppercase and lowercase letters.
Direksyons: Fè yon wonn pè lèt kòrèk "e": lèt majiskil ak lèt miniskil.

eF	Ee	Ec	eC	Qe

 Directions: The uppercase letter "E" is in the first column. Look at the four letters in the row and circle the lowercase letter that matches the uppercase letter "E."
Direksyons: Lèt majiskil "E" se nan premye kolòn nan. Gade kat lèt ki nan ranje a epi antoure lèt miniskil ki koresponn ak lèt majiskil "E".

E	c	e	s	x
E	a	c	d	e
E	e	s	c	w
E	v	g	e	o

 Directions: The lowercase letter "e" is in the first column. Look at the four letters in the row and circle the uppercase letter that matches the lowercase letter "e."
Direksyons: Lèt miniskil "e" se nan premye kolòn nan. Gade kat lèt ki nan ranje a epi antoure lèt majiskil ki koresponn ak lèt miniskil "e".

e	F	E	H	T
e	D	T	E	Y
e	E	D	R	N
e	X	S	F	E

Name: _____ Date: ___/___/_____ Score: _____

Appendix 6.0

Introduction of the Letter F/f

✓ **Lesson Check Point**

 Directions: Circle the correct letter "f" pair: uppercase and lowercase letters.
Direksyons: Antoure lèt ki kòrèk "f" pè: lèt majiskil ak lèt miniskil.

     Fd   fF   Yf   Ef   Bf

 Directions: The uppercase letter "F" is in the first column. Look at the four letters in the row and circle the lowercase letter that matches the uppercase letter "F."
Direksyons: Lèt majiskil "F" se nan premye kolòn nan. Gade kat lèt ki nan ranje a epi antoure lèt miniskil ki koresponn ak lèt majiskil "F".

F	k	f	h	t
F	h	t	p	f
F	f	l	d	h
F	b	k	f	t

 Directions: The lowercase letter "f" is in the first column. Look at the four letters in the row and circle the uppercase letter that matches the lowercase letter "f."
Direksyons: Lèt miniskil "f" se nan premye kolòn nan. Gade kat lèt ki nan ranje a epi antoure lèt majiskil ki koresponn ak lèt miniskil "f".

f	B	F	E	H
f	E	K	L	F
f	F	H	M	E
f	J	F	E	P

Homework

Name: _____ Date: ___/___/_____ Score: _____

Appendix 6.0

Letter Recognition F/f

Uppercase and Lowercase Letter

✓ **Lesson Check Point**

Directions: Read each target word. Read the words in the row and circle the word that begins with a different letter.

Direksyons: Li chak mo sib. Li mo ki nan ranje a epi antoure mo ki kòmanse ak yon lèt diferan.

Target Words				
1. fry	try	fact	foal	fuse
2. flag	folk	fly	house	foam
3. fail	farm	keep	flee	five
4. feed	flame	head	fish	flew
5. flour	love	fox	flesh	fax

Directions: Read the words in the four boxes. Circle two words that start with the uppercase and lowercase letter "f."

Direksyons: Li mo ki nan kat kare yo. Ansèkle de mo ki kòmanse ak lèt majiskil ak lèt miniskil "f".

World	feel
Fawn	drive

boats	Books
Flea	fit

Fit	breeze
Houses	flush

Fetch	fill
Eggs	dove

fret	Keeps
Film	depth

ghost	Flair
draw	flow

Learn To Read English With Directions In Haitian Creole

Homework

 Name: _____ Date:___/___/_____ Score:_____

Appendix 7.0

Introduction of the Letter G/g

✓ Lesson Check Point

 Directions: Circle the correct letter "g" pair: uppercase and lowercase letters.
Direksyons: Antoure lèt ki kòrèk "g" pè: lèt majiskil ak lèt miniskil.

Gj   qG   Gg   Jg   Gp

 Directions: The uppercase letter "G" is in the first column. Look at the four letters in the row and circle the lowercase letter that matches the uppercase letter "G."
Direksyons: Lèt majiskil "G" se nan premye kolòn nan. Gade kat lèt ki nan ranje a epi antoure lèt miniskil ki koresponn ak lèt majiskil "G".

G	j	o	g	l
G	g	y	j	p
G	q	g	z	y
G	y	p	q	g

 Directions: The lowercase letter "g" is in the first column. Look at the four letters in the row and circle the uppercase letter that matches the lowercase letter "g."
Direksyons: Lèt miniskil "g" se nan premye kolòn nan. Gade kat lèt ki nan ranje a epi antoure lèt majiskil ki koresponn ak lèt miniskil "g".

g	O	G	J	L
g	G	Q	O	J
g	O	P	Q	G
g	Q	F	G	O

Homework

 Name: _____ Date:___/___/_____ Score:_____

Appendix 7.0

Letter Recognition G/g

Uppercase and Lowercase Letter

✓ **Lesson Check Point**

 Directions: Read each target word. Read the words in the row and circle the word that begins with a different letter.

Direksyons: Li chak mo sib. Li mo ki nan ranje a epi antoure mo ki kòmanse ak yon lèt diferan.

Target Words				
1. greet	judge	grill	gear	glow
2. good	group	glimpse	paint	gain
3. gang	give	boat	growth	gulf
4. guess	grace	job	get	gill
5. grade	gem	grow	girl	pool

 Directions: Read the words in the four boxes. Circle two words that start with the uppercase and lowercase letter "g."

Direksyons: Li mo ki nan kat kare yo. Ansèkle de mo ki kòmanse ak lèt majiskil ak lèt miniskil "g".

get	jet
Peach	Goat

Pen	boat
Greek	give

ball	Gain
grow	jeans

golf	Gray
plant	deep

place	good
jump	Grant

Gift	pie
gum	Ox

Learn To Read English With Directions In Haitian Creole

Homework

 Name: _____ Date: ___/___/_____ Score: _____

Appendix 8.0

Introduction of the Letter H/h

✓ Lesson Check Point

Directions: Circle the correct letter "h" pair: uppercase and lowercase letters.

Direksyons: Antoure lèt ki kòrèk "h" pè: lèt majiskil ak lèt miniskil.

Hh   bH   Bh   hF   Hk

Directions: The uppercase letter "H" is in the first column. Look at the four letters in the row and circle the lowercase letter that matches the uppercase letter "H."

Direksyons: Lèt majiskil "H" se nan premye kolòn nan. Gade kat lèt ki nan ranje a epi antoure lèt miniskil ki koresponn ak lèt majiskil "H".

H	l	h	g	t
H	h	v	l	q
H	t	b	h	f
H	f	p	t	h

Directions: The lowercase letter "h" is in the first column. Look at the four letters in the row and circle the uppercase letter that matches the lowercase letter "h."

Direksyons: Lèt miniskil "h" se nan premye kolòn nan. Gade kat lèt ki nan ranje a epi antoure lèt majiskil ki koresponn ak lèt miniskil "h".

h	F	H	T	S
h	G	T	H	R
h	H	D	J	T
h	B	H	U	L

Homework

 Name: _____ Date: ___/___/_____ Score: _____

Appendix 8.0

Letter Recognition H/h

Uppercase and Lowercase Letter

✓ Lesson Check Point

 Directions: Read each target word. Read the words in the row and circle the word that begins with a different letter.
Direksyons: Li chak mo sib. Li mo ki nan ranje a epi antoure mo ki kòmanse ak yon lèt diferan.

Target Words				
1. hit	hive	hood	like	hub
2. hike	tape	health	hall	hook
3. heal	hair	horn	leaves	he
4. hard	hole	bath	heap	hand
5. hose	jump	hang	hence	haul

 Directions: Read the words in the four boxes. Circle two words that start with the uppercase and lowercase letter "h."
Direksyons: Li mo ki nan kat kare yo. Ansèkle de mo ki kòmanse ak lèt majiskil ak lèt miniskil "h".

herb	tree
brown	Hoard

pink	teeth
home	Heed

light	Hand
bath	hop

hair	Heal
keep	true

look	Horse
hemp	found

Half	hot
dress	top

Homework

 Name: _____ Date:___/___/_____ Score:_____

Appendix 9.0

Introduction of the Letter I/i

✓ **Lesson Check Point**

 Directions: Circle the correct letter "i" pair: uppercase and lowercase letters.

Direksyons: Antoure lèt ki kòrèk "i" pè: lèt majiskil ak lèt miniskil.

Ii	Ij	iJ	Im	Ti

 Directions: The uppercase letter "I" is in the first column. Look at the four letters in the row and circle the lowercase letter that matches the uppercase letter "I."

Direksyons: Lèt majiskil "I" se nan premye kolòn nan. Gade kat lèt ki nan ranje a epi antoure lèt miniskil ki koresponn ak lèt majiskil "I".

I	j	i	l	y
I	f	j	x	i
I	i	h	t	v
I	t	d	h	i

 Directions: The lowercase letter "i" is in the first column. Look at the four letters in the row and circle the uppercase letter that matches the lowercase letter "i."

Direksyons: Lèt miniskil "i" se nan premye kolòn nan. Gade kat lèt ki nan ranje a epi antoure lèt majiskil ki koresponn ak lèt miniskil "i".

i	K	I	T	J
i	I	L	H	K
i	D	Y	I	L
i	J	G	K	I

Learn To Read English With Directions In Haitian Creole

Homework

 Name: _____   Date: ___/___/_____   Score: _____

Appendix 10.0

Introduction of the Letter J/j

✓ Lesson Check Point

 Directions: Circle the correct letter "j" pair: uppercase and lowercase letters.
Direksyons: Antoure lèt ki kòrèk "j" pè: lèt majiskil ak lèt miniskil.

    jY   yJ   Gj   Jj   jL

 Directions: The uppercase letter "J" is in the first column. Look at the four letters in the row and circle the lowercase letter that matches the uppercase letter "J."
Direksyons: Lèt majiskil "J" se nan premye kolòn nan. Gade kat lèt ki nan ranje a epi antoure lèt miniskil ki koresponn ak lèt majiskil "J".

J	y	g	j	l
J	j	v	y	q
J	p	j	g	b
J	g	y	j	p

 Directions: The lowercase letter "j" is in the first column. Look at the four letters in the row and circle the uppercase letter that matches the lowercase letter "j."
Direksyons: Lèt miniskil "j" se nan premye kolòn nan. Gade kat lèt ki nan ranje a epi antoure lèt majiskil ki koresponn ak lèt miniskil "j".

j	K	J	C	L
j	J	O	G	U
j	Q	C	J	O
j	G	V	U	J

Homework

 Name: _____ Date:___/___/_____   Score: _____

Appendix 10.0

Letter Recognition J/j

Uppercase and Lowercase Letter

✓ Lesson Check Point

Directions: Read each target word. Read the words in the row and circle the word that begins with a different letter.

Direksyons: Li chak mo sib. Li mo ki nan ranje a epi antoure mo ki kòmanse ak yon lèt diferan.

Target Words				
1. jaw	jet	jay	yes	joint
2. join	pie	jean	junk	jade
3. jump	jazz	guess	jar	jog
4. jungle	job	gem	judge	jeep
5. January	jail	jug	joke	years

Directions: Read the words in the four boxes. Circle two words that start with the uppercase and lowercase letter "j."

Direksyons: Li mo ki nan kat kare yo. Ansèkle de mo ki kòmanse ak lèt majiskil ak lèt miniskil "j".

Joke	Goat
yes	juice

just	Jolt
prince	your

youth	June
jock	queen

quest	price
jog	Jam

young	Jail
jot	golf

grand	jump
press	Juicy

Learn To Read English With Directions In Haitian Creole

Homework

 Name: _____ Date:___/___/_____ Score: _____

Appendix 11.0

Introduction of the Letter K/k

✓ **Lesson Check Point**

 Directions: Circle the correct letter "k" pair: uppercase and lowercase letters.
Direksyons: Antoure lèt ki kòrèk "k" pè: lèt majiskil ak lèt miniskil.

kB   Kl   kt   kY   Kk

 Directions: The uppercase letter "K" is in the first column. Look at the four letters in the row and circle the lowercase letter that matches the uppercase letter "K."
Direksyons: Lèt majiskil "K" se nan premye kolòn nan. Gade kat lèt ki nan ranje a epi antoure lèt miniskil ki koresponn ak lèt majiskil "K".

K	l	k	y	p
K	b	f	k	l
K	p	h	d	k
K	k	j	l	p

 Directions: The lowercase letter "k" is in the first column. Look at the four letters in the row and circle the uppercase letter that matches the lowercase letter "k."
Direksyons: Lèt miniskil "k" se nan premye kolòn nan. Gade kat lèt ki nan ranje a epi antoure lèt majiskil ki koresponn ak lèt miniskil "k".

k	K	L	M	Y
k	M	N	K	L
k	J	K	H	B
k	V	N	K	T

Homework

 Name: _____ Date: ___/___/_____ Score: _____

Appendix 11.0

Letter Recognition K/k

Uppercase and Lowercase Letter

✓ **Lesson Check Point**

 Directions: Read each target word. Read the words in the row and circle the word that begins with a different letter.

Direksyons: Li chak mo sib. Li mo ki nan ranje a epi antoure mo ki kòmanse ak yon lèt diferan.

Target Words				
1. kid	kin	house	keel	know
2. knit	keen	knight	king	lace
3. kind	kale	body	key	keep
4. krill	hatch	keg	knock	kick
5. kept	drop	karts	knot	kelp

 Directions: Read the words in the four boxes. Circle two words that start with the uppercase and lowercase letter "k."

Direksyons: Li mo ki nan kat kare yo. Ansèkle de mo ki kòmanse ak lèt majiskil ak lèt miniskil "k".

keep	house
Kiss	Eats

dreams	Know
kind	friends

jumps	home
Knock	kick

laughs	knight
bounce	Keys

Knit	kept
free	tree

Knob	trips
hope	kale

Homework

 Name: _____ Date:___/___/_____ Score:_____

Appendix 12.0

Introduction of the Letter L/l

✓ **Lesson Check Point**

Directions: Circle the correct letter "l" pair: uppercase and lowercase letters.

Direksyons: Antoure lèt ki kòrèk "l" pè: lèt majiskil ak lèt miniskil.

    hL   Lk   lT   Ll   lJ

Directions: The uppercase letter "L" is in the first column. Look at the four letters in the row and circle the lowercase letter that matches the uppercase letter "L."

Direksyons: Lèt majiskil "L" se nan premye kolòn nan. Gade kat lèt ki nan ranje a epi antoure lèt miniskil ki koresponn ak lèt majiskil "L".

L	k	l	f	h
L	j	f	l	b
L	l	h	j	x
L	b	y	k	l

Directions: The lowercase letter "l" is in the first column. Look at the four letters in the row and circle the uppercase letter that matches the lowercase letter "l."

Direksyons: Lèt miniskil "l" se nan premye kolòn nan. Gade kat lèt ki nan ranje a epi antoure lèt majiskil ki koresponn ak lèt miniskil "l".

l	L	K	H	V
l	E	F	L	K
l	M	V	T	L
l	L	H	V	E

Homework

Name: _____ Date: ___/___/_____ Score: _____

Appendix 12.0

Letter Recognition L/l

Uppercase and Lowercase Letter

✓ Lesson Check Point

Directions: Read each target word. Read the words in the row and circle the word that begins with a different letter.

Direksyons: Li chak mo sib. Li mo ki nan ranje a epi antoure mo ki kòmanse ak yon lèt diferan.

Target Words				
1. leaf	lack	lush	town	land
2. link	jump	like	lard	left
3. lead	lift	lance	brown	leg
4. late	lunch	friends	leek	latch
5. lick	dreams	limp	lank	live

Directions: Read the words in the four boxes. Circle two words that start with the uppercase and lowercase letter "l."

Direksyons: Li mo ki nan kat kare yo. Ansèkle de mo ki kòmanse ak lèt majiskil ak lèt miniskil "l".

trees	Lend
fruits	lane

boats	Drops
Line	lash

house	Law
list	drips

Less	lynch
front	dress

Lots	home
bumps	lump

Leak	drive
launch	found

Learn To Read English With Directions In Haitian Creole

Homework

 Name: _____ Date: ___/___/_____ Score: _____

Appendix 13.0

Introduction of the Letter M/m

✓ **Lesson Check Point**

  Directions: Circle the correct letter "m" pair: uppercase and lowercase letters.
Direksyons: Antoure lèt ki kòrèk "m" pè: lèt majiskil ak lèt miniskil.

| Um | Nm | Mw | Mn | Mm |

 Directions: The uppercase letter "M" is in the first column. Look at the four letters in the row and circle the lowercase letter that matches the uppercase letter "M."
Direksyons: Lèt majiskil "M" se nan premye kolòn nan. Gade kat lèt ki nan ranje a epi antoure lèt miniskil ki koresponn ak lèt majiskil "M".

M	n	m	n	h
M	w	n	u	m
M	u	v	m	n
M	m	u	n	o

 Directions: The lowercase letter "m" is in the first column. Look at the four letters in the row and circle the uppercase letter that matches the lowercase letter "m."
Direksyons: Lèt miniskil "m" se nan premye kolòn nan. Gade kat lèt ki nan ranje a epi antoure lèt majiskil ki koresponn ak lèt miniskil "m".

m	N	U	M	W
m	M	V	X	J
m	V	W	Z	M
m	X	M	U	N

Homework

 Name: _____ Date: ___/___/_____ Score: _____

Appendix 13.0

Letter Recognition M/m

Uppercase and Lowercase Letter

✓ Lesson Check Point

 Directions: Read each target word. Read the words in the row and circle the word that begins with a different letter.
Direksyons: Li chak mo sib. Li mo ki nan ranje a epi antoure mo ki kòmanse ak yon lèt diferan.

Target Words				
1. meat	mood	mixed	were	might
2. mind	nail	mince	much	mean
3. moist	mug	meal	vote	miss
4. made	mumps	mouth	mist	nest
5. musk	world	mall	mock	mint

 Directions: Read the words in the four boxes. Circle two words that start with the uppercase and lowercase letter "m."
Direksyons: Li mo ki nan kat kare yo. Ansèkle de mo ki kòmanse ak lèt majiskil ak lèt miniskil "m".

noise	moon
vest	Main

write	noon
most	Maid

Make	news
vowel	mouse

used	mane
Move	numb

Mold	milk
nerve	wrote

mourn	nine
Mail	cause

Homework

  Name: _____   Date: ___/___/_____   Score: _____

Appendix 14.0

Introduction of the Letter N/n

✓ **Lesson Check Point**

 Directions: Circle the correct letter "n" pair: uppercase and lowercase letters.
Direksyons: Antoure lèt ki kòrèk "n" pè: lèt majiskil ak lèt miniskil.

| Nm | Vn | nW | Nn | Mn |

 Directions: The uppercase letter "N" is in the first column. Look at the four letters in the row and circle the lowercase letter that matches the uppercase letter "N."
Direksyons: Lèt majiskil "N" se nan premye kolòn nan. Gade kat lèt ki nan ranje a epi antoure lèt miniskil ki koresponn ak lèt majiskil "N".

N	v	n	u	o
N	y	u	w	n
N	n	j	m	f
N	u	b	n	v

 Directions: The lowercase letter "n" is in the first column. Look at the four letters in the row and circle the uppercase letter that matches the lowercase letter "n."
Direksyons: Lèt miniskil "n" se nan premye kolòn nan. Gade kat lèt ki nan ranje a epi antoure lèt majiskil ki koresponn ak lèt miniskil "n".

n	M	W	N	V
n	N	C	W	X
n	U	H	X	N
n	T	N	Z	U

Homework

Name: _____ Date: ___/___/_____ Score: _____

Appendix 14.0

Letter Recognition N/n

Uppercase and Lowercase Letter

✓ Lesson Check Point

Directions: Read each target word. Read the words in the row and circle the word that begins with a different letter.

Direksyons: Li chak mo sib. Li mo ki nan ranje a epi antoure mo ki kòmanse ak yon lèt diferan.

Target Words				
1. nerve	noon	right	news	noun
2. noise	make	near	night	need
3. neck	nail	nose	nice	rope
4. nine	name	none	moist	next
5. name	numb	note	nest	use

Directions: Read the words in the four boxes. Circle two words that start with the uppercase and lowercase letter "n."

Direksyons: Li mo ki nan kat kare yo. Ansèkle de mo ki kòmanse ak lèt majiskil ak lèt miniskil "n".

mall	you
numb	New

unto	Name
house	nerve

much	Near
need	good

Nap	mops
ran	norm

Null	mock
neat	vote

neck	Nest
race	mom

Learn To Read English With Directions In Haitian Creole

Homework

 Name: _____ Date:___/___/_____ Score:_____

Appendix 15.0

Introduction of the Letter O/o

✓ Lesson Check Point

 Directions: Circle the correct letter "o" pair: uppercase and lowercase letters.
Direksyons: Antoure lèt ki kòrèk "o" pè: lèt majiskil ak lèt miniskil.

| Po | Qo | Oc | Oo | Co |

 Directions: The uppercase letter "O" is in the first column. Look at the four letters in the row and circle the lowercase letter that matches the uppercase letter "O."
Direksyons: Lèt majiskil "O" se nan premye kolòn nan. Gade kat lèt ki nan ranje a epi antoure lèt miniskil ki koresponn ak lèt majiskil "O".

O	o	d	g	s
O	c	s	u	o
O	g	o	c	q
O	d	g	o	c

 Directions: The lowercase letter "o" is in the first column. Look at the four letters in the row and circle the uppercase letter that matches the lowercase letter "o."
Direksyons: Lèt miniskil "o" se nan premye kolòn nan. Gade kat lèt ki nan ranje a epi antoure lèt majiskil ki koresponn ak lèt miniskil "o".

o	D	O	Q	G
o	C	Q	V	O
o	Q	C	O	S
o	O	H	Q	C

Homework

 Name: _____ Date: ___/___/_____ Score: _____

Appendix 16.0

Introduction of the Letter P/p

✓ Lesson Check Point

 Directions: Circle the correct letter "p" pair: uppercase and lowercase letters.

Direksyons: Antoure lèt ki kòrèk "p" pè: lèt majiskil ak lèt miniskil.

| Pd | bP | Dp | Pp | Bp |

 Directions: The uppercase letter "P" is in the first column. Look at the four letters in the row and circle the lowercase letter that matches the uppercase letter "P."

Direksyons: Lèt majiskil "P" se nan premye kolòn nan. Gade kat lèt ki nan ranje a epi antoure lèt miniskil ki koresponn ak lèt majiskil "P".

P	q	b	d	p
P	p	d	g	j
P	g	p	h	f
P	d	g	p	b

 Directions: The lowercase letter "p" is in the first column. Look at the four letters in the row and circle the uppercase letter that matches the lowercase letter "p."

Direksyons: Lèt miniskil "p" se nan premye kolòn nan. Gade kat lèt ki nan ranje a epi antoure lèt majiskil ki koresponn ak lèt miniskil "p".

p	R	P	Q	B
p	P	D	F	D
p	F	K	P	Q
p	B	S	G	P

Homework

Name: _____ Date: ___/___/_____ Score: _____

Appendix 16.0

Letter Recognition P/p

Uppercase and Lowercase Letter

✓ Lesson Check Point

Directions: Read each target word. Read the words in the row and circle the word that begins with a different letter.

Direksyons: Li chak mo sib. Li mo ki nan ranje a epi antoure mo ki kòmanse ak yon lèt diferan.

Target Words				
1. pen	pledge	quote	prince	porch
2. play	years	plug	park	pear
3. pitch	peer	pinch	quartz	pop
4. patch	poise	prompt	place	bond
5. praise	queen	pain	pile	proof

Directions: Read the words in the four boxes. Circle two words that start with the uppercase and lowercase letter "p."

Direksyons: Li mo ki nan kat kare yo. Ansèkle de mo ki kòmanse ak lèt majiskil ak lèt miniskil "p".

beach	Peach
teach	patch

fast	past
last	Pearl

Pad	push
Bad	Dad

Say	Day
pay	Path

Pave	Dave
pop	Have

Deal	meal
peel	Pets

Learn To Read English With Directions In Haitian Creole   278   Copyrighted Material

Homework

 Name: _____ Date: ___/___/_____ Score: _____

Appendix 17.0

Introduction of the Letter Q/q

✓ Lesson Check Point

 Directions: Circle the correct letter "q" pair: uppercase and lowercase letters.
Direksyons: Antoure lèt ki kòrèk "q" pè: lèt majiskil ak lèt miniskil

    Pq   Bq   Qq   Oq   pQ

 Directions: The uppercase letter "Q" is in the first column. Look at the four letters in the row and circle the lowercase letter that matches the uppercase letter "Q."
Direksyons: Lèt majiskil "Q" se nan premye kolòn nan. Gade kat lèt ki nan ranje a epi antoure lèt miniskil ki korespon ak lèt majiskil "Q".

Q	p	d	q	d
Q	g	q	j	b
Q	q	f	g	j
Q	j	y	p	q

 Directions: The lowercase letter "q" is in the first column. Look at the four letters in the row and circle the uppercase letter that matches the lowercase letter "q."
Direksyons: Lèt miniskil "q" se nan premye kolòn nan. Gade kat lèt ki nan ranje a epi antoure lèt majiskil ki korespon ak lèt miniskil "q".

q	D	Q	S	H
q	O	S	R	Q
q	Q	D	C	O
q	C	Z	Q	S

Learn To Read English With Directions In Haitian Creole   Copyrighted Material

Homework

 Name: _____ Date: ___/___/_____ Score: _____

Appendix 17.0

Letter Recognition Q/q

Uppercase and Lowercase Letter

✓ Lesson Check Point

 Directions: Read each target word. Read the words in the row and circle the word that begins with a different letter.

Direksyons: Li chak mo sib. Li mo ki nan ranje a epi antoure mo ki kòmanse ak yon lèt diferan.

Target Words				
1. quiz	jumps	quota	quire	quaint
2. quince	quack	quench	quarrel	guest
3. queen	quick	young	quartz	quit
4. quirk	quote	quest	puppy	quack
5. quench	paints	queen	quartz	quicken

 Directions: Read the words in the four boxes. Circle two words that start with the uppercase and lowercase letter "q."

Direksyons: Li mo ki nan kat kare yo. Ansèkle de mo ki kòmanse ak lèt majiskil ak lèt miniskil "q".

quite	peace
Jupiter	Quiet

qualm	Quality
Opens	jumps

puppy	Quiver
quarter	Cover

Opera	Quiche
dance	quibble

qualify	Over
Quacks	person

people	jelly
Quicken	query

Name: _____ Date: ___/___/_____ Score: _____

Homework

Appendix 18.0

Introduction of the Letter R/r

✓ Lesson Check Point

 Directions: Circle the correct letter "r" pair: uppercase and lowercase letters.
Direksyons: Antoure lèt ki kòrèk "r" pè: lèt majiskil ak lèt miniskil.

rR   Rv   rX   kR   rP

 Directions: The uppercase letter "R" is in the first column. Look at the four letters in the row and circle the lowercase letter that matches the uppercase letter "R."
Direksyons: Lèt majiskil "R" se nan premye kolòn nan. Gade kat lèt ki nan ranje a epi antoure lèt miniskil ki koresponn ak lèt majiskil "R".

R	x	r	f	h
R	g	v	s	r
R	r	x	z	v
R	j	r	a	c

 Directions: The lowercase letter "r" is in the first column. Look at the four letters in the row and circle the uppercase letter that matches the lowercase letter "r."
Direksyons: Lèt miniskil "r" se nan premye kolòn nan. Gade kat lèt ki nan ranje a epi antoure lèt majiskil ki koresponn ak lèt miniskil "r".

r	F	S	T	R
r	R	F	W	E
r	F	C	A	R
r	X	R	H	D

Homework

Name: _____ Date:___/___/_____ Score: _____

Appendix 18.0

Letter Recognition R/r

Uppercase and Lowercase Letter

✓ Lesson Check Point

Directions: Read each target word. Read the words in the row and circle the word that begins with a different letter.

Direksyons: Li chak mo sib. Li mo ki nan ranje a epi antoure mo ki kòmanse ak yon lèt diferan.

Target Words				
1. role	ride	nine	ranch	rope
2. ring	music	rose	right	raise
3. rail	ripe	rough	real	closed
4. rose	rank	cream	rinse	roof
5. run	rhyme	root	noon	read

Directions: Read the words in the four boxes. Circle two words that start with the uppercase and lowercase letter "r."

Direksyons: Li mo ki nan kat kare yo. Ansèkle de mo ki kòmanse ak lèt majiskil ak lèt miniskil "r".

Roach	games	march	rake	ring	Road
numb	rub	cave	Round	need	Peek

Pain	mouth	citizen	rink	Rode	peer
Roast	race	Rent	Person	rice	part

Homework

 Name: _____ Date: ___/___/_____ Score: _____

Appendix 19.0

Introduction of the Letter S/s

✓ Lesson Check Point

 Directions: Circle the correct letter "s" pair: uppercase and lowercase letters.
Direksyons: Antoure lèt ki kòrèk "s" pè: lèt majiskil ak lèt miniskil.

    Sc   sZ   cS   sX   sS

 Directions: The uppercase letter "S" is in the first column. Look at the four letters in the row and circle the lowercase letter that matches the uppercase letter "S."
Direksyons: Lèt majiskil "S" se nan premye kolòn nan. Gade kat lèt ki nan ranje a epi antoure lèt miniskil ki koresponn ak lèt majiskil "S".

S	c	s	x	z
S	z	o	c	s
S	s	j	z	t
S	g	c	s	k

 Directions: The lowercase letter "s" is in the first column. Look at the four letters in the row and circle the uppercase letter that matches the lowercase letter "s."
Direksyons: Lèt miniskil "s" se nan premye kolòn nan. Gade kat lèt ki nan ranje a epi antoure lèt majiskil ki koresponn ak lèt miniskil "s".

s	X	C	T	S
s	O	S	C	Z
s	G	C	S	X
s	S	G	O	U

Homework

 Name: _____ Date:___/___/_____ Score: _____

Appendix 19.0

Letter Recognition S/s

Uppercase and Lowercase Letter

✓ Lesson Check Point

 Directions: Read each target word. Read the words in the row and circle the word that begins with a different letter.

Direksyons: Li chak mo sib. Li mo ki nan ranje a epi antoure mo ki kòmanse ak yon lèt diferan.

Target Words				
1. son	since	cash	skate	scale
2. snow	sketch	shell	seek	chick
3. shape	zoo	sell	shrub	soar
4. sheet	smile	save	slip	mother
5. search	seem	shade	corn	school

 Directions: Read the words in the four boxes. Circle two words that start with the uppercase and lowercase letter "s."

Direksyons: Li mo ki nan kat kare yo. Ansèkle de mo ki kòmanse ak lèt majiskil ak lèt miniskil "s".

court	Sharp
grows	sour

slash	Sale
zipper	Clash

Zoo	silk
Share	clock

house	clowns
Size	sew

shark	cord
Snow	zebra

show	vases
zero	Snore

Homework

Name: _____ Date: ___/___/_____ Score: _____

Appendix 20.0

Introduction of the Letter T/t

✓ **Lesson Check Point**

 Directions: Circle the correct letter "t" pair: uppercase and lowercase letters.
Direksyons: Antoure lèt ki kòrèk "t" pè: lèt majiskil ak lèt miniskil.

| Tl | tZ | tJ | Tt | Tk |

 Directions: The uppercase letter "T" is in the first column. Look at the four letters in the row and circle the lowercase letter that matches the uppercase letter "T."
Direksyons: Lèt majiskil "T" se nan premye kolòn nan. Gade kat lèt ki nan ranje a epi antoure lèt miniskil ki koresponn ak lèt majiskil "T".

T	j	l	t	h
T	l	f	b	t
T	t	h	f	d
T	j	l	t	f

 Directions: The lowercase letter "t" is in the first column. Look at the four letters in the row and circle the uppercase letter that matches the lowercase letter "t."
Direksyons: Lèt miniskil "t" se nan premye kolòn nan. Gade kat lèt ki nan ranje a epi antoure lèt majiskil ki koresponn ak lèt miniskil "t".

t	H	T	J	A
t	L	K	L	T
t	T	A	X	L
t	Y	F	T	H

Homework

 Name: _____ Date: ___/___/_____ Score: _____

Appendix 20.0

Letter Recognition T/t

Uppercase and Lowercase Letter

✓ **Lesson Check Point**

 Directions: Read each target word. Read the words in the row and circle the word that begins with a different letter.

Direksyons: Li chak mo sib. Li mo ki nan ranje a epi antoure mo ki kòmanse ak yon lèt diferan.

Target Words				
1. turn	thirst	fool	train	thorn
2. tool	touch	trunk	love	tent
3. tank	than	tenth	tang	help
4. them	tap	tour	drip	thank
5. truck	hope	tray	third	tare

 Directions: Read the words in the four boxes. Circle two words that start with the uppercase and lowercase letter "t."

Direksyons: Li mo ki nan kat kare yo. Ansèkle de mo ki kòmanse ak lèt majiskil ak lèt miniskil "t".

Thanks	term
lick	Fine

Phone	trace
Toy	home

Left	Tart
boat	tint

Twirl	keen
Rain	tube

trail	leaf
Tone	fun

Kind	dock
Tub	take

Homework

 Name: _____ Date: ___/___/_____ Score: _____

Appendix 21.0

Introduction of the Letter U/u

✓ Lesson Check Point

 Directions: Circle the correct letter "u" pair: uppercase and lowercase letters.
Direksyons: Antoure lèt ki kòrèk "u" pè: lèt majiskil ak lèt miniskil.

    Yu   Uu   Vu   Ou   vU

 Directions: The uppercase letter "U" is in the first column. Look at the four letters in the row and circle the lowercase letter that matches the uppercase letter "U."
Direksyons: Lèt majiskil "U" se nan premye kolòn nan. Gade kat lèt ki nan ranje a epi antoure lèt miniskil ki koresponn ak lèt majiskil "U".

U	j	s	u	v
U	o	g	h	u
U	u	k	v	o
U	v	r	o	u

 Directions: The lowercase letter "u" is in the first column. Look at the four letters in the row and circle the uppercase letter that matches the lowercase letter "u."
Direksyons: Lèt miniskil "u" se nan premye kolòn nan. Gade kat lèt ki nan ranje a epi antoure lèt majiskil ki koresponn ak lèt miniskil "u".

u	U	V	C	X
u	Z	C	U	V
u	Y	E	V	U
u	T	U	N	O

Homework

 Name: _____ Date: ___/___/_____ Score: _____

Appendix 22.0

Introduction of the Letter V/v

✓ Lesson Check Point

 Directions: Circle the correct letter "v" pair: uppercase and lowercase letters.
Direksyons: Antoure lèt ki kòrèk "v" pè: lèt majiskil ak lèt miniskil.

    Cv   Uv   Vv   Xv   Vk

 Directions: The uppercase letter "V" is in the first column. Look at the four letters in the row and circle the lowercase letter that matches the uppercase letter "V."
Direksyons: Lèt majiskil "V" se nan premye kolòn nan. Gade kat lèt ki nan ranje a epi antoure lèt miniskil ki koresponn ak lèt majiskil "V".

V	u	v	x	y
V	v	u	n	s
V	c	b	v	x
V	m	v	u	z

 Directions: The lowercase letter "v" is in the first column. Look at the four letters in the row and circle the uppercase letter that matches the lowercase letter "v."
Direksyons: Lèt miniskil "v" se nan premye kolòn nan. Gade kat lèt ki nan ranje a epi antoure lèt majiskil ki koresponn ak lèt miniskil "v".

v	X	Y	T	V
v	T	V	U	M
v	V	Y	X	S
v	J	F	V	Z

Homework

 Name: _____ Date:___/___/_____ Score:_____

Appendix 22.0

Letter Recognition V/v

Uppercase and Lowercase Letter

✓ Lesson Check Point

 Directions: Read each target word. Read the words in the row and circle the word that begins with a different letter.

Direksyons: Li chak mo sib. Li mo ki nan ranje a epi antoure mo ki kòmanse ak yon lèt diferan.

Target Words				
1. vine	went	view	vogue	verb
2. vault	vent	volt	March	vague
3. vow	keys	vein	vest	vane
4. vamp	valve	water	vote	versed
5. voiced	vile	void	vouch	walk

 Directions: Read the words in the four boxes. Circle two words that start with the uppercase and lowercase letter "v."

Direksyons: Li mo ki nan kat kare yo. Ansèkle de mo ki kòmanse ak lèt majiskil ak lèt miniskil "v".

mean	van
worm	Verse

Vase	sour
root	veil

force	Voice
verge	Wept

Vain	apple
visit	cost

veto	Vice
wake	neck

white	raise
Vex	veer

289

Homework

 Name: _____ Date: ___/___/_____ Score: _____

Appendix 23.0

Introduction of the Letter W/w

✓ **Lesson Check Point**

 Directions: Circle the correct letter "w" pair: uppercase and lowercase letters.
Direksyons: Antoure lèt ki kòrèk "w" pè: lèt majiskil ak lèt miniskil.

    wV   Ww   Uw   Wv   Yw

 Directions: The uppercase letter "W" is in the first column. Look at the four letters in the row and circle the lowercase letter that matches the uppercase letter "W."
Direksyons: Lèt majiskil "W" se nan premye kolòn nan. Gade kat lèt ki nan ranje a epi antoure lèt miniskil ki koresponn ak lèt majiskil "W".

W	v	w	x	y
W	u	t	c	w
W	w	u	v	m
W	n	y	w	f

 Directions: The lowercase letter "w" is in the first column. Look at the four letters in the row and circle the uppercase letter that matches the lowercase letter "w."
Direksyons: Lèt miniskil "w" se nan premye kolòn nan. Gade kat lèt ki nan ranje a epi antoure lèt majiskil ki koresponn ak lèt miniskil "w".

w	V	M	W	N
w	U	W	V	A
w	W	X	C	M
w	X	V	Y	W

Homework

 Name: _____ Date: ___/___/_____ Score: _____

Appendix 23.0

Letter Recognition W/w

Uppercase and Lowercase Letter

✓ **Lesson Check Point**

 Directions: Read each target word. Read the words in the row and circle the word that begins with a different letter.
Direksyons: Li chak mo sib. Li mo ki nan ranje a epi antoure mo ki kòmanse ak yon lèt diferan.

Target Words				
1. what	wedge	wrist	mugs	write
2. wire	which	warm	wreck	voyage
3. wear	warn	noon	wound	went
4. wages	while	wise	weak	Mouse
5. wheeze	vowel	waist	wipe	wrest

 Directions: Read the words in the four boxes. Circle two words that start with the uppercase and lowercase letter "w."
Direksyons: Li mo ki nan kat kare yo. Ansèkle de mo ki kòmanse ak lèt majiskil ak lèt miniskil "w".

want	Nail
Wig	video

Match	Where
wrong	None

With	whack
Merge	Vision

Mud	Verdict
whim	Wart

Nuts	wrung
volcano	White

Wool	Volume
Noise	wet

Learn To Read English With Directions In Haitian Creole

Homework

  Name: _____ Date: ___/___/_____ Score: _____

Appendix 24.0

Introduction of the Letter X/x

✓ Lesson Check Point

  Directions: Circle the correct letter "x" pair: uppercase and lowercase letters.
Direksyons: Antoure lèt ki kòrèk "x" pè: lèt majiskil ak lèt miniskil.

Xz   Kx   Xx   xY   Xk

  Directions: The uppercase letter "X" is in the first column. Look at the four letters in the row and circle the lowercase letter that matches the uppercase letter "X."
Direksyons: Lèt majiskil "X" se nan premye kolòn nan. Gade kat lèt ki nan ranje a epi antoure lèt miniskil ki koresponn ak lèt majiskil "X".

X	x	y	z	s
X	v	x	k	y
X	u	z	a	x
X	x	v	k	z

  Directions: The lowercase letter "x" is in the first column. Look at the four letters in the row and circle the uppercase letter that matches the lowercase letter "x."
Direksyons: Lèt miniskil "x" se nan premye kolòn nan. Gade kat lèt ki nan ranje a epi antoure lèt majiskil ki koresponn ak lèt miniskil "x".

x	K	X	Z	V
x	B	K	V	X
x	X	V	U	Y
x	Y	X	K	F

Homework

 Name: _____ Date: ___/___/_____ Score: _____

Appendix 24.0

Letter Recognition X/x

Uppercase and Lowercase Letter

✓ Lesson Check Point

 Directions: Read each target word. Read the words in the row and circle the word that does not contain a letter "x."
Direksyons: Li chak mo sib. Li mo ki nan ranje a epi fè wonn mo ki pa gen yon lèt "x".

Target Words				
1. axed	vamp	ox	mixing	annex
2. tax	taxi	waxy	cooks	flex
3. max	exit	Texas	yes	reflex
4. mix	next	sixth	foxes	cents
5. extra	toxic	fax	boxes	goats

 Directions: Read the words in the four boxes. Circle two words that start with the uppercase and lowercase letter "x."
Direksyons: Li mo ki nan kat kare yo. Ansèkle de mo ki kòmanse ak lèt majiskil ak lèt miniskil "x".

extra	x-ray
Xylan	vote

cortex	excel
Xylene	xanthate

kind	xenon
vault	Xerox

xeric	Xanadu
kale	nail

x-axis	yours
Xylose	knit

Xiphoid	out
mean	xanthoma

Learn To Read English With Directions In Haitian Creole

Homework

 Name: _____ Date: ___/___/_____ Score: _____

Appendix 25.0

Introduction of the Letter Y/y

✓ Lesson Check Point

 Directions: Circle the correct letter "y" pair: uppercase and lowercase letters.
Direksyons: Antoure lèt ki kòrèk "y" pè: lèt majiskil ak lèt miniskil.

| Yg | Yy | Jy | Yj | Xy |

 Directions: The uppercase letter "Y" is in the first column. Look at the four letters in the row and circle the lowercase letter that matches the uppercase letter "Y."
Direksyons: Lèt majiskil "Y" se nan premye kolòn nan. Gade kat lèt ki nan ranje a epi antoure lèt miniskil ki koresponn ak lèt majiskil "Y".

Y	j	y	x	p
Y	y	g	j	l
Y	g	q	y	j
Y	j	y	g	v

 Directions: The lowercase letter "y" is in the first column. Look at the four letters in the row and circle the uppercase letter that matches the lowercase letter "y."
Direksyons: Lèt miniskil "y" se nan premye kolòn nan. Gade kat lèt ki nan ranje a epi antoure lèt majiskil ki koresponn ak lèt miniskil "y".

y	F	G	Y	X
y	Y	L	M	J
y	B	C	X	Y
y	Y	L	Z	G

Homework

 Name: _____ Date: ___/___/_____ Score: _____

Appendix 25.0

Letter Recognition Y/y

Uppercase and Lowercase Letter

✓ **Lesson Check Point**

 Directions: Read each target word. Read the words in the row and circle the word that begins with a different letter.
Direksyons: Li chak mo sib. Li mo ki nan ranje a epi antoure mo ki kòmanse ak yon lèt diferan.

Target Words				
1. yoke	yield	year	quick	y-axis
2. yeast	peace	yeast	yard	yes
3. yonder	yam	yonder	yak	great
4. Yankee	basket	yuppie	yolk	yo-yo
5. younger	yap	group	yogurt	yonder

 Directions: Read the words in the four boxes. Circle two words that start with the uppercase and lowercase letter "y."
Direksyons: Li mo ki nan kat kare yo. Ansèkle de mo ki kòmanse ak lèt majiskil ak lèt miniskil "y".

Yacht	paid
yes	glimpse

yield	good
jog	Year

jean	yoke
quit	Your

yeast	Yikes
group	joke

purse	yoga
Yard	joint

juice	glue
Yon	young

Homework

Name: _____ Date: ___/___/_____ Score: _____

Appendix 26.0

Introduction of the Letter Z/z

✓ **Lesson Check Point**

Directions: Circle the correct letter "z" pair: uppercase and lowercase letters.
Direksyons: Antoure lèt ki kòrèk "z" pè: lèt majiskil ak lèt miniskil.

zX	Zz	Yz	Zv	zF

Directions: The uppercase letter "Z" is in the first column. Look at the four letters in the row and circle the lowercase letter that matches the uppercase letter "Z."
Direksyons: Lèt majiskil "Z" se nan premye kolòn nan. Gade kat lèt ki nan ranje a epi antoure lèt miniskil ki koresponn ak lèt majiskil "Z".

Z	z	c	x	y
Z	x	t	z	g
Z	c	g	s	z
Z	y	h	z	a

Directions: The lowercase letter "z" is in the first column. Look at the four letters in the row and circle the uppercase letter that matches the lowercase letter "z."
Direksyons: Lèt miniskil "z" se nan premye kolòn nan. Gade kat lèt ki nan ranje a epi antoure lèt majiskil ki koresponn ak lèt miniskil "z".

z	D	Z	X	C
z	Z	C	V	N
z	M	G	B	Z
z	Z	N	W	X

Name: _____ Date:___/___/_____ Score: _____

Homework

Appendix 26.0

Letter Recognition Z/z

Uppercase and Lowercase Letter

✓ Lesson Check Point

 Directions: Read each target word. Read the words in the row and circle the word that begins with a different letter.
Direksyons: Li chak mo sib. Li mo ki nan ranje a epi antoure mo ki kòmanse ak yon lèt diferan.

Target Words				
1. zero	zillion	zone	zeal	sold
2. zebras	zag	wear	zip	zygote
3. zinger	vase	zodiac	zoo	zipper
4. zenith	zinc	zonal	suit	zig
5. zoning	zoom	school	zany	zinc

 Directions: Read the words in the four boxes. Circle two words that start with the uppercase and lowercase letter "z."
Direksyons: Li mo ki nan kat kare yo. Ansèkle de mo ki kòmanse ak lèt majiskil ak lèt miniskil "z".

swing	Nose
Zillion	zero

sugar	zeal
wet	Zebra

zinger	Zoo
strive	water

zig	stream
Zebu	wing

sweet	Zone
zap	mouse

Never	swan
Ziti	zinc

Learn To Read English With Directions In Haitian Creole

Homework

Your Next Step:
Learn To Read English Vowels With Directions In Haitian Creole